POWER AND RESISTANCE

Studies in Critical Social Sciences Book Series

Haymarket Books is proud to be working with Brill Academic Publishers (www.brill.nl) to republish the *Studies in Critical Social Sciences* book series in paperback editions. This peer-reviewed book series offers insights into our current reality by exploring the content and consequences of power relationships under capitalism, and by considering the spaces of opposition and resistance to these changes that have been defining our new age. Our full catalog of SCSS volumes can be viewed at https://www.haymarketbooks .org/series_collections/4-studies-in-critical-social-sciences.

POWER AND RESISTANCE

US Imperialism in Latin America

JAMES PETRAS
HENRY VELTMEYER

Haymarket
Books
Chicago, IL

First published in 2015 by Brill Academic Publishers, The Netherlands.
© 2016 Koninklijke Brill NV, Leiden, The Netherlands

Published in paperback in 2017 by
Haymarket Books
P.O. Box 180165
Chicago, IL 60618
773-583-7884
www.haymarketbooks.org

ISBN: 978-1-60846-712-9

Trade distribution:
In the U.S. through Consortium Book Sales, www.cbsd.com
In Canada, Publishers Group Canada, www.pgcbooks.ca
In the UK, Turnaround Publisher Services, www.turnaround-uk.com
In all other countries by Publishers Group Worldwide, www.pgw.com

Cover design by Jamie Kerry of Belle Étoile Studios and Ragina Johnson.

This book was published with the generous support of Lannan Foundation
and the Wallace Action Fund.

Printed in Canada by union labor.

10 9 8 7 6 5 4 3 2 1

Library of Congress Cataloging-in-Publication Data is available.

MIXTE
Papier issu de
sources responsables
FSC® C103567

Contents

List of Tables

Introduction

Imperialism is commonly understood as the geopolitical project of a state concerned with establishing its dominance over another or others for the purpose of advancing what is deemed to be the national interest. Lenin can be credited with connecting this power dynamic with the history of capitalism—defining imperialism as the most advanced stage of capitalism. But this was in the earliest two decades of the twentieth century when capitalist relations of production were for the first time internationalized, creating what in effect, and in retrospect, we might understand as a world system.

The one problem with Lenin's conception is that imperialism in fact is tied to the capitalist system not just at one particular phase in the evolution of capitalism but at all stages in its development of the forces of production. As is well known the nation state and capitalism are intimately connected in the historic development of the forces of production. But to secure the conditions needed for this development capitalism needs the state in more ways than one. Capitalism needs the state to establish an institutional and policy framework for the capitalist development process and to provide for the security of citizens and private property. But the world system is a critically important adjunct to the capital accumulation and capitalist development process. For one thing, it provides the dominant and ruling capitalist class a much larger pool of productive resources and opportunities for the accumulation of capital based on the exploitation of labour, not to mention the rape and pillage of natural resources.

The projection by the imperial state of its various powers is an essential condition of the development process. Another is the subjugation of people on the periphery of the world system, which allows capital to exploit their labour and to profit from their natural wealth, which is appropriated and transferred to the centre of the system with the assistance of the imperial state.

Although, the development of capitalism as an imperialist world system can be traced back to the late fifteenth century Lenin argued that imperialism can be understood as the most advanced phase in the evolution of capitalism as a world system. As Lenin so understood it, as a particular form of capitalism that emerged in a particular historical context, imperialism can be defined and described in terms of its structural features, namely (i) the fusion of financial capital (the big banks) and industrial capital (firms organized in the form of large corporations), or finance capital; (ii) the export of capital (in the search for productive investments, natural and human resources to exploit, and markets); (iii) the territorial division of the world among the imperialist powers;

and (v) an international division of labour based on the production of goods manufactured by capitalist industry in the centre of the system and exported to the periphery in exchange for a supply of raw materials and primary commodities needed by industrial capital.

Lenin was undoubtedly correct in identifying the highest stage of capitalist development to date with its evolution into a world system with an industrial centre and a periphery that served the centre with a supply of cheap surplus labour, the natural resources and raw materials needed by industrial capitalists, and a market. But in his focus on the structural features of imperialism he failed to identify its strategic or political dimension, i.e. the particular strategies and tactics involved in the deployment of the state's political and repressive apparatus. However, we need to define imperialism not just in terms of its structural features, but also by its actions related to the projection of imperial power.

Prior to World War II the preferred mode of action for US imperialism in support of its strategic interests was military direct intervention. The record of US military interventions before the Second World War is as follows: Cuba: 1898, 1906–09, 1912; 1917–1933; Puerto Rico: 1898; Nicaragua: 1898, 1899, 1910, 1912–25, 1926–33; Colombia: 1902, 1904, 1912, 1913–14; Honduras: 1903, 1907, 1911, 1912, 1919, 1924, 1925; Dominican Republic: 1903, 1904, 1914, 1916–24; Haiti: 1914, 1915–34; Guatemala: 1920; Panama: 1921, 1925; and Mexico: 1913, 1914–17, 1918–19 (Saney, 2015). After the Second World War, however, the imperial state turned towards an alternative, less confrontational and violent way of securing the conditions needed for advancing capitalism, namely, international cooperation with the development and security agenda of the economies and states formed on the periphery of the world system—international development, as it has become known (see Chapter 5).

Throughout the period of state-led development the preferred mode of imperialist projection of power was international cooperation or 'development'. Only when this strategy did not suffice did the US resort to direct action, and then it did so generally not by direct military action but by proxy—via its local allies. Thus the dominant form of US imperialism in this period—in subsequent decades it would change, decade by decade (see Chapter 5)—was 'international cooperation' with the development and security needs of the Latin American state—to strengthen the state capacity to secure both a measure of economic and social development, and security (the latter via funding and training of the state's Armed Forces).

The dynamics of this political development will be elaborated in subsequent chapters, but the point is that it is possible to connect the changing forms taken by US imperialism to the expansion of capital and the evolution of the world capitalist system in stages—different phases in the capitalist development of the forces of production—both in the centre of the system (the so-called 'global north') and its various peripheries in Latin America and the Caribbean, Africa and Asia (the 'global south' in the development divide). And to identify the role of the imperial state in the process, and analyze its dynamics.

The purpose of this book is to trace this development in the specific context of Latin America and the US imperial state. The concern here is with US imperialism—its changing forms in the Latin American context. And the central focus is on the latest phase of capitalist development brought about by and associated with what has been described as the 'neoliberal era', i.e. within the institutional and policy framework of a Washington Consensus on the virtues of the market freed from regulatory constraint and a 'new world order' based on the principles of free market capitalism. The process of capitalist development and the dynamics of US imperialism can be traced out decade by decade—from the 1980s, which saw the installation of the new world order, and the 1990s in which these structural reforms led to a dramatic expansion of capital in the region, to the new millennium, which saw both the demise of the neoliberal model and the emergence of a new form of capitalism and imperialism associated with the extraction of natural resources and their exportation in primary form.

US imperialism assumes different forms in different periods of capitalist development. Part 1 of the book is composed of a series of essays focused on the dynamics of US imperialism in the current context of capitalist development in Latin America, i.e. over the course of the last fifteen years of the new millennium. The concern in these chapters is to rethink the nature of US imperialism in this context.

Over the past decade and a half, a new form of capitalism has emerged within the framework of a post-Washington Consensus on the need for governments to move beyond the neoliberal policy agenda as well as some epoch-defining changes in the global economy. These changes include the rise of China as an economic power and conditions of a primary commodities boom that have provoked a tsunami of resource-seeking foreign investments in the acquisition of land in developing countries and the extraction of natural resources ranging from fossil- and bio-fuels, industrial minerals and precious metals, and agro-food products. Of particular note in this land- and resource-grabbing process is the role played by the multinational corporations as the operating agencies of the world capitalist system, and the actions taken by the powerful states at the centre of the system to advance and in support of this 'resource seeking' or extractivist capital.

The operations of these corporations in advancing what we might term extractive capital, and the facilitating actions and support of the imperial state, have generated a new dynamic of capitalist development and unleashed powerful forces both in support of this process and in resistance. As for the forces behind the advances of extractive capitalism they are engineered and led by a few powerful states with a vested interest in the expected outcome—reactivation of the economic development process within their national boundaries. To ensure this outcome, and to maximize their ability and freedom to manoeuvre within the confines of the world market, the agencies and agents of the imperial state have mobilized the diverse powers available to them in constructing an economic model designed to advance the 'forces of economic freedom' (private property, capital, the market) in the global economy, and the multinational companies within the 'private sector', assigning to them the role of development catalyst of process of sustainable resource development.

However, the relevant model (the private sector as the catalyst of 'inclusive growth' or 'inclusionary state activism') and its institutional and policy framework (free market capitalism vs. the regulated market) have been hotly contested, giving rise to an alternative model based on the inclusionary activism of the post-neoliberal state.

Structure of the Book

In Chapter 1 we criticize contemporary theorizing about imperialism for its economic reductionism and a lack of class analysis and institutional specificity regarding the imperial state and the political dynamics of imperial power. In making this argument we establish the importance of class analysis for grasping the changing dynamics of imperial power and the social basis of imperial politics. We then proceed to argue how specific alignments of class forces in the world economy, in their interactions with existing imperial power configurations, is leading to a realignment of economic power in the world capitalist system that constitutes a major challenge for US imperialism in its Latin American operations. We conclude with a discussion of the discontinuities and continuities in US imperial relations with Latin America, and the potentialities and constraints of these relations on economic growth and development.

In Chapter 2 we turn to an overview of US imperialism in the current phase of capitalist development in Latin America conditions that emerged with the turn into the new millennium. In this particular conjuncture of the development process governments in the region have increasingly turned towards a development strategy of natural resource extraction and the export of these resources in primary commodity form.

Some analysts have written about this extractivist approach towards national development as 're-primarization', pointing towards a trend for the region to return to the role of supplying the world market with raw materials and commodities—oil and gas, minerals and metals, and agro-food products— and turning away from the industrial policy of the era of state-led development. In actual fact (see Chapter 2 for details), except for Mexico and Brazil the region never had been able to break out of this traditional mould as an exporter of primary commodities. But with the opening of economies in the region to the world market under conditions of what has been described as the 'Washington Consensus' (on the need to take the state out of the development process) the resulting invasion of capital in the form of foreign direct investment provided by the multinational corporations turned many economies in the region back towards extractivism and primarization, reinforcing the economic structure of trade and exacerbating a long-term trend.

In the new millennium this trend was accentuated under conditions that included a major realignment of economic power in the global economy; the ascent of China and with a growing demand for natural resources; a resulting primary commodities boom; the advance and expansion of extractive capital in the form of resource-seeking foreign investments; and the turn of many governments (predominantly in South America) towards both the 'new developmentalism' (the search for a more inclusive form of development based on poverty reduction) and a more 'progressive' form of extractivism based on the use of resource rents to finance social programs of poverty reduction.

Chapter 3 explores the policy and political dynamics of this 'new' extractivism, as well as the role of the imperial state—primarily the US and Canada— in clearing the way for and advancing the operations of extractive capital in the region: extractive imperialism, as we see it.

In Chapter 4 we turn towards the economic and political dynamics of what we term 'agro-extractivism'—large-scale foreign investment in the acquisition of land, or, in the terminology of critical agrarian studies, 'land grabbing'; the extraction of land-bound natural resources for the production of agro-food commodities and energy (bio-fuels); and the exportation of these commodities on the world market.

Part 2 of the book is composed of a series of reflections on the political (policy and resistance) dynamics of US imperialism in recent years. Chapter 5 reviews the strategies and tactics adopted by US imperialism in Latin America over the years. These strategies and tactics are traced out in different conjunctures of capitalist development in the region:

1. The 1950–70s—the era of the development state, imperialism in the form of international cooperation for national development (foreign aid, in the lexicon of 'development') as well as armed force and repression by proxy, and anti-imperialism in the form of revolutionary movements and armies of national liberation;

2. The 1980s—installation of the neoliberal world order, imperialism in the form of globalization and structural adjustment of macroeconomic policy;

3. The 1990s—the penetration of multinational corporations whose growing presence and operations in the region were facilitated by the structural reforms imposed on government in the region by the World Bank and the IMF, powerful forces of resistance in the form of peasant and indigenous socio-political movements that managed to hold the neoliberal agenda of many governments at bay, and ultimately totally discredit this agenda; and

4. The 00s—the emergence of a new phase of capitalist development (extractive capitalism) and the post-neoliberal state. The economic and political dynamics associated with this 'development' are not discussed, being the subject matter of Part 1 of the book.

In Chapter 6 we reflect on the dynamics of imperial power in the 21st century, while Chapter 7 reviews the outcome of fifty years of imperial war fought by the US. It is concluded that Imperialism as it has evolved over the past quarter of a century cannot be understood as a 'unified whole' in which the two basic components, military and economic are always complimentary. Divergences have been graphically illustrated by the imperial wars in the Middle East, South Asia and North Africa. Convergences are more obvious in Latin America, especially in Mexico, Colombia and Peru, where 'militarization' facilitated the expansion of extractive capital. The theoretical point is that the nature of the political leadership of the imperial state has a high degree of autonomy in shaping the predominance of one or another strand of the imperial expansion. The capacity for imperial capital to expand is highly contingent on the strength and structure of the collaborator state: militarized imperialism that invades and destroys states and the fabric of civil society has led to disinvestment. In contrast economic imperialism by invitation in neoliberal collaborator states has been at the centre of successful imperial expansion.

Chapter 8 examines the realignments of world power in recent decades and the effect of these realignments on the working of the US imperial state in its efforts to maintain its hegemony over the world system.

Imperial states build networks that link economic, military and political activities into a coherent mutually reinforcing system. This role is largely performed by the operational agencies of the imperial state. Thus imperial action is not always directly economic, as military action in one country or region is necessary to open or protect economic zones. Nor do economic interests decide all military actions if the leading sector of the imperial state is decidedly militarist. Moreover, the sequence of imperial action may vary according to the particular conditions necessary for empire building. Thus, state aid may buy collaborators; military intervention may secure client regimes followed later by private investors. In other circumstances, the entry of private corporations may precede state intervention.

In either private or state economic- or military-led projections of state power in furtherance of empire building, the strategic aim is to exploit the special economic and geopolitical features of the targeted country that allow for the creation of empire-centred networks. In the post-Eurocentric colonial world, the privileged position of the US in its empire-centred policies, treaties, trade and military agreements is disguised and justified by an ideological gloss, which varies with time and circumstances. In the war to break up Yugoslavia and establish client regimes, as in Kosovo, imperial ideology utilized humanitarian rhetoric. In the genocidal wars waged in the Middle East, anti-terrorism and anti-Islamic ideology is central, while against China, democratic and human rights rhetoric predominates. However, in Latin America receding imperial power relies on democratic and anti-authoritarian rhetoric aimed at the democratically elected Chávez-Maduro regime.

Chapter 8 reinforces the point made in Chapter 6, regarding the crucial role of collaborators in the construction of the imperialist world system. Our study of the dynamics of US imperialism has demonstrated that the lowest cost in sustaining imperial domination in the long term is by developing local collaborators, whether in the form of political, economic and/or military leaders operating from client regimes. Overt politico-military imperial rule results in costly wars and disruption, especially among a broad array of classes adversely affected by the imperial presence.

Chapter 9 shifts from the political power dynamics of US imperialism to the dynamics of the resistance—the anti-imperialist struggle. The chapter discusses the paradoxes of anti-imperialist politics, which are detailed in Part 3 of the book in the case of Venezuela, which has emerged as the leading force in the anti-imperialist struggle today.

The complexities of the new political relations in Latin America require that we breakdown what previously were the unified components of anti-imperialist politics. For example in the past, anti-imperialist regimes pursued policies which opposed US military aggression and intervention in Latin America and throughout the Third World; opposed foreign investment especially in extractive sectors; and, not infrequently, expropriated or nationalized strategic sectors; opposed joint military exercises and training missions; supported nationalist liberation movements and extended political-material support; diversified trade and investment to other economic regions and countries; developed regional political organizations which opposed imperialism and formed regional economic organizations which excluded the US.

Today, few if any of the anti-imperialist countries fit these criteria. Moreover, some of the countries 'favoured' by Washington fit all the criteria of an imperial collaborator. For example, among the most prominent 'anti-imperialist regimes' in Latin America today, Bolivia and Ecuador are big promoters and supporters of a development model that relies on foreign multinational corporations exploiting mining and energy sectors. And both regimes, in pursuit of extractive capital accumulation, have dispossessed local indigenous and peasant communities, and entered into a relation of conflict with these communities.

In the chapter we elaborate criteria that allows us to classify both pro- and anti-imperialist regimes. In the state-led era of capitalist development the dominant agency in the anti-imperialist struggle were the revolutionary social movements. In the current context, however, it is the state that has emerged as the central 'actor' in mobilizing the forces of resistance in this struggle. Our reference here is especially to what has been dubbed the 'anti-imperialist quartet' of Venezuela, Cuba, Bolivia and Ecuador, which has aligned itself with Hugo Chávez's project of the Bolivarian Revolution. With this reference we discuss the dramatic changes in the nature and scope of the class struggle over the course of the 21st century to date.

Latin America exhibits all four types of class struggle but in varying degrees of prominence. No single form of class conflict exists independently of other types. However, we identify the most prominent and dynamic forms that are most closely linked to the possibility of bringing about substantive social change or structural transformation, and that are linked to the dynamics of extractive capitalism and imperialism. We identify countries where one or another type of struggle predominates and analyzes the relationship between 'anti-imperialist countries' and types of class struggle in the context of the growth of the extractive capital model.

The chapter concludes with the observation although the forces of resistance in the class- and anti-imperialist struggle are directed against the operational agencies of extractive capital and the imperial state, there are signs that the emerging regional struggles can and will expand beyond the extractive sector.

But as to whether the forces engaged in these diverse struggle could be brought together or unified it is much too early to tell.

Part 3 of the book focuses on what we have termed the 'Venezuela pivot of US imperialism'. US policy toward Venezuela, and US-Venezuela relations, is a litmus test of US imperialism in the region, a microcosm of its broader strategy in regard to Latin America. The aim of this strategy is to reverse the trend in the region towards an independent foreign policy vis-à-vis the US and to restore US dominance; curtail the diversification of trading and investment partners and re-centre economic relations to the US; replace regional integration pacts with US-centred economic integration schemes; and privatize firms that have been partly or wholly nationalized.

Chapter 10 reviews a decade of failed attempts by the US government to bring about regime change in Venezuela by abetting and mobilizing the forces of opposition to Presidents Chávez and Maduro, providing massive financial support to individuals and organizations with the determination and capacity to organize these forces, colluding with the forces of reaction in both the 'private sector' and on the right-wing of the political system to destabilize the economy, and foment a coup d'état. The chapter incudes an analysis of the strengths and weaknesses of the Maduro government in confronting the US offensive, and also a summary review of the dynamics of the US-Venezuela relations over the past fifteen years.

Chapter 11 provides an analysis of the Chávez factor in US-Venezuela relations and US imperialism in the region. This includes an analysis of the advances made and limitations of economic policy in Venezuela over the years of Chávez's presidency. It also includes an analysis of the changing forms of the US's imperialist offensive against Venezuela, as well as permutations of the right-wing offensive against the democratically elected regime and the emergence of a middle-class resistance movement. This is followed by an analysis of the fight-back by the forces in support of the Bolivarian Revolution, and an analysis of the advances and the contradictions of government policy as well as the advances made towards socialist transformation. The chapter ends with a review of the 'soft power' and 'hard power' campaigns against the Venezuela government orchestrated by the US imperial state in collusion with the 'private sector' and the so-called 'democratic opposition' within the country.

In the concluding Chapter 12 we review the political dynamics of the imperialist offensive against Venezuela launched by US President Obama. First, we outline some of the critical features of Chávez's political project related to what he described as 'the socialism of the 21st century'. Our main focus here is on the strategic response of the US to this project and the political dynamics of the associated class struggle. Second, we trace out the changes in the correlation of force in the class and anti-imperialist struggle subsequent to Chávez's death and the transition towards the Madero regime. Our concern here is to establish the diverse forms taken by the class struggle and US imperialism in this conjuncture, and the conditions of a failed attempted coup against a democratically elected regime.

PART 1

Rethinking US Imperialism

∵

CHAPTER 1

Imperialism and Capitalism: Rethinking an Intimate Relationship

In this chapter we are concerned with unravelling the intimate relation of imperialism to capitalism and clearing some confusion surrounding it. There are two major problems in the way these two concepts are often understood and used in the literature. In the liberal tradition of political science the projection of imperial power and associated dynamics are generally disconnected from capitalism and its economic dynamics, reducing imperialism to a quest for world domination based on a lust for power or purely geopolitical considerations by the guardians of the national interest in the most powerful countries. On the other hand, in the Marxist tradition of political economy, among world system theorists of the new imperialism there can be found the opposite tendency in which the institutional specificity of the state as an instrument of class power is ignored, and imperialism is reduced to a purely economic dynamic, essentially confusing imperialism with capitalism.

We argue that capitalism and imperialism are intimately connected but engage distinct dynamics in the geoeconomics and the geopolitics of capital that need to be clearly distinguished. We advance this argument in the Latin American context, with reference to the capitalist development process and associated dynamics in their temporal and spatial dimensions. But first we engage several points of dispute among Marxists in regard to imperialism. We then trace out the salient features of imperialism at various stages in the capitalist development process in Latin America.

The Marxist Debate on Imperialism: Points of Dispute

Almost all theories of contemporary imperialism, both in its (neo)Marxist and (neo)liberal variants, lack any but the crudest sociological analyses of the class and political character of the governing groups that direct the imperial state and its policies (Harvey, 2003; Magdoff, 2003; Amin, 2001; Panitch & Leys, 2004; Foster, 2006; Hardt & Negri, 2000). The same is true for contemporary theorizing about the imperial state, which is largely devoid of both institutional and class analysis. Most theorists of imperialism resort to a form of economic reductionism in which the political and ideological dimensions of imperial power are downplayed or ignored, and categories such as 'investments', 'trade' and 'markets' are decontextualized and presented as historically disembodied entities that are comparable across space and time. Changes in the configuration of class relations and associated dynamics are then accounted for in terms of general economic categories such as 'finance', 'manufacturing', 'banking' and 'services' without any analysis of the political economy of capitalist development and class formation, or the nature and sources of financial wealth— illegal drug trade, money laundering, real estate speculation, etc. (Panitch & Leys, 2004). As for the shifts in the political and economic orientation of governing capitalist politicians representing the imperial interests of the dominant class, resulting in the formation of links with other capitalists and imperialist centres with major consequences in the configuration of world power, they are glossed over in favour of abstract accounts of statistical shifts in economic measures of capital flows.

Contemporary theorizing about imperialism generally ignores the sociopolitical and ideological power configurations of imperial policy, as well as the role of international financial institutions such as the World Bank in shaping the institutional and policy framework of the new world order, which not only provides a system of global governance but the rules of engagement for the class war launched by the global capitalist class against labour in its different redoubts of organized resistance.

The focus of most contemporary and recent studies of the dynamics of imperial power is on the projection of military power in the project of protecting and advancing the geopolitical interests of the United States and the geo-economic interests of monopoly capital in the middle east and other zones of capital accumulation, or on the economic operations of the large multinational corporations that dominate the global economy.

In regard to the Middle East the main issue in these studies is the threat presented by radical Islam (and its forces of international terrorism) to accessing one of the world's greatest reservoirs of fossil fuel as well as the imperialist project of world domination. As for the multinational corporations that dominate the global economy, they are viewed by theorists of the 'new imperialism' as the major operational agency of imperial power in the world capitalist system, having displaced the nation-state in its power to advance the project of capital accumulation and the quest for world domination. While theorists and analysts in the liberal tradition continue their concern with the dynamics US foreign policy in the projection of imperial power, and Marxists in the tradition of international political economy and critical development studies continue to concentrate their analysis on the dynamics of state power, the theorists of the 'new imperialism' concentrate almost entirely on the globalizing dynamics of monopoly capital.

Nevertheless, the dynamics of imperial power relations are political as well as economic, and do engage the political apparatus of the state. As for the economic dynamics, as theorized by Lenin in a very different context, they derive from the search by capital for profit and productive investments as well as cheaper sources of raw materials, labour and markets. In terms of these dynamics, particularly those that relate to the fusion of industrial and financial capital, the export of capital and the emergence of monopoly capital, Lenin theorized imperialism as the highest form of capitalism, a manifestation of its fundamental laws of development. However, while liberal theorists of imperialism tend to emphasize the political, and to isolate the political dimension of imperialism from its economic dynamics, viewing imperialism purely in terms of the quest for world domination or the pursuit of geopolitical strategic concerns and the national interest, Marxist theorists following Lenin recognize that the imperial state is a critical agency of capitalist development and a fundamental source of political and military power pursued in the service of capital, to ensure its dominion.

From this Marxist perspective imperialism is understood in terms of its connection to capitalism, and the agency of the imperial state system—the projection of state power—in securing the conditions needed for capital accumulation. Not that there is a consensus on this point—on imperialism as the bearer of capital, an agency of capitalist development. William Robinson, for example, expands on the argument advanced by Hardt and Negri (2000) and other world system theorists that the "class relations of global capitalism are now so deeply internalized within every nation-state that the classical image of imperialism as a relation of external domination is outdated" (Robinson 2007: 7). Although what these class relations might possibly be is unclear, as is the question as to what form imperialism takes under these circumstances (the dominion of capital over labour?), Robinson argues that in effect "national capitalist monopolies" no longer need to "turn to the state for assistance...." The corollary is that the state no longer needs to assume the responsibility for empire-building and the projection of imperial power is no longer concerned with the dynamics of capital accumulation. In Robinson's formulation "the system of nation-states...is no longer the organizing principle of capitalist development, or the primary institutional framework that shapes social and class forces and political dynamics" (Robinson, 2007: 8).

Another assumption made by Robinson and shared by other world system theorists of transnational capital and 'globally integrated enterprise' is that "if we are to get at the root of 21st century global social and political dynamics" the Marxist tradition of imperialism theory based on the classical statements of Lenin and Hilferding should be discarded. Based on the assumption of a world of rival national capitals and economies, conflict among core capitalist powers, the exploitation by these powers of peripheral regions, and "a nation-state centred framework for analysing global dynamics," this theoretical tradition is entirely useless, incapable—according to Robinson—of grasping the fundamental contemporary dynamics of capitalist development (Robinson, 2007: 6–7).

If, as Robinson contends, capital no longer needs the imperial state does it mean that imperialism will wither away, or does it mean, as argued by Klare (2003: 51–52), that it will take the form of "geopolitical competition...the contention between great powers and aspiring great powers for control over territory, resources, and important geographical positions such as ports and harbours...and other sources of wealth and influence." Or does it mean what Robinson and some—including Amin (2001), Arrighi (2005), Foster (2003) and others in the torrent of "new imperialism" literature that has appeared since 2001—have suggested or contend, namely that imperialism is advanced primarily, if not exclusively, in economic form via the agency of transnational (ized) corporations that represent an empire without imperialism, as Hardt and Negri would have it, or capitalism beyond imperialism, as Robinson sees it.

In opposition to this rather reductionist view of imperialism we hold that imperial power is shaped predominantly by the imperial state and its policies that take as a given that what is perceived as in the 'national interest' coincides with the concerns and interests, both economic and political, of the capitalist class—or the 'private sector' in the official discourse. Notwithstanding arguments to the contrary, and taking into consideration both its economic and political dynamics and its actual operations (investments, production, sales), imperialism now as before is clearly designed and works to advance the project of capital accumulation in whatever and in as many ways as possible—to penetrate existing and open up new markets, exploit labour as humanely as possible but as inhumanely as needed, extract surplus value from the direct producers where possible, and access as needed or process raw materials and minerals. Insofar as the capitalist class is concerned the aim and the agenda of its individual and institutional members is to accumulate capital.

As for the imperial state and its agents and agencies, including the World Bank and the agencies of international cooperation for security and development, the agenda is merely to pave the way for capital, to create the conditions needed for economic and social development. In neither case is uneven development of the forces of production and its social conditions (social inequality, unemployment, poverty, social and environmental degradation, etc.) on the agenda. Rather, these conditions are the unintended or 'structural' consequences of capitalist development, and as such inevitable and acceptable costs of progress that need to be managed and, if and where possible, mitigated in the interest of both security and development.

Under these strategic FDI and structural conditions it is illuminating but not particularly useful to measure the impact of imperialism merely in economic terms of the volume of capital inflows (FDI, bank loans, portfolio investments, etc.) and outflows (profit, interest payments, etc.). This is because imperialism is a matter of class and state power, and as such an issue of politics and political economy—issues that are not brought into focus in an analysis of national accounts. At issue here are not only the structural dynamics of uneven capitalist development (the 'development of underdevelopment', in André Gunder Frank's formulation) but social and international relations of power and competition between imperial and domestic classes, between officials and representatives of the imperial state and the state in 'emerging economies' and 'developing societies'.

Under current conditions of rapid economic growth and capitalist development on the southern periphery of the world system, these relations are very dynamic and changing. By no means can they be described today as relations of domination and subordination. In addition, members of the global ruling class (investors, financiers, big bankers, industrialists, etc.) must compete with each other not only in the same sector but in different countries within the world capitalist and imperialist system. This is not only a question of intercapitalist and intra-imperialist rivalry. It is also a development and political issue embedded in the social structure of the capital-labour relation and the economic structure of international relations within the world system. For example, within the dynamic and changing structure of this complex system of class and international relations officials of the states with a subordinate position in the imperial state system will insist on the transfer of technological, management and marketing knowhow to strengthen the ability of their capitalists to compete and for them to make profit, extract rents and serve their 'national interest'.

As for relations of 'domination' and 'dependence' among nations on the lines of a north–south divide the structure of global production, and international relations of domination and subordination, are dynamic and change over time, in part because the geopolitical and economic concerns of the nation-state subject to imperial power leads to a quest for relative autonomy by state officials and politicians in these countries as well as protection of the national interest. Developments along these lines have resulted in qualitative changes in the relations between established imperial and emerging capitalist states. Therefore, theorizing that is focused only on an analysis of inflows and outflows of capital—as if the 'host' country was a 'blank factor'—or a focus on the structure of global production based on a fixed international division of labour, cannot account for the dynamics of capitalist development in countries and regions on the periphery of the system with those at the centre. Nor can this type of economistic theorizing explain dynamic features of the world capitalist system, for example the shift in economic power from North America and Western Europe towards Asia—China and India, to be precise.

Capitalist Development, Class Struggle and Imperialism

In outlining his conception of Historical Materialism, the foundation of Marxism as a social science, Marx had argued that at each stage in the capitalist development process—the development of the forces of production—can be found a corresponding system of class relations and struggle. For Marx this was a matter of fundamental principle arising out of a fundamental conflict between the forces and relations of production. But he could have added that at each stage of capitalist development can also be found both a corresponding and distinct form of class struggle based on the forces of resistance to this advance, as well as imperialism in one form or the other and distinctly understood as the projection of state power in the service of capital—to facilitate its advance in the sphere of international relations and secure its evolution into and as a world system. That is, the projection of state power in the quest for world domination—to establish hegemony over the world system—is a necessary condition of capitalist development. Capitalism requires the state not only to establish the necessary conditions of a capital accumulation process, but to ensure its inevitable expansion—the extension of the capital-labour relation, and its mechanism of economic exploitation (the extraction of surplus value from the labour of the direct producers)— into a world system.

Lenin had theorized this projection of state power in the service of capital as the most advanced stage in the capitalist development process, which includes a phase of 'primitive accumulation' (in which the direct producers are separated from the land and their means of production) and a process by which the small-landholding agricultural producers or peasant farmers are proletarianized, converted and made over into a working class. As Lenin saw it imperialism so conceived (as the 'highest stage of capitalism') featured:

1.   The fusion of industrial and financial capital;
2.   The export of capital in the search for profitable outlets overseas;

3.   The territorial division (and colonization) of the world by European capitalist powers within the institutional and policy framework of *Pox Britannica* (the hegemony and dominion of the United States); and

4.   An international division of labour based on an international exchange of primary commodities for goods manufactured in the centre of the system. These features encompassed an economic dynamic of capital accumulation, but this dynamic and the economic structure of this system evidently required and was secured politically with the projection of state power, including military force.

Lenin astutely identified the fundamental structural features of the world capitalist system at this stage of development. However, it was misleading to characterise it as 'imperialism' in that the projection of imperial class-based state power was a distinct feature of capitalism in an earlier phase in the evolution of capitalism as a world system, namely mercantilism, a system in which merchant's capital was accumulated through the expropriation of natural resources as much as exploitation of labour as well as state-sanctioned and regulated international trade. And imperialism was also a distinct feature and an adjunct to the capital accumulation process in later periods of capitalist development, as discussed below.

Imperialism in an Era of State-led Capitalist Development (1950–80)

In the wake of the Second World War the United States emerged as an economic super-power, in command of at least one-half of world industrial capacity and up to 80 percent of financial resources or capital for productive investment. Having replaced Great Britain as the leader of what were then described as the 'forces of freedom', and to counter a perceived potential threat from its Russian war-time ally, now the USSR, which had also emerged from the war as an industrial power but representing an alternative socialist system for expanding the forces of national production, the US led the construction of a capitalist world order in the form of the Bretton Woods system (Bienefeld, 2013; Frieden, 2006; Peet, 2003).

This system included two international financial institutions—the International Monetary Fund (IMF) and what would become the World Bank—as well as a General Agreement on Tariffs and Trade (GATT), an institutional mechanism for negotiating agreements in the direction of free trade that would eventually emerge as the World Trade Organization (WTO). This system

provided a set of rules used to govern relations of international trade—rules
that favoured the operations and expansion of what had emerged as a complex
of predominantly US-based multinational corporations and thus the hegemony of US capital. However, it also provided the institutional framework of
a project of international cooperation with the nation-building and development efforts of a large number of countries that were engaged in a war of
national liberation and independence from the colonial powers that had
subjugated them for so long.

In this context capitalism engaged a process of productive and social
transformation—the transformation of an economic system based on agriculture and an agrarian society and social system based on pre-capitalist relations of production into a modern industrial capitalist system based on
capitalist relations of production, or wage labour. The basic mechanism of
this transformation was exploitation of the 'unlimited supply of surplus rural
labour' released in the capitalist development of the forces of production in
the agricultural sector (Lewis, 1954).

This process of capitalist development, and the associated process of productive and social transformation, can be traced out in different countries and
regions at different points of time. But the process unfolded in different ways,
engaging different forces of change and resistance in the class struggle, in the
countries at the centre of the system and those on the periphery. First, in
peripheral regions (Latin America and the Caribbean, parts of Asia and Africa)
were found countries that were struggling to escape colonial subjugation and
imperialist exploitation as well as class rule. Governments in these countries
were in a position to choose between a capitalist and a socialist path towards
nation-building and economic development, a situation that called for a strategic and political response from the guardians of the capitalist world order.
The response: to assist the development process in these countries—for the
states in the developed countries and the international organizations and
financial institutions to provide technical and financial assistance (foreign aid,
in the lexicon of international development) to the undeveloped and less
developed countries on the periphery of the system. In this context it is possible to view the idea and the entire enterprise of international development
through the lens of imperialist theory—as a distinct form of imperialism
(Petras & Veltmeyer 2005a; Veltmeyer, 2005).

There is considerable evidence to suggest that the most powerful states
within the institutional framework and system of what can now be described as
Pax Americana (the hegemony and dominion of the United States) in the post-
war era of capitalism began to deploy the idea of development as a means of
facilitating the entry into and the operations of capital in peripheral countries

in the development of their forces of production and the accumulation of capital in the process. In this context diplomatic pressure and military force were deployed as required or dictated by circumstance, but only secondarily, i.e., as a strategy and tactic of last resort. Thus the projection of military force to achieve the geopolitical objectives of the imperial state used predominantly by the US state in the 1950s and early 60s to maintain imperial order in its backyard—Guatemala (1954), Cuba (1961), the Dominican Republic (1963, 1965), Brazil (1964), Guyana (1953) and Chile (1973). After the military coup engineered in Chile this strategy of direct military invention and sponsored military coups gave way to a war by proxy, which entailed the financing of both the policy-making apparatus regarding social and development programs and the repressive apparatus (the armed forces) deployed by its Latin American allies.

In the same way as the imperialist project of International Cooperation for Development was used in the 1950s and subsequently to discourage those countries seeking to liberate themselves from the yoke of colonialism from turning towards a socialist path towards national development, the US government as an imperialist state resorted to the idea of 'development' as a means of preventing another Cuba and turning the 'rural poor' away from the option of revolutionary change provided by the revolutionary movements that had emerged in Latin America (Petras & Veltmeyer, 2007a).

The class struggle at the time (the 1950–60s) assumed two main forms. The first was as a land struggle waged by the peasantry, most of which had been either proletarianized (rendered landless) or semi-proletarianized (forced to take the labour path out of rural poverty). Many of the proletarianized and impoverished peasants, separated from their means of production and livelihoods, chose to migrate and take the development path of labour staked out by the World Bank (2008) and the modernization theorists of 'development'. However, many others chose to resist rather than adjust to the forces of capitalist development operating on them, to join the revolutionary social movements in the form of 'armies of national liberation'. But by means of a three-pronged strategy and policy of (i) land reform (expropriation and redistributing land to the tiller), (ii) integrated rural development (technical and financial assistance to the small landholding peasant or family farmer), and (iii) repression (use of the iron fist of armed force hidden within the velvet glove of integrated development), the imperial state, via its allies in the local states, managed to defeat or 'bring to ground' the social movements engaged in the land struggle. The one exception was the Revolutionary Armed Forces of Colombia (FARC), which continues to be a powerful force of resistance against the incursions of capital in Colombia to this today.

The second major form of the class struggle at the time had to do with the capital-labour relation, and engaged the working class in an organized labour movement against capital and the state for higher wages and improved working conditions. This struggle was part of a global class war launched by capital in the 1970s in the context of a systemic crisis of overproduction (Crouch & Pizzorno 1978). One of a number of weapons deployed in this war was the power of the state, via its policymaking role, to fatally weaken the labour movement in its organizational capacity to negotiate collective contracts for higher wages and reduce the share of labour in national incomes.

This approach was particularly effective in Latin America, where the imperial state, via the international organizations and financial institutions at its command, was in a position to impose market-friendly 'structural' reforms on the labour movement. As a result of these reforms in the capital-labour relation the share of labour (wages) in the distribution of national income in many Latin American countries was reduced by as much as 50 percent. The purchasing power of the average wage in Argentina, for example, was less in 2010—after six years of economic recovery and export-led rapid economic growth—than it was in 1970. The loss in the purchasing power or value of wages was particularly sharp at the level of the government-regulated minimum wage, which the World Bank throughout the 1980s and 1990s tirelessly argued was the major cause of low income, poverty and informalization in the region. For example, in Mexico, the country that followed the strictures of Washington and the World Bank in regard to deregulating the labour market, from 1980 to 2010, over three decade of neoliberalism, the minimum wage lost up to 77 percent of its value (Romero, 2014).

While the imperial state was indirectly engaged in the land struggle via a program of international cooperation that was implemented by the Latin American state but financed by officials of the imperial state, imperialism vis-à-vis the labour movement took the form of an armed struggle against "subversives" (a broad urban coalition of forces of resistance mobilized by the 'political left'). The struggle was led by the armed forces of the Latin American state, particularly in Brazil and the southern cone of south America (Chile, Bolivia, Argentina, Uruguay), although financed by and (indirectly) under the strategic command of the US, and operating within the framework of an ideology and doctrine (the National Security Doctrine) fabricated within the ideological apparatus of the imperial state. By the end of the 1970s this movement had also suffered defeat, its forces in disarray and disarticulated under the combined weight of state repression and forces generated in the capitalist development process. With the defeat of both major fronts of the class struggle and popular movement, with the resurgence of the Right in the form of a counterrevolutionary political movement and an ideology of free market capitalism, the stage was set for a major turnaround in the correlation of opposing forces in the class struggle. Imperialism would have an important role to play in this process.

Imperialism and Capitalism in an Era of Neoliberal Globalization (1980–2000)

Neoliberalism as an ideology of free market capitalism and a doctrine of policy reform in the direction of free market capitalism—'the new economic model', as it was termed in Latin America (Bulmer-Thomas, 2006)—was some four decades in the making, manufactured by a neoliberal thought collective put together by Van der Hayek (Mirowski & Plehwe, 2009). It was not until the early 1980s that the necessary conditions for bringing these ideologues to state power, i.e., in a position to influence and dictate policy, were available or otherwise created. These conditions included an unresolved systemic crisis of overproduction, a fiscal crisis in the North and an impending debt crisis in the South, and the defeat of the popular movement in the class struggle over land and labour.

Under these conditions the imperial state, via its international organizations and financial institutions, mobilized its diverse powers and forces so as to mobilize the forces needed to reactivate the capital accumulation process. The main problem here—from a capitalist and imperialist perspective—was how to liberate the 'forces of freedom' (to quote from George W. Bush's 2012 *National Security Report*) from the regulatory constraints of the welfare-development state. The solution: a program of 'structural reform' in macroeconomic policy (the vaunted 'structural adjustment program' constructed by economists at the World Bank and the IMF) within the framework of a Washington Consensus (Williamson 1990).

By 1990 all but four major Latin American states had succumbed or joined the Washington Consensus in regard to a program that was imposed on them as a conditionality of aid and access to capital markets to renegotiate the external debt. And in the 1990s, in a third cycle and generation of neoliberal reforms, the governing neoliberal regimes in three of these states—Argentina, Brazil, Peru—had followed suit, generating conditions that would facilitate a massive inflow of productive capital in the form of Foreign Direct Investment (FDI) as well as a substantial inflow of unproductive or fictitious capital seeking to purchase the assets of existing lucrative but privatised state enterprises (Petras & Veltmeyer 2004). What followed was what has been described as the 'Golden

Age of US Imperialism' (viz. the facilitated entry and productive operations of large-scale profit- and market-seeking investment capital), as well as the formation of powerful peasant and indigenous social movements to resist the neoliberal policy offensive and protest the destructive impact of neoliberal policies on their livelihoods and communities—movements no longer directed against the big landlords or corporate capital and agribusiness but against the policies of the local and imperial state (Petras & Veltmeyer 2005a, 2009, 2013).

By the end of the decade these movements had successfully challenged the hegemony of neoliberalism in the region as an economic model and policy agenda. What resulted was a 'red' and 'pink' tide of regime change—a turn to the left in national politics and the formation of regimes oriented towards the 'socialism of the 21st century' (Venezuela, Bolivia, Ecuador) or a post-Washington Consensus on the need for a more inclusive form of development—inclusionary state activism (Argentina, Brazil, Chile, Uruguay). The states formed in the so-called 'red wave' of regime change constituted a new anti-imperialist front in the struggle against US imperialist intervention—another front to the one formed by the social movements in their resistance and direct action.

At the level of national politics the main issue was US intervention in Latin America affairs, including the funding of opposition groups in Venezuela, the economic blockade against Cuba, and the attempt by the US government to orchestrate a free trade agreement, first between the US and both Canada and Mexico, and then a continent-wide agreement (FTAA, or ALCA in its Spanish acronym). The US regime was successful in the first instance, but failed miserably in the second—having encountered powerful forces of resistance in the popular sector of many states, as well as widespread opposition within the political class and elements of the ruling class and the governing regime in countries such as Brazil.

Both imperialism and the anti-imperialist struggle in this conjuncture of capitalist development assumed different forms in different countries, but Colombia was unique in that the most powerful movement in the 1960s land struggle had never been defeated. With land still at the centre of the class struggle the existence and large-scale operations of what we might term narco-capitalism allowed the US imperial state to move with armed force against the major remaining obstacle to the capitalist development of agriculture in Colombia—to make the countryside safe for US capital—under the façade of a drug war waged by the government against the manufacturers of cocaine and the narco-trafficking. The mechanism of this imperial offensive was Plan Colombia, a US military and diplomatic aid initiative aimed at combating Colombian drug cartels and left-wing insurgent groups in Colombian territory.

The plan was originally conceived between 1998 and 1999 by the administrations of Colombian President Andrés Pastrana Arango and US President Bill Clinton, as an anti-cocaine strategy but with the aim of ending the Colombian armed conflict and making the countryside safe for US capital (Vilar & Cottle, 2011).

A third front in the imperialist offensive against the forces of resistance in the popular sector involved international cooperation and the agencies of international development. The strategy employed by these agencies was the same as successfully used in the 1960s and 1970s to dampen the fires of revolutionary ferment in the countryside: to offer the dispossessed peasants and the rural poor a non-confrontational alternative to social mobilization and direct collective action (Veltmeyer, 2005). The strategy had a different outcome in different countries. In Ecuador, home to the most powerful indigenous movement in the region—the Confederation of Indigenous Nationalities of Ecuador (CONAIE)—the strategy of ethnodevelopment orchestrated by the World Bank and the IDB resulted in dividing and weakening the movement, undermining its capacity to mobilize the forces of popular resistance (Petras and Veltmeyer, 2009). For example, in just a few years Antonio Vargas, President of CONAIE and leader of the major indigenous uprising of the twentieth century, had been converted into the head of one of the most powerful NGOs in the region, with the capacity to disburse funds for local development microprojects and a resulting diminution in the power of CONAIE to mobilize the forces of resistance. By 2007, when Rafael Correa, a left-leaning economist, came to power as the country's president, the indigenous movement led by CONAIE was but a shadow of its former self, allowing the political left, in the form of Correa's Citizens Movement, to push CONAIE and the indigenous movement aside in the political project of a 'Citizen's Revolution'.

The outcome was rather different in Bolivia, a paradigmatic case of anti-neoliberalism and anti-imperialism in the current conjuncture of the class struggle. Whereas the popular movement in Ecuador had been pushed aside in the capture of the instruments of state power by the Political Left, in Bolivia an extended process of class conflict and mass mobilization was the prelude and condition of the Political Left's rise to power in the form of the Movement Towards Socialism (MAS). The water and gas 'wars', clashes with the military, and the dismissal of several corrupt and neoliberal governments, were all part of a cocktail that allowed for the emergence of a new political 'actor' or instrument in the form of MAS, and the rise to power of Evo Morales, which was backed by the 'social movements'—that encompassed both communities of indigenous 'peasants', a rural proletariat of landless workers, and diverse sectors of the organized working class (Dangl, 2007; Farthing & Kohl, 2006; Webber, 2010).

CHAPTER 2

Imperialism in an Era of Extractive Capitalism

The neoliberal 'structural reform' agenda of the Washington Consensus facilitated a massive inflow of capital in the form of foreign direct investments directed towards non-traditional manufacturing, financial and high-tech information-rich services, and natural resource extraction. The 1990s saw a six-fold increase in the inflows of FDI in the first four years of the decade and then another sharp increase from 1996 to 2001; in fewer than ten years the foreign capital accumulated by MNCs in the region had tripled (ECLAC, 2012: 71) while profits soared. Saxe-Fernandez, a well-known Mexico-based political economist, determined that over the course of the decade the inflow of FDI had netted enormous profits, reflected in the net outflow of US$100 billion over the entire decade (Saxe-Fernández & Núñez, 2001).

Another major inflow occurred in the first decade of the new millennium in the context of a major expansion in the worldwide demand for natural resources and a consequent primary commodities boom in South America (Ocampo, 2007). As shown by data presented in Table 1 this boom in the export of primary commodities in the energy sector of fossil and bio-fuels (oil and gas), as well as minerals and metals, and agrofood products primarily affected

TABLE 1   *Exports of primary products (percentage of total exports)*

	2004	2006	2008	2011
Argentina	71.2	68.2	69.1	68.3
Bolivia	86.7	89.8	92.8	95.5
Brazil	47.0	49.5	55.4	66.2
Chile	86.8	89.0	88.0	89.2
Colombia	62.9	64.4	68.5	82.5
Ecuador	90.7	90.4	91.3	92.0
Mexico	20.2	24.3	27.1	29.3
Peru	83.1	88.0	86.6	89.3
Venezuela	86.9	89.6	92.3	95.5
Latin America	46.2	51.3	56.7	60.9

SOURCE: ECLAC, 2012.

South America, which led a worldwide trend towards the (re)primarization of exports from the periphery of the system and the expansion of extractive capitalism.

The main targets and destination points for FDI in Latin America over the past two decades have been services (particularly banking and finance) and the natural resources sector: the exploration, extraction, and exploitation of fossil and biofuel sources of energy, precious metals and industrial minerals, and agrofood products. In the previous era of state-led development FDI had predominantly served as a means of financing the capitalist development of industry and a process of 'productive transformation' (technological conversion and modernization), which was reflected in the geoeconomics of global capital and the dynamics of capital flows at the time. However, the new world order and two generations of neoliberal reforms dramatically improved conditions for capital, opening up in Latin America the market for goods manufactured in the North (the US, Canada, and Europe) and providing greater opportunities for resource-seeking capital—consolidating the role of Latin America as a source and supplier of natural resources and exporter of primary commodities, a role that is reflected in the flows of productive investment in the region away towards the extractive industries (see Table 2).

At the turn into the new millennium the service sector accounted for almost half of FDI inflows, but data presented by ECLAC (2012: 50) point towards a steady and increasing flow of capital towards the natural resources sector in South America, especially mining, where Canadian capital took a predominant position, accounting for up to 70 percent of FDI in this sector (Arellano, 2010). Over the course of the first decade in the new millennium the share of 'resource seeking' capital in total FDI increased from 10 to 30 percent. In 2006 the inflow of 'resource-seeking' investment capital grew by 49 percent to reach

TABLE 2   *Percentage distribution of FDI by sector in Latin America*

	2000	2001	2002	2003	2004	2005	2006	2007	2008
Resources	10	12	12	11	12	13	12	15	30
Manufacturing	25	26	38	35	38	37	36	35	22
Services	60	61	51	48	46	48	51	49	47

SOURCE: ADAPTED FROM ARELLANO (2010, TABLE 2), BASED ON ECLAC DATA.

US$59 billion, which exceeded the total FDI inflows of any year since economic liberalization began in the 1990s (UNCTAD, 2007: 53).

Despite the global financial and economic crisis at the time, FDI flows towards Latin America and the Caribbean reached a record high in 2008 (US$128.3 billion), an extraordinary development considering that FDI flows worldwide at the time had shrunk by at least 15 percent. This countercyclical trend signalled the continuation of the primary commodities boom and the steady expansion of resource-seeking capital in the region.

The rapid expansion in the flow of FDI towards Latin America in the 1990s reflected the increased opportunities for capital accumulation provided by the neoliberal policy regimes in the region, but in the new millennium conditions for capitalist development had radically changed. In this new context, which included a major realignment of economic power and relations of trade in the world market, and the growth in both the demand for and the prices of primary commodities, the shift of FDI towards Latin America signified a major change in the geo-economics and geopolitics of global capital. Flows of FDI into Latin America from 2000 to 2007 for the first time exceeded those that went to North America only surpassed by Europe and Asia. And the global financial crisis brought about an even more radical change in the geoeconomics of global capital in regard to both its regional distribution (increased flows to Latin America) and sectoral distribution (concentration in the extractive sector). In 2005, the 'developing' and 'emerging' economies attracted only 12 percent of global flows of productive capital but by 2010, against a background of a sharp decline in these flows, these economies were the destination point for over 50 percent of global FDI flows (CEPAL, 2012). In the same year FDI flows into Latin America increased by 34.6 percent, well above the growth rate in Asia, which was only 6.7 percent (UNCTAD, 2012: 52–54).

The flow of productive capital into Latin America has been fuelled by two factors: high prices for primary commodities, which attracted "natural-resource-seeking investment," and the economic growth of the South American sub-region, which encouraged market-seeking investment. This flow of FDI was concentrated in four South American countries—Argentina, Brazil, Chile, and Colombia—which accounted for 89 percent of the sub-region's total inflows. The extractive industry in these countries, particularly mining, absorbed the greatest share of these inflows. For example, in 2009, Latin America received 26 percent of global investments in mineral exploration (Sena-Fobomade, 2011). Together with the expansion of oil and gas projects, mineral extraction constitutes the single most important source of export revenues for most countries in the region.

The New Geopolitics of Capital in Latin America

As noted, a wave of resource-seeking FDI was a major feature of the political economy of global capitalist development at the turn into the first decade of the new millennium. Another was the demise of neoliberalism as an economic doctrine and model—at least in South America, where powerful social movements successfully challenged this model. Over the past decade a number of governments in this sub-region, in riding a wave of anti-neoliberal sentiment generated by these movements experienced a process of regime change—a tilt towards the left and what has been described as 'progressive extractivism' (Gudynas, 2010).

The political victories of these democratically elected 'progressive' regimes opened a new chapter in the class struggle and the anti-imperialist movement, notwithstanding the fact that the wide embrace of resource-seeking extractive capital has generated deep paradoxes for those progressive regimes in the region committed to addressing the inequality predicament and conditions of environmental degradation that are fast reaching crisis proportions as a result of the operations of extractive capital.

Some political leaders and social movements in this context speak of revolution in the context of moving towards "the socialism of the 21st century"—Venezuela's 'Bolivarian" Revolution, Bolivia's 'democratic and cultural revolution', and Ecuador's 'Citizens' Revolution'—and, together with several governments that have embraced the new developmentalism (the search for a more inclusive form of development), these regimes have indeed taken some steps in the direction of poverty reduction and social inclusion, using the additional fiscal revenues derived from resource rents to this purpose. Yet, like their more conservative neighbours—regimes such as Mexico and Colombia, committed to both neoliberalism and an alliance with 'imperialism'—the left-leaning progressive regimes in the region find themselves entangled in a maze of renewed dependence on natural resource extraction (the 'new extractivism') and primary commodity exports ('reprimarization'). Further, as argued by Gudynas, this new 'progressive' extractivism is much like the old 'classical' extractivism in its destruction of both the environment and livelihoods, and its erosion of the territorial rights and sovereignty of indigenous communities most directly affected by the operations of extractive capital, which continues to generate relations of intense social conflict.

Despite the use by 'progressive' centre-left governments of resource rents as a mechanism of social inclusion and direct cash transfers to the poor, it is not clear whether they are able to pursue revolutionary measures in their efforts to bring about a more inclusive and sustainable form of development, or a deepening of political and economic democratization, allowing the people to 'live well' (*vivir bien*), while at the same time continuing to toe the line of extractive capital and its global assault on nature and livelihoods. The problem here is twofold. One is a continuing reliance of these left-leaning post-neoliberal regimes (indeed, all but Venezuela) on neoliberalism ('structural reforms') at the level of macroeconomic public policy. The other problem relates to the so-called 'new extractivism' based on 'inclusionary state activism' as well as the continued reliance on FDI—and thus the need to strike a deal with global capital in regard to sharing the resource rents derived from the extraction process. The problem here is that in this relation of global capital to the local state the former is dominant and has the power, which is reflected in the tendency of the governments and policy regimes formed by the new Latin American Left, even those like Ecuador and Peru that have taken a 'radical populist form', to take the side of global capital (the multinational mining companies) in their relation of conflict with the communities that are directly affected by the extractive operations of these companies (see the various country case studies in Veltmeyer & Petras, 2014).

Another indicator of the relation of dependency between global extractive capital and the Latin American state is the inability of the latter to regulate the former and the extraordinary profits that are made by the companies that operate in the extractive sector. It is estimated that given very low or, as in the case of Mexico, non-existent royalty rates and the typically lax and low tax regime on the exportation of minerals and minerals—a major factor in the export regime of a number of countries in the region (particularly Chile, Bolivia, Colombia, Peru)—over 70 percent of the value of these minerals and metals on the global market is appropriated by different groups of capitalists in the global production chain. For example, *Financial Times* reported on April 18, 2013 that from 2002 to 2008, during the height of the primary commodities boom, the biggest commodity traders harvested US$250 billion dollars in profits on their 'investments'. At the same time, given the capital intensity of production in the extractive sector it is estimated that workers generally received less than ten percent of the value of the extracted resources. Typically, the benefits of economic growth brought about by the export of Latin America's wealth of natural resources are externalised, while the exceedingly high social and environmental costs are internalized, borne by the communities most directly affected by the operations of extractive capital (Clark 2002; Veltmeyer and Petras, 2014).

The continued reliance on the neoliberal model of structural reform within the framework of a post-Washington Consensus on the need to bring the state back into the development process, together with the turn towards and a continued reliance on extractive capital ('resource-seeking' FDI), constitute serious economic, social and political problems for Latin American states seeking to break away from the dictates of global capital and the clutches of imperial power. However, the turn of the State in Latin America towards regulation in regard to the operations of extractive capital, as well as the growing popular resistance and opposition to their destructive and negative socioenvironmental impacts of these operations, also constitute major problems for global capital. The difference is that the capitalists and companies that operate in the extractive sector are able to count on the support and massive resources and powers of the imperialist state.

In regard to the issue of regulation the states and international organizations that constitute imperialism have been able to mobilize their considerable resources and exercise their extensive powers to create a system of corporate self-regulation in the form of a doctrine of a Corporate Social Responsibility (Gordon, 2010; MiningWatch Canada, 2009). With this doctrine the Latin American states that have turned to or resorted to a strategy of natural resource development have been under tremendous pressure to allow the companies that operate in the extractive sector to regulate themselves. As for the issue of the resource wars and social conflicts that have surrounded the operations of extractive capital, particularly in the mining sector, over the past two decades the imperial state has come to the rescue of extractive capital time and time again. In this regard the Canadian state has been particularly aggressive in its unconditional and relentless support of the Canadian mining companies that dominate foreign investments in the industry—accounting for upwards of 70 percent of the capital invested in this subsector in Latin America. The support of the Canadian government for these companies, via diplomatic pressures exerted on Latin American governments in favour of corporate social responsibility, financial support and assistance in overcoming the widespread resistance to the extractive operations of Canadian mining companies in Latin America, has gone so far as to place the entire apparatus of Canada's foreign aid program at the disposal of these companies (Engler, 2012; Gordon, 2010; Webber, 2008).

Conclusion: Theses on the Imperialism of the 21st Century

The conclusions that we have drawn from our analysis of economic and political developments in Latin America over the past two decades can be summed up in the form of twelve theses:

1. The dynamic forces of capitalist development are both global in their reach and uneven in their outcomes. Furthermore the capital accumulation process engages both the geo-economics of capital—the advance of capital in time and place—and the agency of the imperial state in facilitating this advance: the geopolitics of capital.

2. Class analysis provides an essential tool for grasping the changing economic and political dynamics of imperial power in the various conjunctures of capitalist development. It allows us to trace out different stages in the development of the forces of production and the corresponding relations of production and dynamics of class struggle. These dynamics, which we have traced out in the Latin American context, are both internal and international, implicating both the capital-labour relation and a North-South divide in the world capitalist system.

3. Whereas in the 1980s imperialism was called upon to remove the obstacles to the advance of capital and to facilitate the flow of productive investment into the region in the new millennium it has been called upon to assist capital in its relation of conflict with the communities directly affected by the operations of extractive capital, as well as cope with the broader resistance movement.

4. The shift in world economic power in the new millennium, and the new geoeconomics of capital in the region, have significant implications for US imperialism and US-Latin American relations, reducing both the scope of US state power and the capacity of Washington to dictate policy or dominate economic and political relations. This is reflected *inter alia* in the formation of CELAC, a new political organization of states that explicitly excludes the United States and Canada, the two imperial states on the continent.

5. The new millennium, in conditions of a heightened global demand for natural resources, the demise of neoliberalism as an economic model and a number of popular upheavals and mass mobilizations, released new forces of resistance and a dynamic process of regime change.

6. The centre-left regimes that came to power under these conditions called for public ownership of society's wealth of natural resources, the stratification and renationalization of privatized firms, the regulation of extractive capital in regard to its negative impact on livelihoods and the environment (mother nature), and the inclusionary activism of the state in securing a progressive redistribution of wealth and income. As in the 1990s, the fundamental agency of this political development process were the social movements with their social base in the indigenous communities of peasant farmers and a rural proletariat of landless or

near-landless workers. These movements mobilized the forces of resistance against both the neoliberal agenda of 'structural reform' in macroeconomic policy, the negative socio-environmental impact of extractive capitalism, and the projection of imperial power in the region.

7.   These forces of change and resistance did not lead to a break with capitalism. Instead some of 'centre-left' regimes took power and, benefitting from high commodity prices, proceeded to stimulate an economic recovery and with it an improvement in the social condition of the population (extreme poverty). But the policies of these regimes led to the demobilization of the social movements and a normalization of relations with Washington, albeit with greater state autonomy. In this context Washington in this period lost allies and collaborator clients in Argentina, Brazil, Uruguay, Bolivia, Venezuela and Ecuador—and, subsequently faced strong opposition throughout the region. But Washington retained or regained clients in Panama, Costa Rica, Honduras, Colombia, Peru, Mexico and Chile. Of equal importance, the centre-left regimes that emerged in the region stabilized capitalism, holding the line or blocking any move to reverse the privatization policy of earlier regimes or to move substantively towards what President Hugo Chávez termed "the socialism of the 21st century."

8.   The fluidity of US power relations with Latin America is a product of the continuities and changes that have unfolded in Latin America. Past hegemony continues to weigh heavily but the future augurs a continued decline. Barring major regime breakdowns in Latin America, the probability is of greater divergences in policy and a sharpening of existing contradictions between the spouting of rhetoric and political practice on the political left.

9.   In the sphere of military influence and political intervention, collaborators of the US suffered major setbacks in their attempted coups in Venezuela (2002, 2003) and Bolivia (2008), and in Ecuador with the closing of the military base in Manta; but they were successful in Honduras (2009). The US secured a military base agreement with Colombia, a major potential military ally against Venezuela, in 2009. However, with a change in the presidency in Colombia, Washington suffered a partial setback with the reconciliation between President Chávez and Santos. A lucrative US$8 billion trade agreement with Venezuela trumped Colombia's military-base agreements with Washington.

10. It is unlikely that the Latin American countries that are pursuing an extractivist strategy of national development based on the extraction of natural resources and the export of primary commodities will be able

to sustain the rapid growth in the context of contradictions that are endemic to capitalism but that are sharper and have assumed particularly destructive form with extractive capitalism.

11. The destructive operations of extractive capital, facilitated and supported by the imperial state generated powerful forces of resistance. These forces are changing the contours of the class struggle, which today is focused less on the land and the labour struggle than on the negative socio-environmental impacts of extractive capital and the dynamics of imperialist plunder and natural resource-grabbing.

12. The correlation of forces in the anti-imperialist struggle is unclear and changing, but it is evident that the United States has lost both power and influence. Taken together these historical continuities argue for greater caution in assuming a permanent shift in imperial power relations with Latin America. Nevertheless, there are powerful reasons to consider the decline in US power as a long-term and irreversible trend.

Extractive Imperialism and the Post-Neoliberal State

The purpose of this chapter is to put into perspective, if not settle, an ongoing debate about the meaning and significance of what has been viewed as a 'red' or 'pink' tide of progressive regimes in Latin America in the first decade of the 21st century. More than a few observers and analysts have viewed this development as the beginning of the end of the neoliberal era, auguring a new world of social justice and sustainable development. Some have gone so far as to see in them the makings of a more authentic form of socialism—the 'socialism of the 21st century' as Hugo Chávez would have it. Others have been quick to point out that these 'post-neoliberal' regimes are not what they seem or how they are presented by many leftist observers and analysts.

For one thing, these regimes have mostly turned towards natural resource extraction and primary commodity exports as a national development strategy, which relates to a particularly predatory and backward form of capitalism dominant in the 19th century (Cypher, 2010: 565–638). For another, due to the diverse pitfalls of this strategy and the dependence of the state on the bearers of 'extractive capital', these 'progressive' or 'post-neoliberal' regimes are unable to deliver on their promise of greater social inclusion and equity in the distribution of the society's wealth and the social product, and a development that is socially inclusive, sustainable and protective of the global commons. This chapter brings a Marxist perspective on capitalist development to these debates.

The Politics and Economics of Natural Resource Development

In a recent book on 'the study of natural resource extraction in resource-rich countries', the former director of development research at the World Bank, Paul Collier, and the director of the Oxford Centre for the Analysis of Resource Rich Economies, Anthony J. Venables, conclude that 'often plunder, rather than prosperity, has become the norm in the industry' (Collier & Venables, 2011). In line with the post-neoliberal agenda of improving social outcomes through better governance, Collier and Venables set out to improve the management of natural resources in developing countries by 'highlight[ing] the key principles that need to be followed to avoid distortion and dependence'.

But they do this by narrowly focusing on the decision-making process in the management of natural resources while ignoring the capitalist and imperialist dynamics that generate the distortion and dependence in the first place.

A more sophisticated approach to the economics and politics of natural resource extraction is based on the view that it has to do primarily with economic growth strategies and the politics of international trade, rather than resource pillage and labour exploitation, or even environmental degradation and class conflict. In this view, governing regimes in the developing countries (especially in Latin America) have responded to the growing demand for primary commodities (i.e. raw materials, food products, minerals) and shifted their economic growth strategies to the extraction of natural resources, in response to the high prices for primary commodities on the world market (ECLAC, 2010). The result is a reversion to a trade structure based on the export of these commodities, which, Latin American structuralists had warned, is disadvantageous to countries on the periphery. This growth strategy in Latin America was abandoned when the world market collapsed during the Great Depression in favour of an alternative economic growth strategy based on state-led import-substitution industrialization (ISI). This strategy was designed to overcome what development economists have theorized as a 'resource curse'—i.e. rather than the extraction and exploitation of a country's abundant natural resources, such as minerals and fuels, leading to development more often than not it results in underdevelopment and the impoverishment of the deemed 'owners' of these resources (Acosta, 2009; Norman, 2001).

In the 'new world order' established in the 1980s under conditions of an ongoing overproduction crisis, widespread fiscal crises in the north and an emerging debt crisis in the south, the ISI strategy fell victim to the forces of neoliberal globalization. Under the impact of these forces Latin America reverted to a development strategy based on the export of primary commodities, as state enterprises were privatized and tariffs were lowered, forcing national industries to compete with imports from transnational corporations. The IMF imposed the discipline of free market capitalism on Latin American governments, many of which reverted to a commodity export strategy so as to capture the 'comparative advantages' derived from their wealth of natural resources in order to service their foreign debts. But, with the exception of Chile, this strategy failed to activate the capital accumulation and economic growth process in the region—or at least not until the new millennium when conditions in the global economy changed with the rise of China, and, to a lesser extent, India, and other 'emerging markets'. With favourable commodity prices in the 2000s vis-à-vis the price of imported goods and services, Latin American economies accelerated their shift back toward a growth strategy based on the primarization of exports. Deploying this 'reprimarization' strategy, state officials renewed their focus on the economics of resource extraction, but this time with a better regulatory framework and management of the country's resource extraction industry. This is the so-called 'new extractivism' based on 'post-neoliberal governance' in which renewed state activism is combined with a resource-based growth strategy in order increase social inclusion.

As for the presumed state activism in this post-neoliberal strategy—dubbed 'inclusionary state activism' by Arbix and Martin (2010), a feature of the 'new developmentalism'—it is predicated on the idea that rather than constituting a curse, the exploitation of natural resources such as minerals and hydrocarbons (oil and gas) could be a blessing, generating easily taxable rents that could be used to finance social development. Cases in point: Argentina, Chile and Venezuela, as well as Bolivia and Ecuador, have each witnessed in recent years a major upsurge in primary export-led growth and associated increased fiscal revenues. Thus, Haber and Menaldo (2012), with reference to the increased social development program spending related to this upsurge, conclude that 'natural resources are neither a curse nor a blessing'. Reprimarization combined with increased social spending for poverty reduction typifies the development strategy and policies pursued by the post-neoliberal state in Latin America.

The post-neoliberal literature on resource-based growth and the regulatory state views resource extraction as a matter of the state's capacity to regulate the operations of the mining and oil companies, to exact a better deal from these agencies of global capital, and to hold these companies accountable for the environmental and social impacts of their operations. Exponents of this approach define the issue of resource extraction as a matter of 'politics'— as in the 'politics' or 'political ecology' of natural resource extraction' and the 'international political economy' of resource extraction (Gudynas, 2010).

Here there are two fundamental issues. One relates to the 'economic imperatives [that] compel elites to adapt market opening strategies in response to pressures of global competitiveness' (ibid.). The other is the mechanisms of this adaptation, in these accounts, which are 'development policies [that are]... engineered to cushion the impacts of neoliberal reforms'. As a result, the only cases of 'successful' adaption found by Collier and Venables are based on the transformation of the neoliberal into a post-neoliberal state, in line with a new generation of development theorists and self-styled 'international political economists'. Thus, the 'new extractivism' is predicated on a more interventionist state and regulatory regime, and a post-neoliberal policy agenda (i.e. a softening the social costs of extractivist imperialism)—in what the exponents of this approach term 'post-neoliberal governance', which has both a national and global dimension.

At issue in this debate is the nature and role of the state in the development process—i.e., the transformation of a state that is a handmaiden of foreign investment and capitalist development into a post-neoliberal state, which is more interventionist and disposed to strike a better deal with global capital as well as regulate it in the public interest (for the sake of equity or social inclusion, and protection of the environment). This neo-structuralist and international political economy approach 'place[s] domestic politics within the broader context of the global political economy and show[s] how these models of resource governance are constitutive of state strategies in managing globalization' (Singh, 2012). The aim then is to theorize the transformation of the neoliberal state, based on the much but justly maligned Washington Consensus, into a more sustainable and inclusive development policy (Bresser-Pereira, 2009; Silva, 2009).

In this chapter, we take a different approach, based on a Marxist theory of capitalist development and a secondary focus on imperialism as the fundamental agency for advancing this development. In these terms, and with reference to the expanding literature on the 'new extractivism' and the post-neoliberal state in Latin America, it is argued that these recent developments are better understood via the lens of Marxist class analysis and the underlying theory of the dynamics of capitalist development.

We further contend that the 'progressive' post-neoliberal states formed over the past decade have turned towards and opted for a strategy of resource extraction and export primarization, and have done so by striking a deal with the agents of global extractive capital in a coincidence of economic interests: to share the spoils (windfall profits, enhanced claims on ground rent). In siding with the transnational corporations of extractive capital against the local population and communities that bear the brunt of their offensive these regimes have sown the seeds of a new form of class struggle.

The major protagonists in this struggle are the indigenous communities of peasant farmers and semiproletarianized rural landless workers, who, unlike the traditional proletariat formed under earlier conditions of 'primitive accumulation by dispossession', are engaged in a fundamental struggle to preserve their traditional livelihoods and to protect the global commons of land and water on which these livelihoods depend.

On this point a conceptual clarification is in order. In Marxist theory the traditional proletariat is formed by the capitalist development of agriculture, in which the direct producers (small-landholding peasant farmers in many contexts) are separated from their means of production and converted into a working class of wage-labourers. But in the Latin American context the proletariat and the working class take a different form, as do the dynamics of the class struggle in conditions of extractive capital. Here there is no industrial proletariat, but rather a proletariat composed predominantly of landless or near-landless rural workers and a semiproletarianized peasantry, a growing number of whose family members is forced to work 'off-farm' in the rural areas, migrate to the cities in search of paid labour or to work 'on their own account', to use a Statistics Canada term for self-employed workers in the ubiquitous 'informal sector' (Davis, 2006).

Mine workers in these conditions are in no position to wage a struggle against extractive capital: most are trapped in a relation of dependence on the mine owners for the few available wage-paying jobs—natural resource extraction and mining is notoriously capital-intensive, dependent as it is for its development on the extraction of natural resources rather than the exploitation of labour. The class struggle in this context shifts from the workplace to the community, and the local forces of resistance are organized and mobilized from within the community.

This entire argument is constructed as follows. First, we review the dynamics of foreign direct investment in Latin America in the context of the new world order of neoliberal globalization established in the 1980s. Here we argue that the neoliberal policies of structural adjustment were designed to pave the way for the expansion of capital and a new wave of capitalist development and imperialist exploitation. Secondly, we review the brief history of this 'development' over the past two decades to establish the demise of neoliberalism and the emergence of a new development consensus that has led to the formation of what some have termed the 'post-neoliberal state', focused (under prevailing conditions in the world economy) on the economics and politics of natural resource extraction—the 'new extractivism'.

Here we argue that the post-neoliberal state, the supposed outcome of a sharp turn to the left in national politics and a more socially inclusive form of development, is but the latest twist and turn in the politics of what we term 'extractivist imperialism'. Thirdly, we explore the political economy of this development in terms of an imperialist strategy of natural resource exploitation, and the consequences of this strategy: the accumulation of capital based on the pillage of natural and human resources, the destruction of the environment and livelihoods of the local communities affected by the resource extraction process, and widespread resistance leading to a new and virulent form of class conflict. Here we suggest that the agents of the post-neoliberal state will rally to the defence of global capital as the result of congruent economic interests. The likely or possible outcome of this political development is uncertain but promises to be bloody and fraught with conflict.

Foreign Investment in Latin America: Natural Resource Development or Imperialist Plunder?

The first major wave of FDI to hit Latin America was in the 1960s and 1970s, but the imperialist strategy behind this investment was impeded by the regulatory constraints of the developmental state (Chibber, 2005; Evans, 1995). To liberate the 'forces of economic freedom' from these constraints, the Washington-based agents of imperialist expansion (the World Bank and the IMF, as well as the US Department of Treasury) designed a program of structural reforms in macroeconomic policy imposed via the Third World debt crisis that set the stage for a new wave of capital inflows into Latin America in the 1990s.

Table 3 captures some of the dynamics of these capital inflows, and associated outflows. While the late 1970s saw a massive inflow of capital in the form of bank loans, and the 1980s saw an equally massive net outflow of this capital in the form of debt repayment, the 1990s saw a major inflow of foreign direct investment (FDI), facilitated by the structural reforms mandated by the Washington Consensus on the need for free market capitalism. Responding to these sweeping reforms multinational corporations expanded their investments from $8.7 billion in 1990 to $61 billion in 1998—a sixfold increase in FDI inflows (vs. a 223 percent increase worldwide). Over these years 43 percent of FDI flows from the US to developing countries were routed into Latin America, which, as a result, practically doubled its stock of US-based FDI—close to $900 billion by the end of the decade (CEPAL, 1998: 196–97).

TABLE 3   *Long-Term North–South Financial Flows, 1985–2001 (US$ Billions)*

	'85–89	'90–94	'95–99	'00–01
Official (foreign aid)	200.0	274.6	230.1	74.1
Private	157.0	552.5	1240.4	386.8
FDI	76.0	268.5	772.8	334.9
Portfolio investments	6.0	111.5	165.6	69.4
Other	75.0	172.5	302.0	−18.5
Net resource inflow	357.0	827.1	1470.8	440.9
Profits on FDI	66.0	96.5	163.8	100.7
Debt payments	354.0	356.5	560.9	371.1
Net resource outflow	420.0	453.0	724.7	349.6

SOURCES: IMF, 2000; WORLD BANK, 2002.

Table 3 points towards a shift in the 1990s from an 'official' north–south transfer of 'financial resources' to a reliance on private capital, as well as a rapid expansion of 'asset-seeking FDI', which resulted in a significantly greater ownership stake for global capital in the region's most lucrative wealth-generating assets, and also an increased market share for the multinational corporations that took the road paved by the neoliberal reforms of the Washington Consensus. But it also points toward imperialist exploitation: the massive outflow of capital extracted in the form of bank loan repayments, returns to FDI and repatriated profits, and interests paid on portfolio investments. Although the official statistics (see Table 3) clearly do not fully reflect the scope of the actual capital outflows, including those derived from the operations of 'asset-seeking' FDI (in the acquisition of privatized state enterprises), unproductive speculative investments and capital flight, Saxe-Fernandez and Nuñez (2001) estimate that the operations of global capital and imperialist exploitation in the 1990s resulted in the net transfer of US$100-billion from Latin America to the imperial centres of capital accumulation. And this did not include the extraordinary pillage of natural resources, the hidden transfer of capital in the disguised form of the maquilla industry and intra-firm trade, or the transfer of surplus through the mechanism of unequal exchange. In these terms the 1990s can well be described as the 'golden age of US imperialism'.

The 1990s saw a major expansion of foreign investment in developing countries, dubbed 'emerging markets' by investment bankers. But in Latin America, a substantial part of this capital was 'unproductive' in that it was used primarily to acquire the assets of already existing and in many cases profitable if not lucrative state enterprises. As for the inflows of productive capital in the form of FDI, they were predominantly in three sectors: (i) manufacturing; (ii) resource extraction—exploration for and the production of hydrocarbons (oil and gas) and minerals; and (iii) myriad 'services'—personal, professional, financial and banking, and business. The biggest change in the sectoral distribution of FDI was the shift toward high-tech, financial and business services, accompanied by a relative decline in the share of FDI in natural resources and manufacturing. However, with the growing demand for primary products induced by the ascension of China as an economic power and the associated rise in the price of oil, minerals and other commodities, FDI in the extractive industries of resource-rich countries has rebounded and redoubled in recent years.

Despite a dip in FDI inflows to Latin America in 2006 and again in 2008 under conditions of the so-called 'global financial foreign investment in mining' has remained buoyant. In Chile under Bachelet a relatively high level of mining investments was maintained, while in Peru the government anticipates continued rapid growth in mining FDI, estimated to total at least US$10 billion over the next five years and possibly many billions more if the highly contested (see the discussion below) Congo mine project comes to fruition. In Bolivia, despite uncertainties created by revisions to the country's mining tax regime, most of the foreign mining companies have continued operations.

In 2010, exports of minerals exceeded US$2.4 billion, 23 percent over that of the year before, and the greatest beneficiaries of this export growth were the multinationals and the medium-sized petit bourgeois miners in the cooperative sector, with the government taking a relatively small share of the proceeds. Meanwhile, insistent demands by local communities and popular sector organizations for the governments to revert the concessions made to the multinational companies in the natural resource extraction sector to explore and extract the wealth of the country's natural wealth—demands that are resonating throughout the region, especially in the other Andean countries—in most cases have fallen on deaf ears. As we argue below this is primarily due to the coincidence of economic interests between the post-neoliberal state and global capital: windfall profits for the corporations, additional fiscal revenues for the state. But even though in the context of a commodity boom the governments were in a position to demand and successfully negotiate a greater share of the value of the extracted resources the principal beneficiaries of the commodities boom and the new extractivism have been the transnational corporations that dominate the industry.

By far the highest share of FDI in the extractive industry is in mining and petroleum exploration and production. While FDI stock and capital flow estimates are not available for mining and petroleum separately, data on crossborder mergers and acquisitions (M&AS) suggest to economists at UNCTAD that both these industries have attracted increasing volumes of foreign investment in recent years (UNCTAD, 2011). For instance, two of the five largest crossborder M&A deals in 2006 were in the mining sector. The most recent data show that Mexico and Brazil, with inflows of US$19 billion each, remain the region's leading FDI recipients, followed by Chile and Colombia (ibid., p. 54). That is, foreign investors do not seem to favour one type of regime or the other. On the contrary, recent data shows a predilection of these companies for investing and operating in countries such as Colombia and Mexico, whose overtly neoliberal regimes are less demanding and more open to foreign investment and the operations of extractive capital.

While oil and gas exploration and 'development' is still a favoured outlet for extractive capital the regional sources of the supply of both are relatively few and in the case of Venezuela, with the greatest deposit of oil reserves in the region, more or less inaccessible to foreign capital. As a result, mining-related FDI has accounted for most of the increased inflows of extractive capital in recent years, especially in Peru, which hosts some of largest mining explora-tion projects in the world. In 2009 Latin America received 26 percent of the capital invested globally in mineral exploration, According to the Metals Economics Group (MEG), a 2010 bonanza in world market prices led to another increase of 40 percent in investments related to mineral exploration and min-ing, with governments in the region, both neoliberal and post-neoliberal, com-peting fiercely for this capital.

In South America, the primary locus of the primary commodities boom, income on inward FDI has grown steadily since 2003, the beginning of the boom. In 2006, it grew by 49 percent to reach US$59 billion, exceeding the total FDI inflows of any year since economic liberalization began in the 1990s (UNCTAD, 2011. Figure II.18).

Income on FDI (i.e. profits on capital invested in the resource sector) was particularly high in Brazil and Chile, US$14 billion and US$20 billion respec-tively, leading to a surge in the share of retained earnings in total FDI inflows. In the South American countries for which data are available, income on FDI soared from an average of ten percent in 2000–03 to 61 percent in 2006, the year before the publication of UNCTAD's landmark study of FDI in the extrac-tion industry. A large part of the capital invested in the resource sector takes the form of concessions for exploratory projects, which means that the profits are as yet uncertain and to be realized sometime in the future. Thus, the ability to reproduce capital in the sector with relatively minimal investments demon-strates how exceptionally profitable operations of mining capital actually are.

In the new millennium, in the context of a growing demand in China and the other BRIC countries for agricultural and forestry products, fossil fuels and other sources of energy, and strategic industrial minerals, the sectoral distribution pat-tern of foreign investment has changed, with a greater focus on the acquisition of large tracts of land for agriculture, the production of biofuels, and the extrac-tion of minerals—what has been dubbed 'landgrabbing'. Table 2 points to one particular feature of this change: a relative shift of FDI flows into the developing countries from manufacturing into both services and resource-extraction. As for resource extraction investments are directed primarily towards fossil fuels and metal mining, but recently also towards 'large-scale land acquisition' or 'land-grabbing' (Bebbington, Hinojosa & Humphreys, 2009).

Aggregate statistics do not reveal what is actually going on regarding FDI in the natural resource sector, partly because of the lack of reliable statistics and partly because the overall pattern of investment flows do not show significant regional, sub-regional and country variations in the dynamic pattern of FDI flows, or intra-sectoral distributions. Even so, increases in investment in resource extraction is clearly discernable, particularly (as of 2007) in the case

of Canadian extractive capital, which dominates natural resource development both in Latin America and worldwide. In this regard a study by Arellano
based on ECLAC data shows a doubling of foreign investment in Latin America's
mining sector since 2007, versus a marginal decline in investments service sector investments and a 40 percent decline in investments in the manufacturing
sector. The same study shows that the major recipients of these investments
throughout the last decade (and since 2006 in the case of Colombia) were
Brazil, Mexico, Chile, Colombia and Argentina in that order. Together, these
countries were recipients of CDN$222 billion in Canadian foreign investments
in 2007 and 2008, years that saw an overall decline in the level of foreign investments. These investments compare to CDN$12.7 billion for Bolivia, Peru and
Venezuela over the same period—a pattern that holds up over the decade,
again suggesting a preference for the extraction of minerals over fossil fuels or
energy, and an openness to foreign investment (rather than regime type) as the
most critical factors of investment related decision-making.

From Neoliberalism to Post-Neoliberal Governance

The reprimarization of Latin America's economies began in the 1990s under
conditions of the 'structural reforms' imposed by the new world order of neoliberal globalization. These reforms permitted governments in the region, both
neoliberal and post-neoliberal, to exploit a comparative advantage in natural
resources to increase exports and thus generate the foreign exchange and the
additional fiscal revenues needed to service the accumulated external debts as
well as make some move towards a more inclusive form of development based
on the post-Washington Consensus. Given the relatively low prices for primary
commodities at the time, this did not happen, but the reforms did open up the
region's extractive industries to foreign investment.

Key players in this process were Brazil and Chile. What is striking about
both regimes is that notwithstanding a continuing commitment to a neoliberal structural reform agenda their growth strategy in the resource extraction
sector were led by state enterprises—Petróleo Brasileiro, a.k.a. Petrobras,
in the case of Brazil, and Codelco, in the case of Chile. Chile alone produces
35 percent of the global supply of copper, a strategic industrial commodity.
However, although the world's largest copper mine, Escondida, located in the
Northern Atacama Desert is privately owned (primarily by the Rio Tinto Group
and BHP Billiton), Codelco controls up to 70 percent of the nation's copper
reserves. As for Petrobras, it has proven to be very proficient and efficient in
bringing about advances in offshore drilling technology as well as establishing

a 'culture of innovation', both of which were crucial in the discovery of new offshore oil reserves in 2008. Thus, the state still dominates strategic extractive sectors in Chile and Brazil, copper and oil respectively.

Mainstream analysts claim that neoliberal policies related to resource extraction create: economic dynamism; global competitiveness; technology/ knowledge transfer; and sophisticated techniques in managing environmental and social costs. The 'wisdom of the international epistemic community' (adherents to neoliberal ideology) is that private capital can unlock the hidden potential of natural resource development and unleash a sustainable growth process. However, the experience has been otherwise. Not only has private corporate capital failed to kick-start the economic growth process, it resulted in a massive pillage of natural resources, providing few tangible benefits to the local economy but major negative socioeconomic and environmental costs. The record on this point over the neoliberal era is clear enough albeit not substantiated in this study: the failure to generate promised conditions for stable long-term growth in the forces of production; the plunder and pillage and transfer of natural, human and financial resources; and the destruction of the forces of production with significantly negative environmental and social impacts on the environment and livelihoods of working people and local communities.

Under these and other conditions (such as the concentration in the distribution of productive assets and income, a deepening of social inequalities, new forms of poverty), the forces of resistance to capitalist development and imperialist exploitation have been mobilized in recent years to successfully challenge the hegemony of neoliberal globalization. By the end of the 1990s, two decades into the neoliberal agenda, neoliberalism was very much on the defensive, generating conditions for what many now see as a transition to a post-neoliberal state and governance.

After a short downward turn in the capitalist development process (in 2001– 2002, 1989–2001 in Argentina), the 21st century in Latin America opened with (i) a wave of anti-neoliberal protest and a turn to the Left in national politics (a resurgence of left-of-centre politics) by regimes seeking and able to exploit this sentiment; (ii) an unprecedented primary commodities boom, and resulting rise of 'the new extractivism'.

This was unprecedented in two ways. On one hand, it took place against the backdrop of the failure of neoliberal policies to achieve economic growth and political stability in Latin America. On the other hand, the left-of-centre governments that emerged under these conditions pursued new strategies (resource extractivism and nationalism) to consolidate power and meet the demands of their social bases. This strategy of resource extraction and governance (the 'new extractivism') has been pursued within the framework of the post-Washington Consensus (PWC), and its emphasis on socially inclusive growth to stabilize the neoliberal capitalist development. The coincidence of anti-neoliberal sentiment with a commodities boom led to a post-neoliberal or PWC politics based on a resource extraction growth strategy.

This notion of a post-neoliberal regime is not without controversy. Petras and Veltmeyer, among others, have argued that this turn to the Left was more rhetorical than real while Tockman (2010) writes of 'divergent paths' and 'varieties of post-neoliberalism' in regard to 'natural resource policy'. As for ECLAC (the UN Commission for Latin America and the Caribbean), the institution that over the years has led the debate over the development path that countries in Latin America might or should pursue, the scholars and policy analysts associated with it are evidently ambivalent about this new development path. Concerned about the well-documented and extensively analyzed pitfalls of a resource-led development strategy they nevertheless consider it prudent for governments to take advantage of a moment in which commodity prices are high to extract better deals from multinationals, which could then be used for progressive social policies and to support the gradual conversion of the countries' economic structures towards greater innovation and more sustainable economies.

The Natural Resource Politics of Post-Neoliberal Regimes

The essence of the consensus reached by the G20 at their 2000 summit and at the UN New Millennium conference held soon thereafter was: boost economic growth via a neoliberal macroeconomic policy regime but also to regulate private economic activity (the market, capital) in the interest of a more inclusive form of development. What this meant for many (particularly the economists at the World Bank) was the need for 'good governance' (to engage the participation of civil society) and to move beyond neoliberalism towards a more activist and regulatory state, and a new social policy designed to reduce the rate of poverty via social programs such as conditional cash transfers targeted at the poor. However, for the relatively progressive governments that came to power soon thereafter by riding a wave of anti-neoliberal sentiment it meant a clear rejection of the neoliberal policy agenda, a new form of resource nationalism (for the country to take 'ownership' not only of their own development but of the wealth of natural resources), a more substantive redistribution of the social product, and a more effective and consequential participation of the population in the process of economic and social development.

A belief in free market capitalism, in fact had waned and died as early as 1989, when every development agency in the UN system of international cooperation, including the World Bank, came to the conclusion that they had 'gone too far' in the direction of the unregulated market and, as Rodrik (2005), one of many centrist social liberal critics of neoliberalism, put it, that it was necessary to 'bring the state back in'. The result was a synthesis of neoliberalism and structuralism/social liberalism (= neostructuralism), and a new approach to 'development', what the theorists and architects of the new consensus termed 'the new developmentalism' (Bresser-Pereira, 2009), or 'inclusive development' (Sunkel & R. Infante, 2009).

This notion of a post-neoliberal regime is not without controversy, however. As Fernando Leiva (2008) establishes in his critique of this neostructuralist synthesis and paradigmatic shift, the architects and proponents of this post-Washington Consensus did not manage to create either a post-neoliberal state or a new global governance regime, or even a new economic model. It was left to the centre-left governments that came to power in the turning of the political tide—particularly Argentina, Brazil and Chile in the Southern cone, the plurinational/multiethnic states of Bolivia and Ecuador, and the Bolivarian state of Venezuela—to move decidedly if cautiously in this direction.

However, an analysis of the policy agenda and the policies actually implemented by these regimes since 2002 (as opposed to the populist rhetoric) suggests that Venezuela is the only case of a consolidated or truly post-neoliberal state. Neither Bolivia nor Ecuador, and certainly not Brazil, Chile and Argentina—the three regimes most often thought of as exemplifying a post-neoliberal policy regime—have instituted the anticipated substantive changes required to move beyond neoliberalism, let alone capitalism, which is nowhere on the agenda except for Venezuela.

With the exception of Venezuela no PNL regime thus far has moved beyond a PWC policy regime of social inclusion and direct economic assistance to the poor. Why this might be the case is the question. What we suggest is that the answer can be found not so much at the level of ideology (the argument that the PNL regimes have reached the limit of political change permitted by an effective albeit unstated ideology), or in the politics of development (the correlation of political forces within the country), as in the political economy of these regimes: their embrace of a strategy of natural resource development predicated on a dependence on extractive capital and on the need to negotiate and strike a deal with the operators of this capital as to how to share the proceeds of resource extraction and primary commodity exports. In this context, the purported 'new extractivism' boils down to nothing more than the State striking a better deal with global capital regarding its share of the plundered resources—ground and resource rents in the form of royalty payments and taxes on the extraction and export of the country's wealth.

Despite the populist rhetoric of resource nationalism (the country's resources and wealth belongs to the people) and social inclusion, the relation of the Bolivian state to global capital under the Morales-Linera regime has not substantially changed. Even in regard to hydrocarbon development, where the regime has established the ownership rights of 'the people' in the reserves of oil and gas, and the law was rewritten to ensure that future extraction would be controlled by the Bolivian state (supposedly guaranteeing the state-owned company a 51 percent ownership share), the exploitation of the resources in the sector remain under control of the 29 multinationals that remain in the country (Petras & Veltmeyer, 2009).

While the government in some resource sectors (e.g. iron, lithium) has been holding out for what might be deemed 'structural change'—such as the insistence that the raw material be processed in Bolivia—it has been unable to close the deal or either attract or access the capital needed to change its status as an exporter of raw materials. The result is that all that it has been able to do is cut a better deal—obtain a greater share of the resource rents in an industry that in conditions of the growing global demand for resources has proven to be exceptionally lucrative for the companies operating in the sector.[1]

An egregious case of an evident contradiction between the government's nationalist rhetoric (the country's resources belong to the people, and will be developed by the state, not permitting the multinationals to simply extract the resources and export them in an unprocessed form) and actual practice (letting the multinationals extract these resources and export them for processing overseas) is Mutún, the country's (and region's) major iron mine. Notwithstanding the promise of the mine's operator, Jindal, the giant Indian multinational steel and power producer, at the outset of renegotiations with the current regime of a contract signed under a previous neoliberal regime, that it would process the

---

1   Data on profits are hard to come by, but how lucrative mining can be is illustrated by the case of Canada's Gold Corp's operations in Argentina's Valle de Huasco, which netted the company US$3.3 billion in profits last year. In that year the company anticipated the extraction of between 6 and 8 million ounces of gold, at a cost of US$340-80 an ounce and the market price of US$1,652. What facilitated the company's bottom line was a secret deal with the presidents of Chile and Argentina for the extraction or ore at one of the lowest resource royalty payment regimes in the world (10–15% depending on whether the ore is refined or concentrated) and the washing of the ore in the pristine waters of the glaciers in Argentina's Valle de Huasco via a tunnel at no cost (M. Bonasso, 2010). "El mal: El modelo K y la Barrick Gold. Amos y servidores en el saqueo de Argentina," <http://revistasiigg.sociales.uba.ar/index.php/hicrhodus/article/view/212> (Accessed 02 July 2015).

iron ore in Bolivia and invest in the creation of an industry within Bolivia, seven years on there is no sign of any such investment.

Some studies suggest that while this might indeed be the case regarding Bolivia and Ecuador, both relatively weak states vis-à-vis capital, it is argued, Brazil in particular, but also Chile and Argentina are different. They have managed to institute a new form of 'natural resource politics' based on the effective agency of a competent state company in the resources sector (as mentioned above, oil in the case of Brazil, and copper in the case of Chile), and thus represent a more effective post-neoliberal 'regulatory regime'. This is, in fact, what the notion of a 'new extractivism' hinges on.

However, a closer look at these and other cases of the so-called new extractivism reveals that global capital is very much in command, with the State conceding large tracts of land and territory to the multinationals for their operations under new regulations that do very little to impede them. On this point take the example of Peru, which Bebbington and associates have documented as a key area of mineral extractive industry expansion (Bebbington, et al., 2009: 31–62). President Ollanta Humala came to power in June 2011 with a promise to support local communities against the mining companies (on a platform of 'water before gold'). Local and indigenous communities in Peru have violently opposed the planned major expansion of mining operations by a consortium of Newmont Mining Corporation, Peru's Compañía Minera Buenaventura and the World Bank's International Finance Corporation—and successfully put these plans on hold. But Humala, who after only three months in office sent some 3,000 troops to the conflict zone, made it very clear that although the government agreed to order an outside review of plans for the mine expansion the country could not afford to and would not halt the US$4.8 billion project.

This is by no means an unusual situation or political development. Throughout the region, examples can be found of variations of the same dynamic. In every case—and in this the 'post-neoliberal' regimes in Argentina and Chile are no different than the purportedly resource populist Humala regime in Peru or the decidedly neoliberal regime in Mexico—the state is either favourably disposed toward the mining companies and other multinational corporations, as well as the imperial states that back them up, or it is compelled by a coincidence of economic interests to concede to the demands of the multinational corporations in the extractivist sector. These corporations operate under post-neoliberal paradigm in which they receive a license to explore and extract resources under a regulatory regime designed to protect the environment and the livelihoods of the local communities affected by the mining operations. But in reality the aim of the government in issuing this license, and in demanding an environmental review or impact study, is to find a way to advance projects, in which they have a vital interest while somehow eluding the social conflicts and opposition that they invariably generate. Indeed, it is evidently in the interest of the state, whether neoliberal or post-neoliberal, to maximize the capacity of the foreign companies to extract resources and sell them on the global market, placing the government on the side of capital rather than the population and communities directly affected by these operations.

The Struggle Dynamics of Community-based Resistance

Prior to the 1990s, the class struggle and the popular movement in Latin America was primarily concerned with issues of social class related to the struggle over land in the countryside and the labour movement for wages and working conditions in the urban centres In the 1990s, however, the popular movements, with the agency of class-based and community-based social movements, mobilized against the neoliberal state (and the governing regimes) in resistance against their policies. By the end of the decade a number of these movements, led by proletarianized peasant farmers, rural landless workers and indigenous communities, in a number of contexts (Chiapas, Brazil, Ecuador, Bolivia, etc.) achieved major gains in their struggle, placing the existing neoliberal regimes on the defensive and provoking a legitimation crisis for the neoliberal state. At the turn into the 21st century, to all intents and purposes, neoliberalism was dead, no longer able to serve its legitimating function to naturalize the class structures. With the already observed—and widely reported—left turn in national politics (the so-called pink tide), the regimes that came to power in the wake of widespread disenchantment with neoliberalism each and all, including overtly neoliberal regimes in Mexico and Colombia (and Peru at the time), sought to move 'beyond neoliberalism', at least rhetorically, in the search for a new form of governance, an alternate path towards national development, a new post-neoliberal state. To put not too fine a point on it, the fundamental concern, shared by both the community of development associations and the social democratic centre-left, is to bring back the state so as to preserve the capitalist system from its inner contradictions—from the failures of free market capitalism.

Dynamics of the Class Struggle in the Natural Resources Sector

The agency and key agents involved in this 'politics' (resistance against the imperial incursions of capital in the exploitation of 'natural resources')—at least in the Latin American context—are the predominantly indigenous communities that populate the areas ceded by the different governments (be they neoliberal or post-neoliberal in form) to the foreign mining companies for the exploration and exploitation of the natural resources in their territorial lands. However, they also include a variety of civil society groups and nongovernmental organizations that have been drawn into the conflict between global capital and the local communities. And the forces of resistance to resource imperialism include new social movements formed to protest the damage caused by the resource extraction to the environment, as well as the effects on the health and the livelihoods of the local population and the miners themselves who face life-threatening working conditions and health concerns. In other words, many of these movements are rooted in those 'affected' by the impacts of resource extraction and mining operations (for example, REM— Red Mexicana de Afectados por la Minería; and CONACAMI—Confederación Nacional de Comunidades del Perú Afectadas por la Minería).

According to a forum of peoples, communities and groups 'affected' ('negatively impacted') by the operations of mining capital and the resource extraction industry (Foro de los Pueblos Indígenas Minería, Cambio Climático y Buen Vivir) celebrated in Lima on November 2010, the exploitation of the region's mineral resources in 2009 had reached levels hitherto never experienced. Of particular concern was the Amazon region, whose abundant deposits of gold, bauxite, precious stones, manganese, uranium, etc. are coveted by the multinational companies operating in the mining sector. Another concern was the perceived connection between the multinational corporations in the sector and a host of foundations and NGOs with an alleged humanitarian or religious concern for the environment and the livelihood of the indigenous peoples and communities. In this connection, Eddy Gómez Abreu, President of the Parlamento Amazónico Internacional, declared that they had 'incontrovertible evidence of these transnationals and foundations, under the cover of supposed ecological, religious or humanitarian concerns, collaborated in the effort to "extract diamonds, strategic minerals and genetic" as well as espionage and illegal medical experiments on the indigenous population' (Sena-Fobomade, 2005). In effect, he alleged that the mining companies regularly used foundations and other nongovernmental organizations (NGOs) as one of their tactics to secure the consent of the local population to their projects and operations, and to manipulate them. If this is true, these foundations and NGOs continue the long sordid history of European missionaries in the Americas of expropriating the lands of the indigenous, but in an updated form.

On the one hand, the forces of resistance use tactics such as marches and demonstrations, road and access blockades, and other forms of direct collective action, to impede the mining operations. On the other hand, the tactics of the mining companies include visiting the community for the purpose of gathering information and evaluating the local situation (e.g. the degree of opposition) under false pretexts such as representing themselves as members of an NGO concerned with the welfare of the indigenous; arranging public meetings, with the help of local allies or 'friendly' officials; bribing government officials with the promise of jobs and social development funds; manufacturing a 'social license' by negotiating with a friendly local group supportive of the project, albeit not representative of the 'community'; creating a support group and organization, when a submissive or complaint group does not exist in the community; or seeking support for a proposed mining project by offering gainful employment to unemployed members of the community, work for local contractors or service contracts; purchasing land with access to the concessions; infiltration of the community and spying on the opposition; and strategic litigation against public participation, false accusations, intimidation and death threats, and paramilitary action. And ultimately the mining companies rely on the direct violence of military, paramilitary, and/or police forces to overcome opposition to their highly lucrative mining operations.

At issue in this struggle and these tactics is to defeat the resistance against the operations of mining capital and the extraction of resources for the purpose of capital accumulation. From the perspective of the local communities, however, at issue is not only the health of their members and sovereign control over their national territory, but the environment on which their livelihood and way of life, and life itself, depends. In this regard, Gómez Abreu reported— in a socio-metabolic analysis of the economy—over a million people in the Amazonian basin suffer from diseases derived from exposure to and ingestion of toxic and carcinogenic substances, such as mercury. And the researcher, Edgardo Alarcón, in the same regard, documented the scientific evidence that the Peruvian city of Oroya is one of the ten most contaminated cities in the world, with high levels of lead and sulphur in the air and high levels of mining-based and related carcinogens such as cadmium, arsenic and antinomy in the soil, agriculture-based food products and the water supply—toxins that also were detected in other towns and surrounding communities. Thus, what is a source of profit for the transnational mining corporations represents a 'death sentence' for local communities.

Conacami, one of the major organizations participating in the Forum, denounced the fact that by the end of 2010 the vast majority of ancestral sites in its territory were in the hands of the mining and oil companies (the 'transnationals'), which have been ceded up to 72 percent of Peru's national territory for the purpose of exploration and the exploitation of the country's natural resources. Conacami alerted forum participants of the actions of the government—at that time under the control of Humala's neoliberal predecessor, President Alan García—in declaring 33 mega-projects to be in the 'national interest' and thus without the need for the companies to submit environmental impact studies. Subsequent developments under the ostensibly postneoliberal resource nationalist regime established by Garcia's successor, Ollante Humala, indicate that nothing had changed in this regard—that the government continued to side with extractive capital against the local communities in the project of natural resource development.

These and other such reports reflect the fact that Peru, together with Ecuador, is one of the major Latin American sites of class struggle over the extraction and exploitation of natural resources. A major continuing focal point in this struggle relates to the Conga mine, the largest extraction operation in the country and one of the largest in the entire region. At the point of this writing (March 2012), this mining operation expansion is 'on hold', stalled as a result of the organized resistance of the local communities in the Cajamarca region.

This mine expansion project, known as the Conga Project, a joint project between Denver-based Newmont Mining Corp. and Peru's Buenaventura, would help the company (and the government) meet the goal of producing seven million ounces of gold and 400 million pounds of copper by 2017—a major boost to both the GDP, rents (royalties and taxes) collected by the government, and the company's profits. But, of course, these immense rents and profits would come at the cost of devastating the land, water, and livelihoods of the local indigenous communities surrounding the mining operations.

The chances of the stalled operation proceeding is now in doubt. In February 2012, around the same time that President Cristina Fernandez of Argentina was confronting a similar situation, the on-going resistance to the Conga Project took the form of a national march for 'water and life', a mobilization that gained broad public support as well as the active participation of diverse social groups and sectors. And if the local communities in their struggle against mining capital and the extractive industry were to succeed in stopping a project that the government has declared to be of strategic importance, it would also provide a major boost to the forces of resistance throughout the region. It would be viewed as a major victory for 'the people' in an on-going class struggle against capital—one of very few in recent years. It would signal a shift in the correlation of class forces, one of several reasons why the resistance most likely will not succeed: the stakes are too high—for both the mining companies and the State (both in Peru and elsewhere in the region). The odds are that the government will rally in support of mining capital, and take action to create the conditions that will allow the project to proceed, be it co-optation or repression.

The thousands of protesters who packed Lima's downtown core in the 'March for Water and Life' called on the government to cancel the project over fears that the mine's tailing ponds and reservoirs would seep into local water supplies. "We're here because we don't want foreigners taking our water," one of the protesters declared as he marched down a boulevard in central Lima, with the trademark straw hat of a Cajamarca farmer perched atop his head.[2] "It belongs to Peru," he added. The presence of police in riot gear confronting the march was a frightening reminder of the hostility protesters face from mining proponents.

In December 2011, Humala declared a 60-day state of emergency after a series of violent clashes erupted between police and protesters in Cajamarca as a general strike and roadblocks paralyzed the region. Much of the anger at the time stemmed from a perceived flip-flop by Humala, a former left-nationalist and radical populist in the mould of Evo Morales, who spoke out against foreign mining companies during his election campaign for the presidency and even hinted at the possible nationalization of the industry. However, as predicted by some since taking office last summer, he has sided with the mining companies in their conflict with the indigenous communities. The reason for this supposed flip-flop (in fact, Humala's stance was entirely predictable) is clear enough.

At issue in the conflict—and in this the Conga mine issue is no different from struggles over the decade and throughout the region—is the capitalist development of the country's natural resources, including the rents and taxes collected by government—which, as developments in Bolivia over the last five years suggest, can be considerable, reason enough for a political turn to the right (i.e. a coincidence of economic interests between State and Capital). On this point, there are no end of examples—from Peru and Bolivia to Brazil and Argentina—of an ostensibly anti- or post-neoliberal regime spouting nationalist rhetoric regarding ownership and control of the country's natural resources, but then settling all too quickly (or slowly if need be, as in the case of Peru's Conga Project) with global capital in the exploitation of the country's natural resources to a mutual benefit.

In the case of the Conga mine in the Cajamarca region, the company responsible for the project has pointed out that the project, slated to open in 2015, if allowed to go ahead will create as many as 7,000 construction jobs and 1,600 operation jobs. Further, it will be expected to pay the government close to

---

2   Wallace, Kenyon (2012). "Peruvians take to the streets in Lima to protest mine developments," *Toronto Star*. <http://www.thestar.com/news/world/2012/02/18/peruvians_take_to_the_streets _in_lima_to_protest_mine_developments.html> (Accessed 02 July 2015). 18 February.

US$3 billion in taxes over the next two decades as well as royalties, the proceeds of which will be distributed by the government in an equitable fashion in a policy of social inclusion.

Conclusion

Since the late 1990s across Latin America there has been an increasing incidence of local protests against large private (privatized) mining and oil projects based on foreign capital. With respect to mining, the Observatory of Latin American Mining Conflicts (OCMAL) has registered 155 major socio-environmental conflicts in recent years, most of them in Argentina, Brazil, Chile, Colombia, Mexico and Peru.[3] Diverse 'stakeholders' (to use the development jargon), especially campesinos, indigenous groups and small-scale miners, have resisted new investments and projects that give little (few jobs and development) but take and damage a lot (land, water, air—and livelihoods). The numerous mobilizations against extractive activities focus on land and water rights, territorial claims and the notorious environmental record of extractive industries (North, Clark & Patroni, 2006).

While some of these local protests take place in marginalized areas and receive little external support or attention, other conflicts have become well-known and have achieved online status with the global 'antiglobalization movement': the resistance of Peruvian farmers and other local groups against gold mining in Tambogrande and Yanacocha; the massive protests against Barrack Gold's goldmine operations in Argentina's Valle de Huasco, leading to the disappearance of several glaciers, widespread contamination and drought; the mobilization of Mayan communities against silver and gold mines in Guatemala; and various indigenous protests against extractive activities in the Amazon, including the long history of mobilization against Chevron/Texaco in Ecuador. Many of these local protests have been related to the ecological worldview or growing strength of indigenous movements, or the increasing popular resistance to neoliberalism and globalization in the region. However, most of the all too abundant reports and studies of this resistance have been linked to the struggle for a more participatory politics and an alternative post-neoliberal model of capitalist development, and as a consequence have failed to appreciate its significance in regard to the class struggle against capitalism and imperialism.

---

3   See the Observatory's website <www.olca.cl/ocmal> for details about these conflicts.

In this regard the growing protest movement against mining capital and extractivism has engaged the forces of resistance not just against neoliberalism and globalization, but against the underlying and operative capitalist system. Thus the so-called politics of natural resource extraction is not just a matter of better resource management, a post-neoliberal regulatory regime, a more socially inclusive development strategy or a new form of governance— securing the participation of local communities and stakeholders in decisions and policies in which they have a vital interest.

Given the interests that they represent, and the coincidence of these interests with those of the 'transnational capitalist class' (to use the phrase of some sociologists of globalization), the officials and managers of the post-neoliberal state generally side with capital against labour and have not reacted well to the civil society organizations that criticise or resist their mineral policies or extractive projects. The anti-extractivist protests in the region have received international activist (and academic) recognition as part of a global environmental justice movement, but the agents and progressive officials of the 'post-neoliberal' states simply ignore them—and proceed with their geopolitical project: to advance the exploitation of the country's natural resources by global capital in the public interest. Thus, the politics of natural resource extraction resolves into a matter of class struggle—of combatting the workings of capitalism and imperialism in the economic interests of the dominant class, and mobilizing the forces of resistance against these interests found in the indigenous communities of semi-proletarianized peasant farmers.

Agroextractivist Imperialism

A salient feature of global capitalism over the past decade has been the emergence of a trend towards the rapid expansion of large-scale foreign investment in the acquisition of land, dubbed 'landgrabbing' by the exponents of 'critical agrarian studies' (Borras & Franco, 2010). In this chapter we overview the dynamics of change associated with this transition in both the 20th century and today—the 'agrarian question' then and now. In the early decades of the 20th century the 'agrarian question' involved different national paths of development of capitalism in the countryside and its contributions to industrialization (Bernstein, 1997). Later in the decade the transition took the form of the construction of a world market/economy with a centre and periphery, while in the current context the agrarian question is taking shape as a new form of colonialism (landgrabbing) and extractive imperialism, viz. the imperial state in its active support of extractive capital in its diverse operations in the global south.

The Global Land Grab: A New Enclosure of the Global Commons?

In the current conjuncture of worldwide capitalist development hundreds of rural communities in Africa, parts of Asia and Latin America, are confronted with dispossession or loss of their livelihoods and lands that they customarily presume to be their own. These lands are reallocated by administrative fiat to mainly foreign investors to the tune of an estimated 220 million hectares since 2007, and still rising. Large-scale deals for hundreds of thousands of hectares dominate the process, but deals for smaller areas are not uncommon (World Bank, 2010).

At issue in these developments is a veritable global land rush, triggered in part by crises in oil and food markets over the last decade, and in part by the opportunity to make extraordinary profits by extracting and selling primary commodities for which there is strong demand on the world market. In addition, the financialization of these markets has provided lucrative new investment opportunities to sovereign wealth funds, hedge funds and global agribusiness, the new entrepreneurs with 'accumulated capital burning holes in their owners' pockets'.

In this process global shifts in economic power are evident. While northern and western actors (corporations, investors, governments) continue to dominate as investors and land grabbers, the BRICS (Brazil, Russia, India, China) and food-insecure Middle Eastern oil states are active competitors. A regional bias is beginning to show; China and Malaysia dominate land acquisition in Asia while South Africa shows signs of future dominance in Africa. Two South African farmer enclaves already exist in Nigeria, and Congo Brazzaville has granted 88,000 hectares with promises of up to ten million hectares to follow.

One hundred percent of arable farmland is now in the hands of foreign investors, and negotiations for the acquisition of large-scale landholdings and farmland are ongoing in at least 20 other African states (Hall, 2011).

What foreign governments such as China and other investors primarily seek are lands to meet their security need for agrofood products and energy, while multinational corporations in the extractive sector of the global economy are primarily concerned to feed the lucrative biofuel market by producing oil palm, sugar cane (for ethanol) and soya, increasingly the crop of choice for the conversion of farmland for food into the production of energy to feed the growing appetite for biofuel. Another motivation for the global landgrab is to produce food crops and livestock for home economies, bypassing unreliable and expensive international food markets. Additionally, investors are now seeking to launch lucrative carbon credit schemes. For all this cheap deals are needed: cheap land (US$0.50 per hectare in many cases) as well as duty-free import of their equipment, duty-free export of their products, tax-free status for their staff and production, and low-interest loans, often acquired from local banks on the basis of the new land titles they receive.

This rush for land, and the associated plunder of the host country's 'wealth' of natural resources, is not restricted to the extraction of agrofood products and mining for gold and industrial minerals. Local banks, communications, infrastructural projects, tourism ventures and local industry are also being bought up in a frenzy of privatizations. These ventures are keen to take advantage of the new market liberalization and other 'structural reforms' that the governments of resource-rich but poor countries on the periphery of world capitalism have been pushed into by international financial institutions such as the World Bank as a means of allowing them to benefit from the resulting 'economic opportunities'. For host governments, foreign investment in land and the extraction of natural resources is the new catalyst of 'inclusive economic growth' and sustainable development, here replacing foreign aid—and, it would seem, international trade. While the governments that host this foreign investment in the process collect ground and resource rents, as well as bribes. The promise of jobs is more or less the only immediate benefit to national populations, in exchange for the heavy social and environmental costs (as discussed in other chapters).

But where are the poor and the commons (land, water, natural resources) in all this? The answer is evident. Much of the lands being sold or leased to entrepreneurs are commons, lands that are used by the 'commoners' but to which they have no title. This is not surprising because lands defined as 'commons' in the contemporary development discourse generally exclude permanent farms and settlements. Governments and investors prefer to avoid privately owned or settled lands as their dispossession is most likely to provoke resistance. They also want to avoid having to pay compensation for huts and standing crops, or for relocation. Only the unfarmed commons—the forest/woodlands, rangelands and wetlands, can supply the thousands of hectares large-scale investors want. But most of all, as Borras and others (2011) point out, the commons are deemed 'vacant and available'. This is because the laws of most host lessor states still treat all customarily owned lands and unfarmed lands in particular as unowned, unoccupied and idle. As such they remain the property of the state.

As Borras et al. have emphasized the commons are neither unutilized or idle, nor unowned. In fact, under local tenure norms virtually no land is or ever has been unowned, and this remains the case despite the century-long subordination of such customary rights as no more than permissive possession (occupancy and use of vacant lands or lands owned by the state). In practice, customary ownership is nested in spatial domains, the territory of one community extending to the boundaries of the next. While the exact location of intercommunity boundaries are routinely challenged and contested, Wiley (2013: 5) notes that there is little doubt in the locality as to which community owns and controls which area. Within each of these domains property rights are complex and various'. The most usual distinction drawn today, the author adds, 'is between rights over permanent house and farm plots, and rights over the residual commons' (p. 5). And she continues: '[r]ights over the former are increasingly absolute in the hands of families, and increasingly alienable. Rights over commons are collective, held in undivided shares, and while they exist in perpetuity are generally inalienable'.

The implications of the continuing denial that property ownership exists except as recognized by 'imported' European laws are evident. Not just the commons but occupied farms and houses are routinely lost as investors, ownership or concessions to mine or harvest the natural resources in hand, move in while villagers and farmers are either forcibly relocated or forced to abandon their land and communities as the result of the negative socioenvironmental impacts of the extractive activities that ensue. In some contexts (see the discussion below) communities are merely dramatically squeezed, retaining houses and farms but losing their woodlands and rangelands—a variation of the 'classic' pattern of enclosures described by Marx in his analysis of the dynamics of 'primitive accumulation' in England.

Sometimes villagers tentatively welcome investors in the belief that jobs, services, education and opportunities will compensate for the loss of traditional lands and livelihoods. In such cases—at least in the African context—traditional leaders and local elites are often facilitators of deals, making money on the side at the expense of their communities. Reports abound of chiefs or local elites in Ghana, Zambia, Nigeria and Mozambique persuading communities of the benefits of releasing their commons to investors, and even reinterpreting their trusteeship as entailing their right to sell and benefit from those sales. As in the case of North British Columbia (Veltmeyer and Petras, 2014), government officials, politicians and corporate 'entrepreneurs' (energy and mining companies, in the Case of Canada) are routinely on hand to back them up. Such accounts are repeated throughout Africa, and in some Asian states as well as the Americas. Everywhere the story is more or less the same: territorial and communal rights are ignored and disrespected, farming systems upturned, livelihoods decimated, and water use and environments changed in ways that undermine the sustainability of both the environment and livelihoods.

Evidently, possession in the form of customary use is no more sufficient today than it was for the English villagers of the 17th and 18th centuries enclosures. Only legal recognition of commons as the communal property of communities can afford real protection. A number of states in Latin America (Bolivia, Ecuador) have taken this step, setting aside formal registration as prerequisites to admission as real property as well as enshrining in the Constitution ancestral territorial rights and ownership by the people of the country's resource wealth. But the global land rush reduced the likelihood of such reforms coming to pass but it also raises concern that fragile reformist trends in this direction will not be sustained. Because of the coincidence of economic interests (extraordinary profits for the companies, resource rents/additional fiscal resources for the governments) governing regimes find selling or leasing their citizens' land too lucrative to themselves and the class and elites aligned with them, and too advantageous to market-friendly routes of growth, to let justice or the benefits of the commons, or the forces of organized resistance, stand in their way.

Dynamics of Primitive Accumulation: Capitalist Development as Dispossession

From a world-historical standpoint the history of capitalism begins with a process of accumulation originating with the dispossession of the direct smallholding agricultural producers, or peasants, from the land and thus their means of production. Under conditions of this development, secured by diverse means ranging from enclosure of the commons to forceful eviction or expropriation by legal means or by administrative fiat under colonial rule, the capitalist development of the forces of production proceeded apace, and with it a process of productive and social transformation—historically the conversion of an agrarian society based on a precapitalist relations of production and a traditional communalist culture into a modern industrial capitalist system in which relations of direct production are replaced by the capital-labour relation (an exchange of labour power for a wage).

Within the framework of development economics this transformation or transition towards capitalism was theorised as a process of structural change—modernization and industrialization—based on the exploitation of the 'unlimited supply of surplus labour' generated by the capitalist development of agriculture. But within a Marxist political economy framework the transition towards capitalism was conceptualized as the 'agrarian question', in which reference is made to the following processes:

1.   The commodification of land and labour;
2.   The concentration of property in landholdings and capital, with fewer and larger landholdings and units of production at one pole and the proletarianization of the small peasant farmers at the other, converting them into a class for hire or proletariat (Marx, 1979: 5054);
3.   The internal differentiation of the peasantry, with the conversion of some medium-sized peasant landholders into rich peasants and capitalist farmers, and the impoverishment of large numbers of medium- and small-landholding peasant farmers;
4.   The transition, by diverse paths, towards capitalist agriculture based on the exploitation of the countryside by capital in cities;
5.   The proletarianization and impoverishment of increasing numbers of small agricultural producers and poor peasant farmers—what Marx in his theory of the General law of Capital Accumulation (GLCA) conceived as the 'multiplication of the proletariat'; and;
6.   A process of industrialization and modernization based on the exploitation of surplus agricultural labour and its incorporation into the capitalist development process.

This process unfolded with different permutations more or less as theorized from both a development economics and a political economy perspective, leading large numbers of dispossessed peasants—viewed by the agencies of 'development assistance' as the 'rural poor'—to abandon both their rural communities and agriculture, a process that was facilitated by several pathways out of rural poverty—labour and migration—opened by the agencies of development (World Bank, 2008).

While some of the 'rural poor', mostly dispossessed peasant farmers and rural landless workers, initially (in the 1960s and 1970s) took up arms in the land struggle and others were cajoled by the agents of 'development' to stay on their farms with assistance provided through programs of integrated rural development, others in large numbers migrated to the cities and urban centres in search for work, fuelling a process of rapid urbanization and capitalist development of the forces of production, and with it the depopulation of the rural communities and the capitalist development of agriculture. By the end of the first decade into the new millennium this process had resulted in the urbanization of most of the population—now over 70 percent.

This entire process unfolded if not quite according to the planning models of development theorists then more or less as theorized by development economists such as Walt Rostow (1960) who saw as the end point of the modernization process the creation of prosperous centres of modern capitalist industry and middle class societies of high income earners and mass consumption. But in the 1980s on the periphery of the system—in Latin America, for example— the capitalist development process began to unfold in quite if not an entirely different form. Behind or at the base of this peripheral capitalist development process was the installation of a new world order, a new set of rules used to govern international relations of trade and the flow of investment capital. The new rules required governments to implement a program of 'structural reforms' (privatization, deregulation, liberalization, decentralization) designed to open up the economy to the forces of 'economic freedom' (the market liberated from regulatory constraint, capitalist enterprise in the private sector, and the flow of private capital), to unleash thereby a process of 'economic growth' and 'prosperity'. However, the outcome was rather different than theorized or expected.

Opening up local and national economies in peripheral regions to the 'forces of economic freedom' resulted not in economic growth but in the destruction of the productive forces in both industry and agriculture—as well as a decade 'lost to development' marked by economic stagnation, increased social inequalities in the distribution of wealth and income, new forms of poverty (urban rather than rural), and the emergence in the urban economies of an informal sector in which rural migrants were forced to work on their own account on the streets rather than in factories and industrial plants, and offices, for wages (Klein & Tokman, 2000).

As for the rural economy and society the capitalist development process continued to generate what development economists conceptualized as 'unlimited supplies of surplus labour' for the urban labour market, and what Marxists viewed similarly as 'proletarianization' (the transformation of small-scale impoverished agricultural producers or peasants into an industrial proletariat or working class), with its 'industrial reserve army' of proletarianized peasants whose labour is surplus to the requirements of capital. On this process in the Latin American context see Nun (1969) and Quijano (1974). Regarding the associated process of social transformation there emerged a major debate in Latin America between the 'peasantists' (Esteva, 1983) and the 'proletarianists' (Bartra, 1976) as to the fate of the peasantry. At issue in this debate was whether the forces of change unleashed by the capitalist development of agriculture would result in the disappearance of the peasantry. Roger Bartra and other proletarianists argued that the forces of capitalist development would lead to the disappearance of the peasantry and any form of precapitalist forms of production just as it had in manufacturing and other sectors. On the other hand 'peasantists' argued that there were limits to the capitalist development process in its capacity to subsume the labour of the direct producers and that the economy of small-scale agriculture could survive within the interstices of the capitalist system.

The debate took place in the 1970s, but it would take 'developments' in the 1980s to more or less settle it. The 'development' that advanced if not settled the debate was the emergence of an urban proletariat of informal street workers and a large rural semi-proletariat of near-landless rural workers with one foot as it were in the urban labour market and the other in the rural communities and agriculture.

It was not until well into the 1990s that mainstream development economists took cognizance of this 'development'—the emergence of a dualist two-sector economic structure, each with its own structural features and social conditions—by adapting their development strategy vis-à-vis the rural poor, and adjusting the theory used to inform this strategy. Up to this point the theorists and practitioners of development encouraged the outmigration of the rural poor, encouraging them to abandon agriculture in favour of labour in on one form or the other—to take the labour and migration pathways out of rural poor. The role assigned to the state, or the government, in this process was to facilitate the process by capacitating the poor to take advantage of the opportunities available to them in the urban labour markets—to provide the services and programs (education, health, social welfare) designed to this end, and to generate or strengthen the human capital of the poor.

But by the mid-1990s and the turn into the 21st century it was evident that the operating theory of economic development (modernization, industrialization, capitalism), as well as the associated strategy and policies, had to be 'adjusted' to prevailing conditions. For one thing, neoliberal policies based on free market capitalism or the Washington Consensus were simply not working—they neither delivered on the anticipated economic growth, and led to excessive inequalities in the access to productive resources and the distribution of income, and with these inequalities a worsening of poverty and the emergence of social discontent that threatened to undermine and destabilize the system. Also it was evident that both labour and migration had begun to reach if not exhaust their limits in the capacity to expand the forces of production.

With an increasingly restrictive labour market for employment in the private or public sector—up to 80 percent of jobs in the 1980s were generated in the informal sector—and the limited capacity of the informal sector to generate productive forms of self-employment, labour no longer was the pathway out of poverty that it had been theorized to be. Not only did the expanding urban economies generate unsustainable levels of employment, but they featured high levels of un- and under-employment, low income, social disorganization and crime, not to mention the 'planet of have' that bred these conditions (Davis, 2006).

Under these conditions of modernity and deindustrialization several new social categories of individuals emerged in peripheral social formations: an urban proletariat of street workers and large numbers of youth who neither studied nor worked. The reason for this was the contradictory dynamic of uneven capitalist development based on the town-countryside relation: at some point the system will exhaust its capacity to absorb the masses of surplus workers, the rural proletariat of landless or near-landless rural workers (or from another perspective, the 'rural poor'), expelled from the countryside and forced to migrate in the search for work. At the same time, even international migration was reaching or had evidently exceeded its capacity to absorb surplus labour.

The result of these contradictory 'developments' was a shift in thinking among development economists and policymakers in the direction of seeking to slow down rather than encourage rural outmigration—to look for ways to keep the rural poor in their communities. This led to or played into the ongoing search for a new development paradigm—for a more inclusive and participatory form of development based on what rural sociologists would conceptualize as the 'new rurality' (Kay, 2009). This 'new rurality' made reference to the response of the rural semiproletariat and the poor to the forces of capitalist development and social change operating on them, which was to seek to diversify their sources of household income. Other responses included an adjustment to these forces in the form of outmigration in the search for greater opportunities and improved conditions in the world of work. This remained the strategy of a large number of rural households. But another response was to resist rather than adjust to the forces of change by forming or joining a social movement designed and aimed at mobilizing the resistance against the policies that released these forces and resulting conditions, and to take direct collective action against them.

This was a major response of the dispossessed peasantry and rural proletariat to the forces of peripheral capitalist development in the 1960s and 1970s, and again in the 1990s, when the indigenous communities in a number of countries joined the rural semiproletariat in the class struggle for land reform. In both contexts the guardians of the prevailing social and economic order turned towards 'development' as a way of dampening the fires of revolutionary ferment—to provide the rural poor a less confrontational and alternative agency and form of social change. In the 1990s, however, this development process took a different form. Instead of state-led rural development in the form of micro-projects (based on a strategy of 'integrated rural development') 'development' in the 1990s increasingly took the form of local development in which the active agent was the 'community'—community-based organizations run by the poor themselves, by those among the poor who were empowered to act for themselves with 'international cooperation' and 'social participation' (the mediation of NGOs funded by international donors or the government). Development in this form was geared to diverse efforts, and the 'project' of ensuring that the inhabitants of rural society are able to subsist and stay in their communities and are not forced to migrate. The solution: a strategy of diversifying sources of household income.

Evidently agriculture is not a development pathway out of rural poverty given that peasant agriculture is deemed to be the structural source of rural poverty (low productivity) and that very few 'peasants' have the capacity or the wherewithal to be transformed into a capitalist entrepreneur—to access the needed capital, modern technology and markets. However, it behoves the near-landless rural proletariat and semiproletariat to retain access to some agriculture, if only for self-subsistent food production. But the sustainability of rural households is predicated on accessing alternative and additional sources of income, particularly derived from labour—working off-farm or for some household members to migrate week-days, or seasonally, or for longer periods. Sociological studies into household income have determined that today, and as of the mid-1990s, over half of the income available to rural households in the region is derived from one form of labour or the other. However, food gardening and labour/migration by themselves would not relieve the pressure on the 'rural poor' to migrate and abandon their communities. Additional sources of household income, facilitated by state-supported 'development' and international cooperation, today include migrant remittances and conditional direct income transfers to the poor, as well as income-and employment generating development micro-projects.

This rural household survival strategy and associated conditions of community-based development (the 'new rurality') constituted the reality lived by much of the rural proletariat on the periphery of world capitalism at the turn into the 21st century. But conditions would soon change as these rural communities were swept by the changing tides of capitalist development—with the penetration of resource-seeking foreign investments and the expanded operations of extractive capitalism.

The New Geoeconomics of Capital and Associated Dynamics of Agrarian Change

As noted above the 21st century opened up with changes in the global economy driven by the growing demand for natural resources, both fossil fuels and other sources of energy, industrial minerals and precious metals, but also agro-food products. This demand not only led to a primary commodities boom, as governments in resource-rich countries responded to this demand by increasing their exports of these commodities, but to a global land- and resource-grab in the search for improved direct access to these resources.

An important but not well-documented by-product of this expansion of foreign investments into land and agribusiness, as well as exploration for and the mining of fossil fuels and industrial minerals, has been the concentration of capital in the natural resource sector (metal mining, oil and gas, agriculture) as well as increased foreign land ownership (Borras et al., 2011: 9)—what FAO prefers to term 'foreign investments in large-scale land acquisitions'—and also the rapid expansion of extractive industries that require the capture or control of lands.

By a number of accounts and any measure the scale of these foreign investments in both the acquisition of land and natural resource assets, and the rights to explore and extract these resources, is enormous. At the macro-level it is reflected in a significant shift in the 'sectoral distribution of foreign investments' (see Table 2). While resource-seeking investments (in land and natural resource development) constituted only ten percent of FDI flows into Latin America in 2000, by 2010 it represented over 30 percent (Arellano, 2010).

By some accounts the change in the sectoral distribution of FDI has been even greater in Africa, with a larger proportion of these investments being in the acquisition of land rather than in investing in the extraction of natural resources. In either case, the outcome has been the same—a process described by Harvey (2005) as 'accumulation by dispossession'.

One outcome and a major feature of this global land grab is increased foreign ownership of land as well as the concentration of capital in the agricultural sector (UNCTAD, 2011: 110–111), adding another twist to the century-long land struggle. Other dimensions of the landgrabbing process include:

1. The privatization and commodification of land, and with it the transformation of a system of customary rights in regard to land usage into legal and written titles to land ownership;

2. The rationalization of the use of such demarcated landed property as a form of capital (land as a commodity) at the service of 'original' and expanded capital accumulation;

3. The proletarianization of the direct agricultural producers in the form of rural outmigration—by reducing nonmarket access to food and self-sustenance and creating a mobile global proletariat concentrated in the urban centres of what has become the world economy; and, more specifically in regard to extractive capitalism.

4. The forced displacement of inhabitants of the rural communities contiguous to the major sources of natural resources by the negative impacts of extractivist operations—damaging the health, and destroying the environment and livelihoods of the inhabitants of these rural communities.

Under contemporary conditions of this transition—i.e. within the new world order of neoliberal globalization—peasants have been and are, so to speak or write, 'on the move' in three different senses. One is in the form of spatial relocation—migration from diverse rural localities and communities to the urban metropolis and beyond. The dynamics of this well-documented response to the forces of capitalist development are much in evidence, manifest in the uprooting and displacement from the countryside of huge numbers of landless producers, their families and their households. The vast majority of these migrants are absorbed into the urban economy at the level of work or economic activity as a mass of informal workers, working 'on their own account' on the streets, rather than for wages in industrial plants and factories, in private and public sector offices, or in transportation or construction. At the level of living and residence, these rural migrants and landless workers are incorporated into what Mike Davis has dubbed 'a planet of slums'.

Migration is a well-defined and documented response of the rural proletariat to the forces of social change generated in the capitalist development process and the social antagonism between the city and the countryside is present in all societies that have developed under the capitalist mode of production. The World Bank in its 2008 *World Development Report* conceives of this response as a 'pathway out of rural poverty'. Another option available to the rural proletariat—also conceived by World Bank economists as a 'pathway out of poverty'—is 'labour': basically an exchange of labour-power for a living wage. Responses along this line, also understood as a matter of individual decision-making, are represented in the resulting process of social transformation, which for the individual small-scale agricultural producer or 'peasant' means entry into a relation of work or labour under whatever conditions might be available.

This type of response or pathway out of poverty has resulted in the formation of a sizeable semiproletariat with links to both land and wage-labour, allowing peasants to secure the livelihood of their households; and, at a different level, to constitute what Marx in a different context termed an 'industrial reserve army' of workers whose labour is held in reserve without capital having to assume the costs of its reproduction (Veltmeyer, 1983). As for the World Bank's interpretation of this response it is reflected in the category of 'labour-oriented household' that has adopted 'labour' (wage-labour in agriculture and industry, self-employment) as a strategic pathway out of rural poverty—from 45 percent of all households in predominantly rural/agriculture-based societies such as Nicaragua to 53 percent of households in societies such as Ecuador considered to be 'urbanized' or 'transforming' (World Bank, 2008: 76).

The economists behind the 2008 *World Development Report* on Agriculture for Development identify 'farming' as the third strategic response of the rural poor to the forces of social change. This pathway out of rural poverty is predicated on the modernization of agriculture and the capitalist development of production. But a more consequential strategic response, not identified by the World Bank given its ideological focus on possible forms of structural adjustment, takes a 'political' rather than a 'structural' form (the outcome of economic decisions made by countless individuals). It is to organize a social movement as a means of mobilizing the forces of resistance within agrarian society against the processes of primitive accumulation and proletarianization—against the loss of land and the destruction of their livelihoods, against forced migration and the subsumption and exploitation of labour, against the depredations of global capital and imperialism, against the policies of the neoliberal state and its governing body in the global economy ('the international bourgeoisie').

In a sense, both sides of the argument regarding the process of the capitalist development and agrarian transformation are supported by some of the 'facts' and thus able to explain some of the changes taking place in the Latin American countryside, on the periphery of the expanding capitalist nucleus in the urban centres. This is because, under conditions of what some have conceptualized as 'peripheral capitalism', the peasantry is being transformed in part but not completely, emerging as what we have described as a 'semiproletariat' of near-landless rural workers or landless 'peasants. Under these conditions rather than the 'disappearance of the peasantry' what we have is its reproduction in diverse forms. Many self-defined 'peasants' or family farmers in these circumstances emerge as a rural semiproletariat of landless workers forced to combine direct production on the land with wage-labour—working off-farm to secure the livelihood of their households and families; and an urban proletariat of workers in the informal sector of the urban economy, to work 'on their own account' in the streets and live in the slums formed on the periphery of this economy.

There is little 'new' about this process. Its diverse permutations can be traced out in the dynamics of productive and social transformation all over the world in different geographical and historical contexts. But what is new or distinctive about the transition towards capitalism in this context is that the associated process of productive and social transformation has been arrested or stalled in its tracks as it were, with both modernity and capitalism taking a distinct peripheral form in the formation of a semiproletariat of rural landless workers forced into seasonal or irregular forms of wage-labour. Under these conditions, together with the politics of resistance against the neoliberal 'structural reform' agenda responsible for them, there is no question of the peasantry disappearing into the dustbins of history as predicted by structuralists in both the development economics and Marxist camps. The problem is to determine the particular form taken by the class struggle under these conditions and under the new conditions that have emerged over the past decade of extractive capitalism and extractivist imperialism.

The devastating and painful consequences of this process are reflected in the detritus of grinding poverty left behind in the countryside as well as the negative socioenvironmental impacts of extractive capitalism. As for the issue of poverty the concerted efforts of the international organizations engaged in the fight against 'global poverty' and those governments that have embraced the post-Washington Consensus and the 'new developmentalist' policy agenda appear to have succeeded in reducing the incidence of poverty—at least in some cases (Brazil, Chile, Venezuela) and in these cases by as much as 40 percent. Nevertheless, notwithstanding these advances on the anti-poverty front, and notwithstanding the emergence in the 1990s of poverty as an urban phenomenon, 75 percent of the world's poor today still live in the rural areas.

In this regard, the century-long class struggle for land has been transformed into a broader struggle for sustainable livelihoods and for maintaining a 'traditional' way of life and culture associated with small-scale agricultural production. This struggle, as well as the struggle by organized labour for improved wages and working conditions, has also been broadened and transformed into resistance against the policies of the neoliberal state and the forces of 'globalization'— integration into a global economy in which the forces of 'economic freedom' (investment capital, trade in goods and services) have been liberated from the regulatory constraints of the development-welfare state. And in the new millennium, as discussed below, a new phase in the capitalist development of the forces of production on a global scale—extractivist imperialism—would bring about another major change in both the form taken by the forces of resistance and the correlation of forces in the broader struggle.

Food Versus Energy: The Political Economy of Biofuels Capitalism/Imperialism

Agricultural extractivism rakes a number of forms, but in the current context what has dominated the debate—apart from the dynamics of landgrabbing— has been what we might term the political economy of biofuels capitalism: the conversion of farmland and agriculture for food production into the production of biofuels. What set off the debate was the change in land use in Brazil in the use of corn from a food and feedlot product into ethanol. However, what sparked the current debate has been the large-scale change in the use of farmland to convert it from food production into the production of soy as a biofuel form of energy. It would appear that biofuels production and related financial speculation is a major impetus behind landgrabbing, particularly in Argentina and Brazil, where enormous swathes of farmland have been given over to soy production.

The conversion of agriculture (sugarcane and soya) production of food into energy evidently drives agrarian change in countries such as Argentina and Brazil. However, as emphasized by Novo et al. (2010) regarding Brazil, biofuels production must be understood in the broader context of the new geoeconomics of capital (extractive capitalism), not just than in terms of the recent expanded global demand for energy. Agrarian change in this context includes not only increased large-scale land grabs and a process of accumulation by dispossession, but a process of economic concentration in addition to changes in land use and the destruction of traditional economies that have sustained generations of farming families and local food markets, the destruction of the livelihoods of millions of small landholding producers for local food markets, and, more broadly a sharp rise in the price of food and with it the onset of a global food crisis.

Environmentalists have criticized the massive conversion of forestland and other yet non-arable land into biofuel production, and have called into question its supposed environmental efficiencies and the overall effect of biofuels on reducing greenhouse gas emissions. But development-oriented arguments have suggested that the biofuel agenda in rich countries, supported with heavy government subsidies, were driving up food prices and competing with other forms of land use, and also when biofuel production is planned on supposedly 'marginal' lands, because these are often important for the livelihoods of the poor (OXFAM, 2008). These arguments have shifted views within some decision-making bodies of the EU and the FAO. The FAO (2008), for example, has concluded that the rise of food prices is indeed an effect of the expansion of biofuel production and that whether biofuels will help to reduce or increase greenhouse gas emissions depends on the precise conditions. But to date, there seem to be few empirical studies of competing claims on land use, even though these seem to be central to the biofuel controversy.

In the controversial debate about biofuels, Brazil is pivotal in that it is the second largest liquid biofuel producer in the world with a complete biofuel social-technical configuration and a full chain from producing sugarcane and ethanol to flex-fuel cars that run on biofuels, supported by government subsidies, a regulatory system, technical research and finance arrangements (Novo et al., 2010). Another such case is Argentina, where the government has actively promoted opening up the country to large-scale investments in the production of soy to fuel both the domestic and the global economy.

Class Struggle on the Global Commons

An interesting but as yet not well-documented by-product of this expansion of FDI into exploration and mining of oil, gas, and minerals has been the concentration of capital in the sector as well as increased foreign land ownership based on land-grabbing (Borras et al., 2011: 9)—what FAO prefers to term 'large-scale foreign investments in land acquisition'—and the rapid expansion of mineral extractive industries that require the capture or control of lands. But yet another outcome of this territorial development has been the emergence of new forms of class struggle and forces of resistance on what we might view as the 'global commons' of land, water and associated natural resources on the expanding frontier of extractive capitalism.

Boaventura de Sousa Santos, a professor of sociology at the School of Economics at the Portuguese University of Coimbra, points out that more than 80 percent of natural resources and the biodiversity that humanity requires for its subsistence in the future belong to indigenous and peasant communities, a significant number of which are found in Latin America. The indigenous people and peasants everywhere existed for millennia prior to colonialism and were capable of sustaining their livelihoods and communities on the basis of a traditional culture that respected both the integrity of mother earth or nature (known as *Pachamama* in the Andes) and the intimate symbiotic relationship of their agrarian societies with nature.

Indigenous Peoples in Argentina and Brazil: A Struggle for Survival[1]

While the indigenous peoples of Argentina, according to Giarracca and Teubal (2014) were the first to resist having their communities cornered and harassed by old or new corporations, such as the old sugar mills or Benetton in the Patagonia, they were not the first to appear in the media or the public arena. In Argentina, they note—and there is nothing particular to Argentina here— there is a long practice of ignoring or 'invisibilizing' the pre-existing inhabitants of these territories, unlike in neighbouring Brazil, especially in Mato Grosso do Sul, where the indigenous population were ruthlessly expelled from the land by 'farmers' and ranchers anxious to expand into the rich farmland of the agribusiness frontier in both the Amazonian region and the southern Pampas. In two countries in which the old agro-export capitalist economy is entrenched and widely celebrated, the idea that there may be other uses for the national territory—better uses of land and other ways of producing food-is difficult to imagine.

The indigenous population in these areas is widely viewed by large land-owning farmers, ranchers and corporations as an anachronism, a nuisance and an obstacle to progress. In the long and continuing struggle of the indigenous groups and communities to resist the advance of the large soy and sugar-cane plantations and agribusiness in their territories they have been either systematically pushed off the land, invisibilized or exterminated as dictated by circumstances.

An emblematic case study of these symptomatic conditions and the resulting struggle for land respect for territorial rights and survival is that of the Kolla

---

1   The following discussion relies heavily on the account given by Giarracca and Teubal in Veltmeyer & Petras (2014).

in the north-western provinces of Argentina. The Kolla are organized and live in communities that extend from the Bolivian border into the Argentine province of Salta. These communities have a long history of intense and violent struggle to reclaim territories that were usurped by a sugar mill belonging to one of the main oligarchic families of the north. Among other actions they led a series of '*caravanas*' or large-scale displacements of indigenous populations to the cities, where they encamped and made their claims. In February 2009, the Supreme Court of Justice, in response to a claim presented in 2008 by the indigenous communities and peasants of the departments of San Martín, Orán, Rivadavia and Santa Victoria in Salta, ordered suspension of a deforestation project authorized the previous year. In ordering this suspension the court invoked the precautionary principle set out in Article 4 of the *Ley General del Ambiente, No. 25,675*.

At this time the Kolla communities of Salta organized the *Coordinadora de Organizaciones Kollas Autónomas*, which included virtually all the communities in the province of Qullamarka, thus strengthening the resistance and their protest actions for their territorial rights and autonomy. This permitted them to take action in defence of their livelihoods, including the deforestation of their territories. Once the Supreme Court presented its ruling the Qullamarka also denounced the advance of mining in their territory, repudiating the pillage of resources and contamination of the commons. The Qullamarka in this struggle defended a territory of more than a million hectares against diverse projects, including mining and tourism, that involve what Harvey has termed a process of 'accumulation by dispossession' as well as a plundering of the territory's wealth of natural resources. In fighting for its customary rights and communal title to the land the Qullamarka have also had to contend with the interventions of the state and NGOs (Giarracca & Teubal, 2014).

Giarracca and Teubal document similar struggles in Chaco and Formosa, where communities of the Qom, Wichí and Mocoví led important mobilizations for the purpose of instigating a public debate over the situation affecting the indigenous populations in these provinces, namely their displacement in a context of landgrabbing and deforestation. In a context in which important and profound transformations are taking place in social structures and productive systems access to land has become one of the main claims structuring the historical demands of these and other indigenous communities in the country.

The struggles of the Mapuche ('people of the land'), who straddle the border between Argentina and Chile in the South of both countries warrant special consideration. These indigenous communities have organized themselves in recent decades in order to recuperate their lands and defend their territorial and customary land rights. The border area is a region with a wide biodiversity, including minerals and petroleum, and consequently it has been the object of diverse confrontations with economic interest groups that are the main agents of plunder and dispossession in the territory. These groups act with the complicity of the provincial government, which are not disposed to protect the communities or to regulate the indiscriminate sale and concession of lands and goods.

As a result of the complicity of government officials with the landgrabbers and extractive capitalists, and because of the futility and delay involved in legal procedures for restitution of their territory, a number of communities have taken direct action, provoking class conflict over access to the commons. Giarracca and Teubal make reference to several noteworthy landmarks in this regard. In the mid-1990s, 42,000 hectares were recovered in the locality of Pulmarí in the province of Neuquén after a long process of land occupation and legal actions that lasted over a decade. The conflict concerned the continuing nonfulfillment of a statute, according to which the *Corporación Interestadual Pulmarí* (which included national and provincial authorities as well as representatives of the Mapuche) was to take charge of the combined administration of a parcel of land of 110,000 hectares. Also in Neuquén the Mapuche have opposed and continue to resist the activities of oil companies in their territory, both the Spanish-owned Repsol-YPF and now the nationalized YPF, mostly because of their use of new technologies that are even more contaminating and destructive than fracking.

Giarracca and Tuebal (2014) have studied a number of cases of extractive capitalism, colonialism and imperialism—and the struggles engendered by the activities involved in the process of capitalist development. However, Brazil provides an even more advanced setting for a series of case studies into this process and associated struggles. One of these cases is set in the Brazilian state of Mato Grosso do Sul, home to a small number of tribal and farming communities with ancestral rights to a vast territory found on a new but rapidly expanding frontier for extractive capital and agribusiness. In their resistance against the incursions of extractive capital, big landowning 'farmers and agribusiness corporations into their territory a number of tribal groups and communities have fought back by occupying farms and ranches set up by these agrarian capitalists' (Glusing, 2014). In occupying the farms and ranches these groups are fighting for their land, protecting the borders of their reservations, resisting the construction of hydroelectric power plants in their regions and protesting against the advance of the agricultural industry, which is destroying their homeland.

What is particularly instructive about this case of resistance by the Terena tribal group is how that it illustrates so clearly the relation between capital and the state in the development process of extractive capital in Brazil, as well as (more concretely) the power of the big farmers lobby and the subordination of the PT regime under Rousseff to the large landowning agrarian elite who constitute a decisive power bloc in the legislative assembly and have a virtual stranglehold over the regime's agricultural policy.

The Peasantry

In their documentation of the land struggle in Argentina Giarracca and Tuebal (2014) make particular reference to the work of several organizations involved in the *Mesa Nacional de Organizaciones de Productores Familiares*, and that currently form part of the *Movimiento Nacional Campesino Indígena* (MNCI). These organizations, they note, have employed tactics such as preventing evictions in diverse actions to reclaim the land and their territories, as well as direct confrontations with soy producers and land invaders. Within the movement it appears that several organizations are particularly active, including the *Movimiento Campesino de Santiago del Estero-Vía Campesina*, the *Movimiento Campesino de Córdoba,* the *Unión de Trabajadores Sin Tierra* (Mendoza), the *Red Puna (Jujuy)* and the *Encuentro Calchaquí*. Several urban organizations in Buenos Aires and Rosario that are close to regional peasant organizations and movements such as the *Coordinadora Latinoamericana de Organizaciones del Campo* (CLOC) and *Vía Campesina* are also incorporated into the movement and actively participate in the struggle, coordinating their actions and mobilizations.

Their main propositions and demands of these organizations and movements are:

1. an effective and comprehensive agrarian reform, to democratize the control over the means of production and redress the problem of poverty in the countryside and the city;
2. food sovereignty, in opposition to agribusiness and defense of a productive culture that provides healthy food for the population, by means of adherence to the principles of *comercio justo* (Fair Trade);
3. the respect of peasant and indigenous territorial rights and territories, recognizing community use and ownership of land as well as the commons;
4. respect of the 'social function' of land, which implies respect for the biodiversity of the environment and the social rights of workers, and food production in the context of the right to a dignified life; and
5. respect for the collective organizations of peasant famers and indigenous communities, such as the *Coordinadora de Comunidades Indígenas y Trabajadores Rurales de Argentina*.

The latter organization is the result of the amalgamation of different organizations with different collective identities but who all form part of CLOC, such as the *Consejo Asesor Indígena,* the *Unión de Campesinos Poriajhú* (in Chaco) and the *Campamento de Trabajo* (Córdoba). As with the organizations mentioned above the land struggle and confrontations with agribusiness are the main aspects of their protests and resistance.

As for the land struggle the main issue over the years has been land reform—redistribution of the land, which in most of Latin America is highly skewed in terms of ownership (Moyo & Yeros, 2005). Over the past decades, especially in the 1960s and 1970s, this structure led to large waves of rural migrants, peasant farmers forced to abandon their communities and agriculture, and move to the cities in search for a better way of life. It also led to and fed a growing movement of rural landless workers in Argentina as well as Bolivia modelled on the Brazilian example. Another option exercised by these landless 'peasants' or 'rural landless workers', an alternative to both outmigration and the land struggle, has been to rebuild local food markets that have been decimated by decades of capitalist development and nefarious US trade and aid policies.

In this context mention can also be made of the resurgence of the *Ligas Agrarias* (Agrarian Leagues), which is intent on recapturing the experiences of the peasant movement in the 1970s, an experience shared with peasants in Brazil. This movement is promoted by the ex-leaders of the previous *Ligas Agrarias* in the provinces of Chaco, Santa Fe and Corrientes. The structure assumes a regional character and is inserted into national organizations that coordinate peasant action. This organization has established itself as a civic association and some of its members occupy public office.

Finally worth mentioning is the *Asamblea Campesina e Indígena del Norte Argentino* (ACINA), a coordinating body and assembly of diverse peasant and indigenous organizations in Argentina's North formed in 2006. Some of the organizations brought together by ACINA, with extensive experience of land and class struggles dating back to the 1980s, also participate in the *Frente Nacional Campesino,* a national front of peasants formed in the class struggle for land. The presence of powerful groups such as the *Unión de Pequeños Productores del Chaco,* as well as the *Mesa de Organizaciones de Pequeños Productores del Chaco,* which integrates all the organizations of the province, is also significant. The importance of ACINA is in its creation of a regional organizational and political space that contributes to the generation of other organizations and relationships among indigenous communities and peasant organizations at the provincial and national level.

Conclusion

Our analysis of the contemporary dynamics of agrarian extractivism—landgrabbing for energy, minerals, and metals, and agrofood—leads us to conclude that Bernstein (2010: 82–84) was substantially correct in the propositions that he established regarding the impact of globalization on agriculture and the agrarian question today. These propositions are that:

1. the policy of trade liberalization, implemented within the framework of the Washington Consensus, has led to a shift in global trade patterns of agricultural commodities (increased south–north flows);
2. futures trading in agricultural commodities, i.e. speculation spurred by financialization, has resulted in an increase in the price of agrofood products on different markets;
3. the removal of subsidies and other forms of support to small farmers in the south together with the promotion of 'export platforms' (especially of animal feeds and high-value commodities) and large-scale foreign investment in the acquisition of land for extractive purposes;
4. the increasing concentration of global corporations in both agri-input and agro-food industries, marked by mergers and acquisitions and the economic power of fewer corporations commanding larger market shares;
5. introduction of new organizational technologies deployed by these corporations along commodity chains from farming (harvesting and feeding) to retail distribution (the 'supermarket revolution');
6. the push by these corporations to patent intellectual property rights in genetic material, particularly as regards terminator seeds and other genetically modified products, with a devastating impact on the environment, the health of the population, biodiversity in agricultural production, rural livelihoods based on small-scale production and farming, and access of small family farmers and peasants to seeds, and food security;
7. a new technical frontier of engineering plant and animal genetic material (genetically modified organisms or GMOs), together with specialized monoculture, has contributed to a significant loss of biodiversity;
8. a new profit frontier of agrofuel production, dominated by agribusiness corporations, with a consequent loss of food security and food sovereignty;
9. the negative health consequences of the corporate agribusiness model of agriculture and the rising level of toxic chemicals in industrially grown

and processed foods—contributing to a trend toward nutritional diet deficiencies, obesity-related illness, and growing hunger and malnutrition; and

10. the environmental costs of the industrialization of food farming, including increased levels of fossil-fuel use and their carbon emissions.

Another conclusion that can be drawn from our analysis of the dynamics of agricultural extractivism, a conclusion that Bernstein might have but did not reach, is that each twist and turn in the capitalist development process generates different forces of resistance, and that in the current context the dynamics of class struggle have shifted from the demand for land reform and higher wages/improved working conditions, and resistance against the neoliberal policy agenda, towards a defence of the commons (of land, water and natural resources) and an organized resistance against the socioenvironmental impacts of extractive capitalism—including environmental degradation and forced abandonment. The class struggle, in short, has moved away from workplaces to the streets and in some contexts the sites of extractive operations and the communities that are directly and negatively affected by these operations.

PART 2

Policy and Resistance Dynamics of US Imperialism

∵

US Imperialism in Latin America: Then and Now

In the wake of a second world war as the dominant economic power in the 'free world', the US strove assiduously to consolidate this power at the level of foreign policy. Under prevailing conditions that included the potential threat posed by the USSR and the fallout from a spreading and unstoppable decolonization movement in the economically backward areas of the world, US policymakers decided on, and actively pursued, a foreign policy with three pillars. One of these pillars was a strategy of economic reconstruction of an economically devastated Europe and the capitalist development of the economies and societies on the periphery of the system. A second pillar of the post-war order was what would become known as the 'Bretton Woods system', composed of three institutions (a Bank of Economic Reconstruction and Development—known today as the International Monetary Fund; and a General Agreement on Tariffs and Trade that would morph into the World Trade Organization (WTO) 50 years on) and the mechanism of the US dollar, based on a fixed gold standard, as the currency of international trade. The third pillar would become the United Nations—a system of international organizations designed to provide the necessary conditions of (capitalist) development and collective security, a system of multilateral conflict resolution.

The motivating force behind this foreign policy was clear enough: to advance the geopolitical and economic interests of the United States as a world power, including considerations of profit and strategic security (to make the world safe for US investments and to reactivate a capital accumulation process). It was to be an empire of free trade and capitalist development, plus democracy where possible, a system of capitalist democracies backed up by a system of international organizations dominated by the US, a military alliance (NATO) focused on Europe in the protection of US interests and collective security, and a more global network of military bases to provide logistical support for its global military apparatus.

Within the institutional framework of this system and international order the US was particularly concerned to consolidate its power and influence in Latin America and the Caribbean, regarded by policymakers and many politicians as a legitimate sphere of undue influence—the exercise of state power in the 'national interest'. This chapter will elaborate on the economic and political dynamics of the efforts pursued by the US to pursue these interests via the projection of state power—and the resulting 'informal empire' constructed by default.

US Imperialism in Latin America—Forms and Dynamics

The US has always been imperialistic in its approach to national development in Latin America, but in the wake of World War II the situation that it found itself in—commanding, it is estimated, half of the world's industrial capacity and 80 percent of its financial resources; and already an occupying power of major proportions—awakened in US policymaking circles and its foreign policy establishment its historic mission regarding the Americas and also the dream of world domination, provoking the quest to bring it about in the preferred form of an 'informal empire'. A key strategy to this purpose was to institute the rules for what would later be termed 'global governance'—for securing its economic and geopolitical strategic interests in a world liberated from colonial rule (i.e., competing empires). The resulting world order, dubbed Bretton Woods I by some, provided an institutional framework for advancing the geopolitical strategic interests of the US in the context of a 'cold war' waged against the emerging power of the USSR, and for advancing cooperation for international development, a policy designed to ensure that the economically backward countries seeking to liberate themselves from the yoke of European colonialism would not succumb to the siren of communism, that they would instead undertake a nation-building and development process on a capitalist path.

This development project required the US to assume the lead but also share power with its major allies, strategic partners in a common enterprise organized as the OECD and a united Europe, with a system of United Nations institutions to provide a multilateral response to any security threats—and that prevented any one country for embarking on the path of world domination via unilateral action. This was the price that the US had to pay for national security under conditions of an emerging threat presented by the USSR—Soviet communism backed up by what was feared to be a growing if not commanding state power.

In this context the US began to construct its empire, and it did so on a foundation of six pillars:

1. consolidation of the liberal capitalist world order, renovating it on neoliberal lines in the early 1980s when conditions allowed;

2. a system of military bases strategically located across the world, to provide thereby the staging point and logistics for the projection of military power when needed, and rule by military force when circumstances would dictate;

3. a project of cooperation for international development, to provide financial and technical assistance to countries and regimes willing to sign on

the project—to provide a safe haven for US economic interests and pave the way for the expansion of capitalism and democracy, the bulwarks of US imperialism;

4. implementation of a neoliberal agenda of policy reforms—to adjust the macroeconomic and development policies to the requirements of a new world order in which the forces of freedom would be released from the constraints of the welfare-development state;

5. regional integration—construction of regional free trade agreements to cooperate with, and not discriminate against, US economic interests regarding international trade; and

6. globalization—the integration of economies across the world into the global economy in a system designed to give maximum freedom to the operating units of the global empire.

Each strategy not only served as a pillar of imperial policy but provided the focal point for the projection of state power in different forms as circumstances required or permitted. Together they constituted what might be termed *imperialism*. Each element of the system was, and is, dynamic in its operations but ultimately unstable because of the countervailing forces that they generated.

Rule by Armed Force: War in the Informal Empire

Within ruling class circles in the US since at least 2000 there is an open acceptance that theirs is an imperial state and that the US should maintain or act to restore its dominant position in the 21st century by any means available, and certainly by force if need be.

The whole tenor of the debate over US foreign policy in the past two decades, Mann (2007) notes, is framed in these terms. In this connection, Richard Hass, the current director of Policy Planning in the State Department, wrote an essay in November 2000 advocating that the US adopt an 'imperial' foreign policy. He defined this as 'a foreign policy that attempts to organize the world along certain principles affecting relations between states and conditions within them'. This would not be achieved through colonization but thorough what he termed 'informal control' based on a 'good neighbour policy' backed up by military force if and when necessary—harking back to the 'informal empire' of a previous era (McLean, 1995; Roorda, 1998).

Mechanisms such as international financial markets and structural reforms in macroeconomic policy, and agencies such as the World Bank, the WTO and the IMF, would work to ensure the dominance of US interests, with the military iron fist backing up the invisible hand of the market and any failure in multilateral security arrangements.

This system of 'economic imperialism', maintained by US hegemony as leader of the 'free world' (representing the virtues of capitalist democracy), was in place and fully functioning from the 1950s throughout the 1980s and the reign of Ronald Reagan. In the 1990s, with the disappearance of the threat of the Soviet Union and international communism, this system of economic imperialism, based as it was on the hegemony of 'democracy and freedom' as well as multilateralism in international security arrangements, did not as much break down as it was eclipsed by the emergence of the 'new imperialism' based on the unilateral projection of military force as a means of securing world domination in 'the American century'.[1]

This conception of 'new imperialism', a 'raw imperialism' that would not 'hesitate to use [coercive] force if, when and where necessary' (Cooper, 2000), based on 'aggressive multilateralism' or the unilateral projection, and strategic use, of state power including emphatic military force, was advanced in neo-conservative circles over years of largely internal debate, and put into practice by a succession of regimes, both Democratic and Republican. It achieved its consummate form in George W. Bush's White House, in the Gang of Four (Donald Rumsfeld, Paul Wolfowitz, Condoleeza Rice, Dick Cheney), and its maximum expression in a policy of imperial war in the Middle East and the Gulf region. Although the US also projected its military power in other theatres of imperial war such as Yugoslavia and Colombia (viz. the covert Colombia-centred class war 'on subversives' against the FARC-EP and the overt regional 'war on drugs') the policy of imperial war and the strategy of military force were primarily directed towards the Gulf region.

In the academic world the issue as to the specific or dominant form taken by imperialism has not been generally framed as a matter of when and under what circumstances military force might be needed or legitimately used (generally seen as a 'last resort' but as the necessary part of the arsenal of force available to the state, conceived of as the only legitimate repository of the use of violence in the 'national interest'). Rather, the issue of armed force in the imperialist projection of military power has been framed in terms of an understanding, or the argument that an imperial order cannot be maintained by force and coercion; it requires 'hegemony', which is to say, acquiescence by the subalterns of imperial power achieved by a widespread belief in the legitimacy of that power generated by an overarching myth or dominant ideology— the idea of freedom in the post-World War II context of the 'cold war' against

---

1 The 1992 Wolfowitz Report asserted explicitly that the US had to maintain a military machine so powerful as to discourage local or global rivalries. Under George W. Bush this doctrine was converted into policy.

communism and the idea of globalization in the new imperial order established in the 1980s. Power relations of domination and subordination, even when backed up by coercive or armed force, invariably give rise to resistance, and are only sustainable if and when they are legitimated by an effective ideology—ideas of 'democracy' and 'freedom' in the case of the American empire or 'globalization' in the case of the economic imperialism that came into play in the 1990s.

It is no accident that the 1990s saw the advent of a new—military—form of imperialism. For one thing, the idea of globalization, used to legitimate and justify neoliberal policies of stabilization and structural reform, had lost its commanding force—its hold over the minds of people, particularly among classes within the popular sector. As a result, the 1990s in Latin America saw the advent and workings of powerful forces of resistance to the neoliberal policy agenda and the machinations of US imperialism. To combat these forces of resistance state officials resorted to different strategies and tactics as dictated by circumstances, generally by combining development assistance and outright repression.

How this worked in practice can be illustrated in the case of Paraguay in recent years. In 1996 the then-government presided over by Nicanor Duarte decreed as legal the presence of military and paramilitary forces in the countryside because the police were unable to contain the peasant struggle. At the same time and in the same context the regime authorized the presence of American troops, giving them immunity for any violation of the country's laws that might occur in the process of their 'humanitarian assistance' (counterinsurgency training) provided to Paraguayan troops. It was alleged by the peasant organizations that some of the nongovernmental organizations operating in the area and financed by USAID are also enlisted to provide assistance in controlling the population; diverting the rural poor away from the social movements; and having them opt for local micro-development projects instead. In this sense, what is happening in Paraguay is in the time honoured US tradition of combining the iron fist of armed force with the velvet glove of local development on the front lines of rural poverty.

Elsewhere in the global US empire neither neoliberalism in policy or resistance in the form of social movements was as virulent as they were in Latin America. As a result, the idea of 'globalization' had more currency in other macro-regions of the empire than it ever had in Latin America. It would require the events of 9/11, and the resurrection and reconstruction of the US's global mission (to defend the free world) for the administrators of the empire under George W. Bush to escape the confines of 'globalization' and dispense with its constraints, allowing the administration to institute the 'new imperialism' with as much overt force and military power as the state could dispose, multi-laterally if possible but unilaterally if necessary.

International Development

Overseas Development Assistance (ODA)—foreign aid, in more common parlance—is widely viewed as a catalyst of economic development, a boost to 'developing societies' economies to assist them in following the path towards progress and prosperity traced out by the club of rich or advanced capitalist countries. But is possible to look at foreign aid in a very different way—as a means of advancing the geopolitical and strategic interests of the governments and organizations that provide this aid. In 1971, at the height (but impending crisis) of the Bretton Woods world economic order, this view was expressed in the notion of 'imperialism as aid' (Hayter, 1971).

The purpose of aid was essentially geopolitical: to ensure that the former colonies of British-led European imperialism upon achieving national inde-pendence would not fall prey to the lure of communism and to ensure that they would follow a capitalist path towards their national development.

In the wake of the Cuban Revolution the US redirected its 'development' efforts and its entire strategy away from nation building towards the countryside in various 'developing societies' where there was a build-up of revolutionary ferment. In Latin America, where this new strategy was concentrated, this entailed the construction of the 'Alliance for Progress'—a new policy and insti-tutional framework of international cooperation for rural development, a proj-ect aimed at the rural poor—to turn them from the confrontational politics of the social movements and opt instead for local development (Veltmeyer, 2005).

In the 1960s and 70s, a combination of this approach with a strategy of co-optation of the leadership of the social movements, and strategic use of its repres-sive apparatus, resulted in the defeat of the impulse towards social revolution among the rural poor and destruction of the armies for national liberation that had sprouted throughout the Latin American countryside under conditions of imperialist and class exploitation. The Revolutionary Armed Forces of Colombia—the People's Army (FARC-EP)—was one of the very few such revolutionary orga-nizations in the region that survived. The occasional fragile unity of the forces of resistance mounted by organized labour in the cities and the proletarianized peasants in the countryside was everywhere broken, and the remaining forces of resistance were demobilized and went to ground, awaiting more favourable con-ditions. As it turned out, such conditions only materialised in Chiapas, allowing the grounded forces of resistance to reappear under changed conditions—erupting, in this case, on January 1, 1994, the day in which the North American Free Trade Agreement (NAFTA), a new offensive in the imperialist war, was launched.

This particular offensive, as it turned out, would also be ultimately defeated— not by armed force but by a policy of strategic isolation and encirclement. In other contexts—particularly in Brazil, Ecuador and Bolivia—the forces of resistance against neoliberalism and US imperialism were more successful. Indeed, the social movements in these countries succeeded in either halting, slowing down and even, in some cases, reversing the neoliberal agenda, placing state officials in these countries, as well as the agencies of US imperialism, on the defensive. It would take another decade of concerted actions against these movements to hold them at bay. Again it was not armed force but the project of international cooperation for 'development', implemented within the new policy framework of the post-Washington Consensus, that was primarily responsible for dampening the forces of revolutionary change in the region.

The political Left, having abandoned the revolutionary struggle, was complicit in this defeat of the social movements. Certain elements took up positions within the development project on the basis of what Holloway (2002) views as a 'no power' approach to social change (to bring about change without taking power). Other elements of the Left opted for what used to be termed the 'parliamentary road' to state power, namely democratic elections. By 2005, with the notable exception of Bolivia, where the revolutionary forces were actively mobilized in the struggle to prevent the privatization of the country's strategic natural resources, the wave of social movements that had washed over the neoliberal state in the 1990s had ebbed, weakened and was forced into retreat by the very centre-left that had achieved state power in the wake of widespread disenchantment with neoliberalism (Petras & Veltmeyer, 2009, 2011).

The Neoliberal Agenda

The neoliberal agenda, a prominent feature of the economic imperialism of recent years, had been decades in the making but it was not until the early 1980s, in the vortex of two crises, that the conditions needed for its implementation became available. The fiscal crisis provided the political conditions of a conservative counterrevolution in development thinking and practice—for the advent of neoliberalism. On the other hand was the debt crisis, which provided a lever for adjusting government policies to the requirements of this new world order.

While the World Bank and the IMF might be considered the operational units of the economic imperialism, its brain trust, as it were, is constituted by an array of neoconservative and neoliberal institutions, including the Pelerin Society, a neoliberal thought collective constituted to advance free-market capitalism at the level of national policy (Mirowski & Plehwe, 2009). It also includes the Council on Foreign Relations (CFR), a complex of policy forums and Washington-based foundations. The institutional structure of this 'new world order' encompasses the World Bank, the IMF and the WTO, the latter stillborn in 1944 negotiations, not constructed until 1994 in a major shift in imperial strategy manifest in and coinciding with the institution of NAFTA.

The impetus behind the call for a 'new world order' in the 1980s was to resolve the fiscal and production crisis, to advance capitalist development on a global scale, and create a policy agenda for advancing these interests, which are represented most directly in the operational units of this system, namely the multinational corporations which could be defined as the crack troops of US economic imperialism. The dynamics of these institutions, viz. globalization and structural adjustment, and the role in the design and implementation of macroeconomic policy, are well documented, much more so than the operations of the CFR and even more so of the MPS, whose members have played a major role in the promotion of neoliberalism, to finance research centres and policy forums to promote (i) free enterprise and the free market; (ii) economic integration in the form of regional free trade agreements; (iii) macroeconomic policy in the form of structural reform.

This project, based on a neoliberal agenda, can be traced back to the 1940s, to ideas promulgated at the time by members of the Pelerin Society, but was only seriously advanced in the 1980s when political conditions for a counter-revolution in development theory and practice—a new world order—were favourable.

In the mid-1980s the neoliberal agenda for 'structural reform' was advanced in the form of globalization, the ideology constructed as a means of mobilizing support for this policy agenda, presenting it as a consensus and a development program, the only way forwards to general prosperity—and to establish hegemony over the whole system. By the end of the decade, however, the idea of globalization fractured and succumbed to forces of resistance. It no longer served as an effective ideology to justify and mask the neoliberal policy agenda, leading to a major revision in the agenda, an effort to provide it for a human face—present it as the policy framework for a more inclusive form of national and local development, designed to empower the poor, capacitating them. By the new millennium, this PWC was achieved in the form of a more pragmatic form of neoliberalism pursued by the centre-left regimes in the region that had assumed and remain in power.

Regionalism

The first projection of an imperial strategy of regional free trade arrangements was in the immediate post-war period in which the US was constrained in its own national interest to push for the integration of Europe—the creation of a strong economy and a system of cross-Atlantic state alliances that would provide an important market for the US as well as a bulwark against communism and the growing power of the USSR.

Subsequently, the decade saw an important twist if not turn in imperial policy—towards the creation of free markets in the form of NAFTA, instituted in 2004, and later the unsuccessful project of the FTAA—defeated by the forces of resistance in the region. The impetus behind this strategy, certainly in the case of Latin America, was to reverse the large and growing trade deficit with countries in every region except, as it happens, in Latin America. In fact, Latin America was a crucial factor in offsetting a growing deficit on its global trade account, and NAFTA (and later FTAA) was viewed, and used, as a mechanism of economic imperialism.

The now defunct Latin America Free Trade Agreement (LAFTA) was a key element of Washington's empire-building project in Latin America—an extension of NAFTA, CAFTA-DR and its bilateral agreements with Chile, Colombia and Peru. The FTA, if it had succeeded, would have given US multinational corporations (MNCs) and banks unrestrained access to markets in the region, as well as raw materials and labour, while limiting European and Japanese entry and protecting US markets. This neomercantilist imperialist device was another unilateral initiative, taken in agreement with the client states such as Colombia and Peru in the region without any popular consultation. Given the high levels of discontent already in the region, under the neoliberal regimes, the imposition of neomercantilist imperialism would likely have led to explosive social conditions and the re-emergence of nationalist and socialist alternatives. As it is the alternative trade agreement advocated by Hugo Chávez, ALBA (*Alianza Bolivariana para los Pueblos de Nuestra América*/Bolivarian Alliance for the Americas) has provided a major counterpoint and countervailing force to US imperialism in the region.

The Dynamics of Empire Building in Latin America

The informal US Empire, constructed in the post-war years, extended into and held sway in five macro-regions. The dynamics of these forces and the working of imperialism in each region are substantively different. But in this chapter we are only concerned with Latin America, where the US Empire was extended from its original base in Central America and Mexico to points further south to encompass virtually the entire region.

The workings of empire in the region can be traced out in three phases that more or less correspond to empire-building efforts elsewhere.

1945–79: US Imperialism in an Era of State-led Capitalist Development

In the American hemisphere after the Second World War the informal US empire remained largely unchanged, although it began to creep further southward. The region was seen as having relatively low strategic and economic value, and received less economic or military attention from the US than other regions. The bigger states in the hemisphere pursued their own development path while the US was content to influence the smaller states in its backyard through *comprador* regimes that shared US preference for authoritarian regimes and conservative forms of capitalism.

However, these regimes more often than not were confronted by populist force of resistance, by workers in the cities and peasants in the countryside, demanding and actively mobilizing for social change. If and when these forces achieved power as they did in Cuba in 1959, they drove a hard bargain with American corporations and financial interests as well as the ruling classes—threatening US 'interests', leading US officials to brand them as 'communists', enemies of the 'forces of freedom and democracy'. Alternatively, where local class conflict intensified, the US perceived a danger of escalation to 'chaos' and then perhaps to 'communism'. Both outcomes were perceived to threaten US interests. In response, or in some conjunctures in anticipation of this threat, the US mobilized its military assets in attempting/succeeding to overthrow regimes deemed to be antithetical to its 'interests'—Arbenz in Guatemala (1954), Fidel Castro in Cuba (1961), Bosch in the Dominican Republic (1963), Goulart, a moderate nationalist, in Brazil (1964), the Dominican Republic (1965), Jagan in Guyana (1953) and then Allende in Chile (1973).

Arbenz was overthrown by US-funded 'rebels' but the dismal failure of this tactic in Cuba (viz. the Bay of Pigs debacle) led the US to elaborate and pursue an alternative strategy of sponsoring military coups and a concerted regional strategy of a 'dirty war' by proxy against subversives, using the armed forces of the countries in question, arming them and training them within the framework of a National Security Doctrine (NSD) constructed to the purpose. In 1964 this strategy was successful in removing Goulart from power in Brazil because of his nationalist threat to US interests—to nationalize US assets and property. Within one hour of his removal from power by the US-trained Armed Forces, the new self-proclaimed President of the country was congratulated by President Johnson for 'restoring democracy' to Brazil. A decade later, Salvador Allende, also democratically elected but unlike Goulart a proclaimed 'socialist', was removed from power by means of a violent coup engineered and financed by the US, allowing the subsequent military dictator Augusto Pinochet to implement a neoliberal agenda at the level of national policy—as well as 'teach the world a lesson in democracy'. Other NSD-based military coups, all supported by the US, took place in Bolivia (1911), Uruguay (1972) and Argentina (1976).

In this period, the US launched several open military interventions but far more covert or proxy ones. It was an informal empire, mixing gunboats with proxies but without colonies. It was generally justified or legitimated as the spread of freedom and democracy, with communism presented as the antithesis of democracy, as the enemy of freedom. But this mission statement was undercut by the clear US preference for authoritarian allies and the sponsoring as well as support and propping-up of military dictatorships in the region.

In reviewing the dynamics of US imperialism in this period there was essentially two major strategies pursued, each with appropriate tactics. The two-pronged strategy included use of the 'iron fist' of military force within the velvet glove of development assistance or foreign aid. The resort to military force has already been alluded to in the sponsoring or support of military coups across the region from 1964 to 1976. However, an equally important use of imperial power took the form of rural development—NGO-mediated assistance to the rural poor to prevent them from joining or forming social movements pressing for revolutionary change.

The state was assisted in this struggle but in the wake of the Cuban Revolution the US redoubled its efforts on the ground, using community development activists and organizations to penetrate the countryside and turn the rural poor away from social revolution, to teach them the virtues of democracy, capitalism and reform. By these means, and a deployment of nongovernmental organizations on the frontline of the war on rural poverty, the agents of the state managed to dampen the revolutionary ferment in the Latin American countryside. Where this effort did not suffice in demobilizing the forces of revolutionary change the state stepped in with its repressive apparatus. By the end of the 1970s virtually every army of national liberation had been destroyed or decapitated—FARC in Colombia a notable exception. In many cases, as in Mexico (Guerrero and Chiapas) the revolutionary movement went to ground, was held at bay or, as in the case of Chiapas, took time and space to rebuild, awaiting more favourable conditions.

1980–1990: Imperialism under the Washington Consensus

By 1980, the countryside was more or less pacified and labour was very much on the defensive in a long class war waged against it by capital and the state, its leadership co-opted, its forces in disarray, its ties to the peasant movement for land disarticulated, and its capacity to organize and negotiate with capital reduced. At the macro-level virtually very government has to contend with the conditions of a decade-long production crisis and an emerging fiscal crisis, as well as pressures to restore democracy, not in the authoritarian bureaucratic or military form pushed by the US but as the rule of law and civilian elected administrations responsive to demands from 'the people', not a preserve of the political elite. As for the fiscal crisis, and the detritus of the 1970s production crisis in the form of stagnant production and runaway inflation, in the early 1980s it combined with conditions derived from US high interest rate policy and an unfavourable turn in the export markets to produce a scissor-squeeze on fiscal resource to precipitate a decade-long debt crisis and create conditions for launching the new world order.

Unfortunately for the revolutionaries in Nicaragua, these conditions also coincided with their capture of state power, provoking the Contra affair, as the US government struggled and used its proxies to launch covert military operations against the revolutionary regime. As it turned out this would be the last military adventure of US imperialism, its agents resorting instead to structural reform of macroeconomic policy (to create conditions for a renewal of foreign investment and reactivation of an accumulation process), international cooperation for local development (to demobilize or turn the rural poor away from the social movements), and co-opting 'civil society' organizations in the responsibility of restoring order—'good governance' in the lingo of the new imperialism.

The emergence of neoconservative regimes in the US, the UK and elsewhere in the North, formed under conditions of a fiscal crisis, facilitated the implementation of the neoliberal agenda under the Washington Consensus on correct policy. Under these conditions US imperialism turned away from the generals, allowing them to be shunted back to the military barracks, and turned away from armed force towards the officials of the IMF and the World Bank, essential adjuncts of US state imperialism, to help make Latin America safe for US capital.

It would take close to a decade for this to happen. But developments in the 1990s tell the tale: the privatization of key economic sectors and lucrative state enterprises; a major influx and reflux of capital, netting the empire, it is estimated, over US$100-million dollars in profit (net financial resource transfer) over a decade of neoliberal policies (Saxe-Fernández & Núñez, 2001).

The 'Contras affair' closes one chapter in US imperialism and the installation of a new world order (i.e. implementation of a 'new economic model'—neoliberal globalization) opens another—a chapter characterized not by armed force, projection of military power, but rather what we might term 'economic imperialism'—the engineering of free market 'structural reforms' in national policy, the penetration of foreign capital in the form of MNCs (the shock troops of the old imperialism) and a free trade regime implemented in diverse regional contexts. The agents of this economic imperialism included the IMF and the World Bank and the WTO—the 'unholy trinity' (Peet, 2003)— as well as the host of neoconservatives, neoliberal economists and policy makers that serve the 'global ruling class' as described by Pilger (2002).

The new imperial order of neoliberal globalization was made possible, and facilitated, not only by a political turn towards neoconservatism but by new reserves of ideological power: the idea of globalization, presented as the only road to 'general prosperity', the necessary condition for reactivating a growth and capital accumulation process. The idea of globalization was launched in mid-decade, used to justify and advance the neoliberal agenda, as noted above, and came to replace the widespread call for a new world order. The World Bank's 1995 World Development Report, *Workers in an Integrating World*, could be seen as one of its most important programmatic statements, a capitalist manifesto on the need to adjust to the requirements of a new world order in which the forces of freedom would hold sway over the global economy.

The call for a new world order was led by the Heritage Foundation and other Washington-based foundations and policy forums that, together with the US Treasury and Wall Street exemplified what became known as the 'Washington Consensus' (although it also represented the wisdom of 'the City' in London and finance capital everywhere). These banks and international financial institutions would bail out the indebted countries, agreeing to 'restructure' their loans in return for deep economic reforms—an austerity program of cutting central and local government spending, imposing high interest rates, stabilizing the currency, privatizing state-owned enterprises, abolishing tariffs, freeing labour markets from union restrictions, and opening up local capital markets and business ownership to foreign business. This was backed by a rhetorical neoliberalism declaring that morality and efficiency alike required reducing the power of governments, communal land ownership and labour unions. The freedom of markets and private property rights must rule.

As for the political adjustment to the 'new world order' the US was constrained by its own declared mission to spread democracy and make the world safe for freedom, to support the widespread movement in diverse regions towards political democracy. As for Latin America, the US adapted to the spread of democracy across the hemisphere, conducting a policy of 'democracy by applause' from the sidelines, as Latin Americans made their own democratic gains in a process of redemocratization based on the negotiated retreat of the generals to their barracks.

The structural adjustment programs as implemented in the 1980s were unpopular to say the least, with the core opposition coming from organized labour and those dependent on the state. In some contexts, democratic governments were reluctant to sign up and most programs were introduced by authoritarian regimes, as they were in Latin America in the 1970s, which made the IMF appear to favour dictatorships over democracies, just as the US did politically and militarily in this period (Biersteker, 1992: 114–6; Vreeland, 2003; 90–102). However, in Latin America, the SAP, representing a second round of neoliberal reforms, were generally implemented by civilian regimes or democratic governments that came to power after the first experiments in neoliberalism crashed and burned in the early 1980s.

In the academic circles of the US empire there was a similar 'adaptation' to reality, and to the ideology of free-market democracy, in a reversal of the hitherto prevailing belief among political scientists in the liberal tradition that political authoritarianism provides a better fit and conditions for economic liberalism and development than democracy. In short order in the 1980s this idea gave way to the idea that economic liberalization would lead to political liberalization or vice versa, and that both were conditions of 'development'.

The 1980s paved the way for what could be regarded as the golden age of US imperialism in Latin America: a decade of pillage facilitated by a program of Washington-mandated structural reforms in national policy. Under these conditions in the 1980s all but four major governments in the region (especially Bolivia, Chile, Mexico, Jamaica) followed the Washington Consensus or succumbed to direct pressures exerted by the IMF and the World Bank to structurally adjust their economies. In the following decade, three of the major holdout countries in this 'development'—Argentina, Brazil, Peru—made the belated transition towards neoliberalism. In Venezuela the memory of *caracazo*, a violently repressed wave of riots and protests in Caracas in 1989, was enough to hold back if not derail the neoliberal agenda of the governments of the day. It also helped created the political conditions that took form in the presidency of Hugo Chávez and the Bolivarian Revolution.

1990–1999: US Imperialism and the Post-Washington Consensus

The 1990s can be viewed as a decade of major gains for the social movements in their resistance to the neoliberal agenda of governments in the region and the operations and machinations of US imperialism. Already in the 1980s the push towards neoliberal policies had generated widespread opposition and protest, which in the case of Venezuela had resulted in a major social and political crisis—the *caracazo* of 1989—in which hundreds of protesters against the high price of food and IMF policies were massacred by the state. More generally, conditions of structural adjustment across the region generated widespread opposition and resistance in the form of protest movements. They also led to a reorganization and mobilization of the forces of resistance in the popular sector. By the 1990s these organizations took form as antisystemic social movements formed on the social base of indigenous communities, landless workers and peasants.

The rural social movements represented the most dynamic forces of resistance to the policies of neoliberal globalization and US imperialism. In a number of cases these movements managed to halt and even reverse the policies implemented under the neoliberal agenda. In the context it is even possible to name the decade as a decade of major gains for the movements.

However, the neoliberalism at issue in this resistance was not the same as it was in the 1980s, modified as it was by the search for a more socially inclusive form of development, By the end of the 1980s it was widely recognised by the architects and the guardians of the new world order that neoliberalism was economically dysfunctional and more important unsustainable, generating as it does forces of resistance that could be and were mobilized against the system. The solution was a more socially inclusive form of neoliberalism—to give the structural adjustment process a human face—a new development paradigm and social policy targeted at the poor, empowering and capacitating them to act on their own behalf, in taking advantage of their 'opportunities' for self-advancement (Sandbrook, Edelman, Heller & Teichman 2007; World Bank, 2007).

In this context, the 1990s saw a major shift in the correlation of class forces, mobilized in support of, or against, capitalist development in its neoliberal form. On the left, the political class was on the defensive, unable to make gains under condition of a divided and demobilized working class, and few ties to the new forces of resistance. The Left materialised basically in the form of social movements and, to some extent, social organizations for local development mobilized against the neoliberal regimes that were loath to accept the PWC and against new imperialist offensives such as NAFTA—and beyond Latin America the 1994 Agreement on Trade-Related Aspects of Intellectual Property Rights (TRIPS).

Most Latin American regimes at the time (the mid-1990s) were still aligned with the US. But the US, seeking to reverse major setbacks in Asia and other parts of the world, was rapidly losing influence and the capacity to dictate policy in the region or to counter the growing power of the social movements. The major exception here was Colombia, where the US continued with a major military presence. The governments of Mexico and Peru, and El Salvador in Central America, were (and are) also similarly aligned with the US.

2000–15: US Imperialism under the Davos Consensus

The first decade of the new millennium opened and is closed with an involution in capitalist production, a region-wide crisis in the first case, and a crisis of more global proportions in the second. The years betwixt and between, some six years under the presidency of George W. Bush and a shift in the political tide towards the centre-left in South America, the region actively participated in a primary commodities boom on the world market, a development that for some six years changed and to some extent reversed a historic pattern in the terms of north–south trade, bringing with it windfall profits for the private sector in agro-export production and unanticipated windfall gains in fiscal revenues for the centre-left regimes that had formed in the wake of a spreading disenchantment and turning away from neoliberalism. Unfortunately for the Left and the popular sector organizations that had pinned their hopes on these regimes the opportunity to change the course of national development in a popular or populist direction was missed. Apart from Chávez's Venezuela no change in national policy could be discerned.

It would take the onset of crisis in October 2008 to bring about a change in fiscal policy, but even then not in the interest of a more equitable distribution of the social product but as part of a counter-cyclical strategy to boost demand. Throughout the decade what prevailed was a development policy program designed as a means of saving capitalism from itself—from a propensity towards crisis and from widespread forces of resistance held in abeyance by the centre-left in power. In addition to this post-Washington Consensus on development policy, which was implemented to different degrees by virtually every government in the region, what prevailed—and still prevails—is what *The Economist* (January 22, 2011: 13) describes as the 'Davos Consensus': the belief in the need to boost economic growth with free market capitalism (pro-growth policies of 'structural reform'—privatization, deregulation, liberalization), and to reduce the incidence of extreme poverty, via a strategy of enhancing human capital and targeted social expenditures.

As for US-Latin American relations, the Obama regime in the US has attempted to reconstruct them in an effort to reverse the decline in US power and influence over the past decade, a decline facilitated by the overriding concern of the George W. Bush administration with developments elsewhere in the empire. In the context of what might well be described as a 'new military empire' based on 'aggressive unilateralism' or unilateral action, officials of the US imperial state in the 1990s was forced to turn its attention to greater priorities in other macro-regions—East Asia and even Europe (Kosovo), but especially the Middle East and gulf region. Except for a military invasion of Panama in December 1989, which could be used to date its beginnings—and an earlier skirmish in Grenada launched by Reagan in 1983 against the small island state in the Caribbean—the new military imperialism was almost entirely engaged elsewhere in the world, providing governments, parties and movements in the region space and time to conduct their affairs with relatively little concern or interference from the US.

In this context of US-Latin American relations, countries in the region can be placed into three categories: (i) Chile, Peru, Colombia-Mexico—aligned with the US; (ii) Venezuela—to some extent Bolivia, Ecuador, Argentina, Brazil, even Honduras and Nicaragua—in the US's backyard as it were—pursuing a path of relative autonomy and alternative integration; (iii) other countries lie some-where in between—relatively autonomy but commercially competitive—not an ally to be counted on, yet still very much 'client states'.

US Imperialism in Latin America Today: Peru and Honduras

One of the ironies of the often commented on but generally misunderstood pat-tern of regime change—i.e. a supposed red or pink tide in national politics—over the course of the past decade has been a weakening of the forces of resistance against neoliberalism, a retreat of the social movements in a context of revived dynamism of the Right—a weakening of the Left and the strengthen-ing of the Right. In part this is the result of misplaced views of the Left that these regimes are 'on their side'—anti-neoliberal in economic policy and anti-imperialist in their relations with the US. However, this is clearly not the case. Except for Venezuela, and of course Cuba, and to some extent Bolivia and Ecuador, these regimes are not in the least or only formally 'populist' and can best be characterized as 'pragmatic neoliberal'. In some cases, particularly in the case of Peru, Colombia and Mexico, the current and recent regimes can even be described as dogmatically neoliberal—not even as in the case of Chile, Argentina and Brazil, concerned with adapting neoliberal agenda to the post-Washington Consensus on the need for a more inclusive form of neoliberalism.

A clear example of this is Peru, where the efforts of the government to pro-tect the economic interests of US capitalism in June 2009 resulted in a major confrontation with the indigenous communities adversely affected by these interests, leading the government to resort to its repressive apparatus, result-ing in the deaths of 24 police and 10 indigenous persons. On the day after Alan Garcia announced a new cabinet in response to the growing wave of social and class conflict, and a month into the wave of conflict arising from the confronta-tion with the indigenous communities, thousands of workers had taken to the streets to demand a change in the government's neoliberal policies in the interest of US imperialism. At a time in which the *Defensoría del Pueblo* had identified up to 226 'active' social conflicts in the country, transport and public sector workers were on strike, joining in the march organized by the General Confederation of Workers (CGTP), the major Workers' Central in the country. At the same time on the periphery of Lima numerous street blockades were reported, harking back or pointing towards the quasi-revolutionary situation or insurrection that emerged in Ecuador in 2000 and in Bolivia at various points between 2000 and 2005.

Similar situations are brewing in other countries in the region. But none of these are as meaningful for US imperialism as the situation in Honduras brought about by the actions of the ruling class against the sitting and democratically elected President of the country. For US imperialism, Honduras represents not so much a political crisis, a crisis in US-Latin American relations, as a crossroads in imperial power and policy—in the way the US administration under President Obama sought to recover its position and influence in Latin America.

Today US imperialism in the region is at another crossroads. Whereas the primary commodities boom of 2002–08, at a time in which the US administration was seriously distracted by the greater game in Eurasia and security concerns in the Gulf region, and too overstretched to attend to its Latin American affairs, 2008 saw the emergence of an entirely new context for US-Latin American relations.

It is in this context that Honduras took centre-stage for a time, eclipsing efforts of the regime to repair its relations with former client states and re-assert its influence if not dominance. The successful coup engineered in Honduras, and actively supported and even encouraged by the US administration, followed various similar interventions over the past decade—in Venezuela (unsuccessful) and Haiti (successful). In Bolivia, US intervention in Latin American affairs, in an effort to reassert its waning influence and declining power, took a different albeit not unconventional form: the financing of NGOs and active support of oppositional forces with the explicit subversive aim of destabilizing the regime. In this context, US foreign policy in the region, aimed at reasserting its dominance, was focused on Colombia, its chief ally in the region and central to its empire rebuilding project. The significance of Honduras in this context is that it represented an opportunity for the US to counter the growing influence of Hugo Chávez and his Bolivarian Revolution project in the region, particularly in its Central American domain, where Nicaragua and even El Salvador, not to mention Honduras, were vulnerable and at risk of being lost. In this context, Chávez, more than Raúl Castro, is perceived by the US to be the major obstacle in its efforts to restore its dominion, and this in part because of the financial resources

Chávez is able to command but also because of the ideological attraction of his policies—particularly his project of 21st-Century Socialism—in some circles, particularly among the popular classes.

In 1992, within hours of being deposed from power in a coup engineered by elements of Venezuela's ruling class, the US administration recognized the de facto regime. But it was soon forced to backtrack from this support when masses of poor urban workers rallied to Chávez's defence and forced his return to power. However, in the case of Honduras, given the immediate and definitive response of the OAS and its demand that Zayala be restored to office, the US had no choice in public but to join the demand for Zalaya's return. Needless to say, the coup succeeded with the active, albeit covert, support of the US administration. Neither Honduras' ruling class, in control of the military apparatus as well as the legislature and the judiciary if not the government, nor the US administration had any intention to allow Zayala to track Chavez's path towards some new form of socialism. The US had no intention to allow this if it could be helped, and it is safe to assume that the State Department will stop at nothing in its efforts to prevent another Chávez. Democracy and capitalism have to be defended at all cost, regardless of any sensibilities regarding sovereignty, human rights or the freedom of a country to pursue its own development path.

Conclusion

Apart from Honduras, which provided the US both a challenge and an opportunity to recover lost political space, other issues on the agenda of the Obama administration include Cuba and how to counter the leftist tilt in national politics and an incipient-but-growing nationalism vis-à-vis control over natural resources and trade. Since 2001, a growing number of countries in the region have taken and are taking positions on policy and trade issues (the search to diversify trade relations, joining ALBA) that are not in the US national interest, and Obama has undoubtedly been briefed as to how to respond to this challenge to US power and influence. Of particular concern for US imperialism is the movement of more and more countries in its immediate backyard and former sphere of influence, the Caribbean and Central America, towards and into the Chávez orbit (Petrocaribe, etc.). In this panorama, Honduras too provides favourable conditions for a Washington-made solution—a US military base, intimate regular day-to-day relations with Armed Forces personnel, a malleable and supportive Congress and Supreme Court, a ruling class that shares its concerns about the actual and possible forces of subversion in the country and region.

In some ways the situation confronted by Obama in Central America is similar to that faced by President Reagan in the early 1980s regarding Nicaragua. But Reagan had on his side a number of cronies and dictators—Alvarez in Uruguay, Videla in Argentina, Pinochet in Chile, and Stroessner in Paraguay. In this regard at least the political landscape in Latin America has indeed changed. The majority of countries in the region might be described as centrist and pragmatic in terms of macroeconomic policy, rather than leftist (national populist) or rightist (neoliberal), but are also concerned to maintain a line of independence vis-à-vis the US on matters of foreign relations and policies.

What this means for the current Obama administration might be gauged by its reaction to the nomination of Insulza, a social democrat close to, and a nominee of, Chile's Bachelet, for the position of OAS Director. It seemed that the US was implacably opposed to his nomination, apparently (according to several Washington 'insiders') because of Insulza's support for Cuba's entry into the OAS, his campaign against the 'golpistas' in Honduras and his earlier denunciation of US intervention in Venezuela. If this be the attitude and position of the US vis-à-vis a noted progressive and liberal social democrat, a representative of a centrist and pragmatic position in Latin American politics and the nominee of a country supportive of the US and allied with it at the level of bilateral trade, what might the position of the Obama administration be regarding relations with regimes seeking to strike a more independent line and steer a leftward course?

Obama's administration at the outset made various overtures to governments in the region such as Lula's in Brazil with which previous US administrations had strained relations, but how the Obama administration copes with an emergent push in the region for greater independence, how it relates to Chávez and to the right-wing opposition in countries such as Honduras, Bolivia and Venezuela, and how it dealt with the 'Honduras question', provided a clear sign of the direction that US imperialism is taking in the region. If the Obama regime's current mix of strategies and tactics fails to bear fruit, and if politics in the region tilt or turn further to the right as it appears to be doing (witness developments in Chile), then the US might well return to its historic policy of direct intervention in Latin American affairs and support for military coups—this time not as matter of choice but as a 'last resort'.

CHAPTER 6

US Global Power in the 21st Century: Military or Economic Imperialism?

Despite vast amounts of imperial data to the contrary, the great majority of writers on imperialism continue to describe and analyze US imperialism strictly in economic terms, as an expansion of 'capital accumulation', 'accumulation on a world scale'. In fact the major and minor US imperial wars have more to do with 'capital dis-accumulation', in the sense that trillion dollar flows have gone out from the US, hundreds of billions of dollars in profits from resource sites have been undermined, markets for exports have been severely weakened and exploitable productive labour has been uprooted. At the same time the US imperialist state 'dis-accumulates capital', multinational corporations, especially in the extractive sector are expanding, 'accumulating capital' throughout Latin America.

This new configuration of power, the conflicting and complementary nature of 21st century US imperialism, requires that we anchor our analysis in the real, existing behaviour of imperial state and extractive capitalist policymakers. The basic premise informing this essay is that there are two increasingly divergent forms of imperialism: military driven intervention, occupation and domination; and economic expansion and exploitation of resources, markets and labour by invitation of the 'host country'.

We proceed in this chapter by examining the choices of imperial strategy, in a historical—comparative framework and the alternatives that were selected or rejected. Through an analysis of the practical decisions taken regarding 'imperial expansion' we can obtain insights into the real nature of US imperialism. The study of imperial strategic choices, past and present, state and corporate, requires three levels of analysis: global, national and sectoral.

Global Strategies: US Imperial State and the Multinational Corporation

The US imperial state invested trillions of dollars in military expenditures, hundreds of thousands of military personnel into wars in the Middle East (Iraq, Yemen, and Syria), North and East Africa (Libya, Somalia), South Asia (Afghanistan) and imposed sanctions on Iran costing the US hundreds of billions in 'capital dis-accumulation'.

The US corporate elite, driven out of Iraq, Syria, Libya and elsewhere where US military imperialism was engaged, chose to invest in manufacturing in China and extractive sectors throughout Latin America. In other words, the US imperial state strategists either chose to expand in relatively backward areas (Afghanistan, Pakistan, Somalia and Yemen) or imposed under-development by destroying or sanctioning lucrative extractive economies (Iraq, Libya, Iran).

In contrast the MNCs chose the most dynamic expanding zones where militarist imperialism was least engaged: China and Latin America. That is, 'capital did not follow the flag'; it avoided it. Moreover, the zones where extractive capital was most successful in terms of access, profits and stability were those where their penetration was based on negotiated contracts between sovereign nations and CEOs—economic imperialism by invitation.

In the priority areas of expansion chosen by imperial state strategists, entry and domination was by force, leading to the destruction of the means of production and the loss of access to the principle sites of extractive exploitation. US military driven imperialism undermined energy companies' agreements in Iraq and Libya. Imperial state sanctions in Iran designed to weaken its nuclear and defense capabilities undercut US corporate extractive, public-private contracts with the Iranian state oil corporations. The drop in production and supply in oil in Iraq, Iran and Libya raised energy prices and had a negative impact on the 'accumulation of capital on a world scale'.

If imperial state decision-makers had followed the direction of economic rather than military driven policymakers they would have pivoted to Asia and Latin America rather than the Middle East, South Asia and North Africa. They would have channelled funds into economic imperialist strategies, including joint ventures, high and medium tech trade agreements, and expanded exports by the high-end manufacturing sector, instead of financing 700 military bases, destabilization campaigns and costly military exercises.

Twentieth century military imperialism stands in stark contrast to late twentieth century economic imperialism. In the mid 1960s the US announced a vast new economic program in Latin America: the Alliance for Progress that was designed to finance economic opportunities in Latin America via joint ventures, agrarian reform and investments in the extractive sector. The imperial state's military policies and interventionist policies were designed to secure US business control over mines, banks, factories and agro-business. US backing for the coups in Chile, Bolivia, Brazil, Uruguay and Peru led to the privatization of key resource sectors and the imposition of the neoliberal economic model.

US policy in Asia under Nixon was directed first and foremost to opening economic relations with China, expanding trade agreements with Japan, Taiwan and South Korea. The 'pivot from war' to free trade led to a boom in US exports as well as imports, in private investments and lucrative profits. Military expenditures declined even as the US engaged in covert operations in Afghanistan, Angola, Nicaragua and El Salvador.

Imperial intervention combined military and economic expansion with the latter dictating policy priorities and the allocation of resources.

The reversal set in with the US military backing of the jihadist extremists in Afghanistan and the demise of the USSR. The former set the stage for the rise of the Taliban to power and the emergence of the Al Qaeda terrorist organization. The latter led US imperial strategists to pursue wars of conquest with impunity—Yugoslavia and Iraq during the 1990s.

Easy military conquests and visions of a 'unipolar' world dominated by US military supremacy, encouraged and fostered the emergence of a new breed of imperial strategists: the neoconservative militarists with closer ties to Israel and its military priorities than to the US extractive oil capitalists in the Middle East.

Military versus Economic Imperialism at the National Level

In the post-Cold War period, the competition between the two variants of imperialism was played out in all the nations subject to US intervention.

During the first Iraq war the balance between militarists and economic imperialists was in play. The US defeated Iraq but did not shred the state, nor bomb the oil fields. Sanctions were imposed but did not paralyze oil deals. The US did not occupy Iraq; it partitioned the north—so-called 'Kurdish' Iraq but left the secular state intact. Extractive capital was actively in competition with the militarist neo-conservatives over the future direction of imperial policy.

The launch of the second Iraq war and the invasion of Afghanistan marked a decisive shift toward military imperialism: the US ignored all economic considerations. Iraq's secular state was destroyed; civil society was pulverized; ethno-religious, tribal and clan warfare was encouraged. US colonial officials ruled by military fiat; top policymakers with links to Israel replaced oil-connected officials. The militarist 'war on terror' ideology replaced free market, free trade imperialism. Afghanistan killing fields replaced the China market as the center of US imperial policy. Billions were spent, chasing evasive guerrillas in the mountains of a backward economy while the US lost competitive advantages in the most dynamic Asian markets.

Imperial policymakers chose to align with sectarian warlords in Iraq over extractive technocrats. In Afghanistan they chose loyal ex-pat puppets over influential Taliban leaders capable of pacifying the country.

Extractive versus Military Imperialism in Latin America

Latin American neoliberalism went from boom to bust in the 1990s. By the early 2000s, crises enveloped the region. By the turn of the century, US-backed rulers were being replaced by popular nationalist leaders. US policymakers stuck by their neoliberal clients in decline and failed to adapt to the new rulers who pursued modified socially inclusive extractivism. The US military imperialists longed for a return of the neoliberal backers of the 'war on terrorism'. In contrast international multinational extractive corporations were realists— and adapted to the new regimes.

At the beginning of the new millennium, two divergent tendencies emerged at the world level. US military imperialism expanded throughout the Middle East, North Africa, South Asia and the Caucuses, while Latin American regimes turned in the opposite direction—toward moderate nationalism, and populism with a strong emphasis on poverty reduction via economic development in association with imperial extractive capital

In the face of these divergent and conflicting trends, the major US extractive multinational corporations chose to adapt to the new political realities in Latin America. While Washington, the imperial state, expressed hostility and dismay toward the new regimes' refusal to back the 'war on terror' (military imperialism) the major MNCs' robust embrace of economic imperialism, took advantage of the investment opportunities opened by the new regimes' adoption of a new extractivist model, to pour billions into the mining, energy and agricultural sectors.

Extractive Imperialism in an Era of Neoliberal Decline

Extractive imperialism in Latin America has several specific characteristics that sharply demark it from earlier forms agro-mineral imperialism.

1. Extractive capital is not dominated by a single imperial country-like the Spanish in the 18th century, the British in the 19th century or the US in the 20th century. Imperial extractive capital is very diverse: Canadian, US, Chinese, Brazilian, Australian, Spanish, Indian and other MNCs are deeply involved.
2. The imperial states of the diverse MNC do not engage in 'gun boat diplomacy' (with the exception of the US). The imperial states provide economic financing and diplomatic support but are not actively involved in subverting Latin American regimes.

3.   The relative weight of US MNCs, in the new imperial extractivism is much less than it was a half-century earlier. The rise of diverse extractive MNCs and dynamism of China's commodity market and deep financial pockets have displaced the US, the IMF and World Bank and established new terms of trade with Latin America.

4.   Probably the most significant aspect of the new imperial extractivism is that its entry and expansion is by invitation. The Latin American regimes and the extractive MNCs negotiate contracts—MNC entry is not unilaterally imposed by an imperial state. Yet the 'contracts' may result in unequal returns; they provide substantial revenues and profits to the MNC; they grant large multi-million acre tracts of land for mining or agriculture exploitation; they obligate the national state to dispossess local communities and police repress the displaced. But they also have allowed the post-neoliberal state to expand their social spending, to increase their foreign reserves, to eschew relations with the IMF, and to diversify their markets and trading partners.

In regional terms extractive imperialism in Latin America has accumulated capital by diverging from the military imperialism practiced by the US in other regions of the world political economy. Over the past decade and a half, extractive capital has been allied with and relies both on post-neoliberal and neoliberal regimes against petty commodity producers, indigenous communities and other anti-extractive resistance movements. Extractive imperialists do not rely on 'their' imperial state to quell resistance; they turn to their national political partners.

Extractive imperialism by invitation also diverges from the military imperial state in its view toward regional organizations. US military imperialism placed all its bets on US-centered economic integration, which Washington could leverage to political, military and economic advantage. Extractive capital, in the great diversity of its 'national identity', welcomed Latin American-centred integration that did not privilege US markets and investors.

The predominance of economic imperialism, in particular the extractive version, however, needs to be qualified by several caveats.

US military imperialism has been present in several forms. The US-backed the military coup in Honduras overthrowing the post-neoliberal Zelaya government; likewise it supported an 'institutional coup' in Paraguay.

Secondly, even as multinational corporations poured capital into Bolivian mining and energy sectors, the US imperial state fomented destabilization activity to undermine the MAS government, but was defeated and the agencies and operatives were expelled. The crucial issue in this as well as other instances is the unwillingness of the MNCs to join forces with the military imperialists, via boycotts, trade embargoes or disinvestment. Clearly the stability, profitability and long-term contracts between the Bolivian regime and the extractive MNC counted for more than their ties to the US imperial state.

US military imperialism has expanded its military bases, and increased joint military exercises with most Latin American armed forces. Indoctrinated military officials can still become formidable potential allies in any future 'coup', if and when the US 'pivots' from the Middle East to Latin America.

US military imperialism in its manifest multiple forms, from bankrolling NGOs engaged in destabilization and street riots in Venezuela, to its political support of financial speculators in Argentina and right-wing parties and personalities in Brazil, has a continuous presence alongside extractive imperialism. The success of the latter and the eclipse of the former is based in part on two contingent circumstances. The US serial wars in the Middle East diverts attention away from Latin America; and the commodity boom fuels the growth of extractive capital. The economic slowdown in China and the decline of commodity prices may weaken the regimes in opposition to US military imperialism.

Paradoxically, the weakening of the ties between the post-neoliberal regimes and extractive imperialism resulting from the decline of commodity prices is strengthening the neoliberal socio-political forces allied with US military imperialism.

Latin America's Right Turn: The Cohabitation of Extractive and Military Imperialism?

Throughout Latin America the post-neoliberal regimes which ruled for the better part of a decade and a half face serious challenges—from consequential social opposition at the micro-level and from aggressive political and economic elites at the macro-level. It is worthwhile to survey the prospects for a return to power of neoliberal regimes allied with military imperialism in several key countries.

Several factors are working in favour of a return to power of political parties and leaders who seek to reverse the independent and inclusive policies of the post neoliberal power bloc.

First the post-neoliberal regimes development strategy of depending on foreign extractive capital, perpetuated and strengthened the economic basis of imperialism: the 'colonial style' trade relation, exporting primary commodities and importing finished goods, allowed the agro-mineral elites to occupy key positions in the politico-social structure. With the decline in commodity prices, some post-neoliberal regimes are experiencing fiscal and balance of payments shortfalls. Inflation and cuts in social expenditures adversely affect the capacity of the post-neoliberal regimes to retain popular and middle class electoral support.

The divergence between post-neoliberals and economic imperialism is accentuating with return of the neoliberal right. The agro-mineral sectors perceive an opportunity to rid themselves of their power and revenue sharing agreements with the state and to secure even more lucrative arrangements with the advance of the neoliberal right which promises tax and royalty reductions, deregulation and lower wage and pension payments.

Secondly, the post-neoliberal regimes' alliances with the building, construction, and other bourgeois sectors, was accompanied by corruption involving payoffs, bribes and other illicit financial transactions designed to finance their mass media based electoral campaigns and patronage system that ensured electoral majorities. The neoliberal right is exploiting these corruption scandals to erode the middle class electoral base of the post-neoliberal regimes.

Thirdly, the post-neoliberal regimes increased the quantity of social services, but ignored their quality—provoking widespread discontent with the inadequate public educational, transport, and health services.

Fourthly, inflation is eroding the decade long advance of wage, pension and family allowances. The post-neoliberal regimes are caught between the pressures to 'adjust'—to devalue and impose fiscal 'austerity' as proposed by the international bankers and lose mass support, or to engage in deeper structural changes which require among other things, changes in the extractive dependence model and greater public ownership. The crisis of the post-neoliberal regimes is leading to irresolution and opening political space for the neoliberal right, which is allied to military and economic imperialism.

Military imperialism, which was weakened by the popular uprisings at the turn of 20th century is never absent. US military imperialism is first and foremost powerfully entrenched in two major countries: Mexico and Colombia. In both countries neoliberal regimes bought into the militarization of their societies, including the comprehensive and deep presence of US military-police officials in the structures of the state.

In both states, US military and economic imperialism operates in alliance with paramilitary death squads, even as they proclaimed a 'war on drugs'. The ideology of free market imperialism was put into practice with the elimination of trade barriers, widespread privatization of resources and multi-million acre land grants to MNCs.

Through its regional clients, US imperialism has a springboard to extend its influence. Mexican style 'militarized imperialism' has spread to Central America; Colombia serves as a launchpad to subvert Venezuela and Ecuador.

Where dissident regimes emerged in regions claimed by militarized imperialism, Honduras and Paraguay, military and civilian coups were engineered. However, because of the regional concentration of US military imperialism in the Middle East it relies heavily on local collaborators, political, military and economic elites as vehicles for 'regime change'.

Extractive imperialism is under siege from popular movements in many countries in Latin America. In some cases, the political elites have increasingly militarized the contested terrain. Where this is the case, the regimes invite and accept an increased imperial military presence, as advisers, and embrace their militarist ideology, thus fostering a 'marriage' between extractive and military imperialism. This is the case in Peru under Humala and Santos in Colombia.

In Argentina and Brazil, the moderate reformist policies of the Kirchner and Lula-Rousseff regimes are under siege. Faltering export earnings, rising deficits, and inflationary pressures have fuelled a neoliberal offensive, which takes a new form: populism at the service of neoliberal collaboration with military imperialism. Extractive capital has *divided*: some sectors retain ties with the regime, others, the majority is allied with rising power of the right.

In Brazil, the Right has promoted a former environmentalist (Silva) to front for the hardline neoliberal financial sector—which has received full support from local and imperial mass media. In Argentina, the imperial state and mass media have backed hedge fund speculators and have launched a full-scale economic war, claiming default, in order to damage Buenos Aires' access to capital markets in order to increase its investments in the extractive sector.

In contrast in Bolivia the extractive model par excellence, has moved successfully to oust and weaken the military arm of imperialism, ending the presence of US military advisers and DEA officials, while deepening and strengthening its ties with diverse extractive MNCs on the one hand, and on the other consolidating support among the trade unions and peasant-indigenous movements.

In Ecuador the extractive regime of Correa has diversified the sources of imperial capital from the US to China, and consolidated Correa's power via effective patronage machinery and socioeconomic reforms. While the US-Colombian military threat to both Ecuador and Venezuela has diminished and peace negotiations with the FARC are advancing the regime now faces trade union and Indian-peasant opposition with regard to its extractive strategy and corporatist labour reforms. In both Ecuador and Bolivia, imperial militarism appears to lack the vital strategic military-civilian allies capable of engineering a regime change.

The case of Venezuela highlights the continuing importance of imperial militarism in shaping US policy in Latin America. The pivot to a military policy was taken by Washington prior to any basic social reforms or economic nationalist measures. The coup of 2001 and lockout of 2002 were backed by the US in response to President Chavez' forceful rejection of the 'War on Terrorism'. Washington jeopardized its important economic stake, petrol investments, in order to put in place a regime conforming to its global military strategy.

And for the next decade and a half, the US imperial strategy totally ignored investment, trade and resource opportunities in this wealthy petrol state; it chose to spend hundreds of millions in financing opposition NGOs, terrorists, electoral parties, mass media and military officials to effect a regime change. The extractive sector in the US simply became a transmission belt for the agencies of the militarized imperial state. In its place, Russia and China, interested especially in the extractive sector signed multi-billion dollar contracts with the Venezuelan state: a case of extractive imperialism by invitation—for economic and security reasons.

Apart from the ideological conflict over US militarist expansion, Venezuela's promotion of Latin American centred regional integration weakened US leverage and control in the region. In its struggle against Latin American centred regional organizations and to regain its dominance, US imperialism has upgraded its economic profile via the Trans-Pacific Alliance, which includes its most loyal neoliberal allies: Chile, Peru, Colombia and Mexico. The global eclipse of economy-driven imperial expansion in favour of the military has not totally displaced several key economic advances in strategic countries and sectors in Mexico, Colombia and Peru.

The privatization and denationalization of the biggest and most lucrative public petrol company in Latin America, PEMEX, the Mexican giant, opens up enormous profitable opportunities for US MNCs. The rapid appropriation of oil fields by US-based MNCs will enhance and complement the militarization of Mexico undertaken by the US military-security apparatus.

The Mexican example highlights several features of US imperialism in Latin America. Imperial militarization does not necessarily preclude economic imperialism if it takes place within an existing stable state structure. Unlike the imperial wars in Iraq and Libya, the military imperialist policies in Mexico advanced via powerful local political clients willing and able to engage in bloody civil wars costing over 100,000 civilian deaths in over a decade. Under the aegis and guidance of US imperial rulers, the US and Mexican military devastated civil society, but safeguarded and expanded the huge mining and manufacturing enclaves open to economic imperialist exploitation. Militarization contributed to weakening the bargaining rights of labour—wages have declined in real terms over the decades and the minimum wage is the lowest in the hemisphere.

Mexico highlights the crucial role that collaborator elites play in imperial capital accumulation. Mexico is an excellent example of imperialism by invitation—the political agreements at the top, impose 'acquiescence' below. The extraordinary levels of corruption that permeate the entire political class, solidify the longstanding links between Mexican political-business elite, the MNC and the security apparatus of the imperial state. Extractive imperialism is the principal beneficiary of this 'triple alliance'. In the case of Mexico, militarized imperialism laid the groundwork for the expansion of economic imperialism.

A similar process involving 'triple alliances' is operative in Colombia. For the past decade and a half, militarized-imperialism poured over six billion dollars in military aid (Plan Colombia) to finance the dispossession, assassination, arrest and torture and of over four million Colombians, including the killing of thousands of trade union and social movement leaders.

The scorched earth policy, backed by a substantial US military mission operated through the existing state apparatus and with the active support of the agro-mineral and banking elite, aided by nearly 40,000 member paramilitary death squads and drug traffickers laid the groundwork for the large scale entry of extractive capital—particularly mining capital.

Military imperialism preceded the long-term and large-scale 'invasion' by economic imperialism in the form of a free trade agreement and multi-million acre land grants to mining companies. This general pattern was repeated in Peru. The 'war on terror' under Fujimori and the subsequent liberalization of the economy, under three subsequent presidents, culminated in the massive primarization of the economy under President Humala who deepened and extended the expansion of imperial extractive capital.

The economic downturn in some of the post-neoliberal economies, namely Brazil, Argentina and Venezuela, and the rightward moving political spectrum, has opened a window of opportunity for US economic imperialism to work in tandem with the rising neoliberal political opposition. The military option, a military coup or US military intervention is not on the horizon for the present time. The central focus of imperial state decision makers regarding regime change is a combination of overt electoral and covert 'street intervention': adopting 'populist', moralist and technocratic rhetoric to highlight corruption in high offices, inefficiency in the delivery of social services with claims of bureaucratic interference in the operations of the market. Business disinvestment, financial speculation on the currency and negative mass media propaganda has coincided strikes and protests against shortages and lag between wage and price increases.

Despite costly and failed imperial wars in the Middle East, despite a decade of military retreat in Latin America, economic imperialism is advancing via the electoral route; it already has established a formidable array of allies among the political regimes in Mexico, Colombia and Peru and is posed to re-establish neoliberal allies in Brazil, Argentina and Venezuela.

Conclusion

Imperialism as it has evolved over the past quarter of a century cannot be understood as a 'unified whole' in which the two basic components, military and economic are always complimentary. Divergences have been graphically illustrated by the imperial wars in the Middle East, South Asia and North Africa. Convergences are more obvious in Latin America, especially in Mexico, Colombia and Peru, where 'militarization' facilitated the expansion of extractive capital.

The theoretical point is that the nature of the political leadership of the imperial state has a high degree of autonomy in shaping the predominance of one or another strand of the imperial expansion. The capacity for imperial capital to expand is highly contingent on the strength and structure of the collaborator state: militarized imperialism that invades and destroys states and the fabric of civil society has led to disinvestment. In contrast economic imperialism by invitation in neoliberal collaborator states has been at the centre of successful imperial expansion.

The ambiguities and contradictions intrinsic to the post-neoliberal extractivist based development model have both constrained the military component of imperialism while expanding opportunities for economic imperial accumulation. Accumulation by invitation, and accumulation by dispossession are simply moments in a complex process in which political regime changes intervene and establish the locations and timing for refluxes and influxes of capital.

The rise of new economic imperialist powers like China competing with established imperial powers like the US, has led to alternative markets and sources of financing, which erodes the effectiveness political, military and diplomatic instruments of imperial coercion.

Regional variations in political configurations, imperial priorities and choice of instruments of power, have deeply influenced the nature and structure of imperialism. And as the world historic record seems to argue, military driven empire building in the Middle East has been a disaster while economic driven imperialism shows signs of rapid recovery and successes in Latin America.

Fifty Years of Imperial Wars: Results and Perspectives

Over the past 50 years the US and European powers have engaged in countless imperial wars throughout the world. The drive for world supremacy has been clothed in the rhetoric of 'world leadership.' The consequences have been devastating for the peoples targeted. The biggest, longest and most numerous wars have been carried out by the United States. Presidents from both parties direct and preside over this quest for world power. The ideology that informs imperialism varies from 'anti-communism' in the past to 'anti-terrorism' today.

Washington's drive for world domination has used and combined many forms of warfare, including military invasions and occupations; proxy mercenary armies and military coups; financing political parties, NGOs and street mobs to overthrow duly constituted governments. The driving forces in the imperial state behind the quest for world power vary with the geographic location and socio-economic composition of the targeted countries.

What is clear from an analysis of US empire building over the last half century is the relative decline of economic interests, and the rise of politico-military considerations. In part this is because of the demise of the collectivist regimes (the USSR and Eastern Europe) and the conversion of China and the leftist Asian, African and Latin American regimes to capitalism. The decline of economic forces as the driving force of imperialism is a result of the advent of global neoliberalism. Most US and EU multinationals (MNCs) are not threatened by nationalizations or expropriations, which might trigger imperial state political intervention. In fact, the MNCs are invited to invest, trade and exploit natural resources even by post-neoliberal regimes. Economic interests come into play in formulating imperial state policies, if and when nationalist regimes emerge and challenge US-based MNCs as was the case in Venezuela under President Chávez.

The key to US empire building over the past half-century is found in the political, military and ideological power configurations that have come to control the levers of the imperial state. The recent history of US imperial wars has demonstrated that strategic military priorities—military bases, budgets and bureaucracy—have expanded far beyond any localized economic interests of global capital in the form of the MNCs. Moreover, the vast expenditures and long term and expensive military interventions of the US imperial state in the

Middle East have been at the behest of Israel. The takeover of strategic political positions in the Executive branch and Congress by the powerful Zionist power configuration within the US has reinforced the centrality of military over economic interests

The 'privatization' of imperial wars—the vast growth and use of mercenaries contracted by the Pentagon—has led to the vast pillage of tens of billions of dollars from the US Treasury. Large-scale corporations that supply mercenary military combatants have become a very 'influential' force shaping the nature and consequences of US empire building.

Military strategists, defenders of Israeli colonial interests in the Middle East, mercenary military and intelligence corporations are central actors in the imperial state and it is their decision-making influence which explains why US imperial wars do not result in a politically stable, economic prosperous empire. Instead their policies have resulted in unstable, ravaged economies, in perpetual rebellion.

We proceed by identifying the changing areas and regions of US empire building from the mid-1970s to the present. We then examine the methods, driving forces and outcomes of imperial expansion. We then turn to describe the current geo-political map of empire building and the varied nature of the anti-imperialist resistance. We conclude by examining the why and how of empire building and more particularly, the consequences, and results of a half century of US imperial expansion.

Imperialism in the Post-Vietnam Period: Proxy Wars in Central America, Afghanistan and Southern Africa

The US imperialist defeat in Indo-China marks the end of one phase of empire building and the beginning of another: a shift from territorial invasions to proxy wars. Hostile domestic opinion precluded large-scale ground wars. Beginning during the presidencies of Gerald Ford and James Carter, the US imperialist state increasingly relied on proxy clients. It recruited, financed and armed proxy military forces to destroy a variety of nationalist and social revolutionary regimes and movements in three continents. Washington financed and armed extremist Islamic forces worldwide to invade and destroy the secular, modernizing, Soviet backed regime in Afghanistan, with logistical support from the Pakistan military and intelligence agencies, and financial backing from Saudi Arabia.

The second proxy intervention was in Southern Africa, where the US imperial state financed and armed proxy forces against anti-imperialist regimes in Angola and Mozambique, in alliance with South Africa.

The third proxy intervention took place in Central America, where the US financed, armed and trained murderous death squad regimes in Nicaragua, El Salvador, Guatemala and Honduras to decimate popular movements and armed insurgencies resulting in over 300,000 civilian deaths.

The US imperial state's 'proxy strategy' extended to South America: CIA and Pentagon backed military coups took place in Uruguay (Alvarez), Chile (Pinochet) Argentina (Videla), Bolivia (Banzer) and Peru (Morales). Empire building by proxy, was largely at the behest of US MNCs which were the principal actors in setting priorities in the imperial state throughout this period.

Accompanying proxy wars were direct military invasions: the tiny island of Grenada (1983) and Panama (1989) under Presidents Reagan and Bush, Sr. Easy targets, with few casualties and low cost military expenditures: dress rehearsals for re-launching major military operations in the near future.

What is striking about the 'proxy wars' are the mixed results. The outcomes in Central America, Afghanistan and Africa did not lead to prosperous neo-colonies or prove lucrative to US multinational corporations. In contrast the proxy coups in South America led to large-scale privatization and profits for the American MNCs.

The Afghan proxy war led to the rise and consolidation of the Taliban 'Islamic regime' which opposed both Soviet influence and US imperial expansion. The rise and consolidation of Islamic nationalism in turn challenged US allies in South Asia and the Gulf region and subsequently led to a US military invasion in 2001 and a prolonged (15 year) war (which has yet to conclude), and most probably to a military retreat and defeat. The main economic beneficiaries were Afghan political clients, US mercenary military 'contractors,' military procurement officers and civilian colonial administrators who pillaged hundreds of billions from the US Treasury in illegal and fraudulent transactions.

Pillage of the US Treasury in no way benefited the non-military MNCs. In fact the war and resistance movement undermined any large-scale, long-term entry of US private capital in Afghanistan and adjoining border regions of Pakistan.

The proxy war in Southern Africa devastated the local economies, especially the domestic agricultural economy, uprooted millions of labourers and farmers and curtailed US corporate oil penetration for over two decades. The 'positive' outcome was the de-radicalization of the former revolutionary nationalist elite. However, the political conversion of the Southern African 'revolutionaries' to neoliberalism did not benefit the US MNCs as much as the rulers turned kleptocratic oligarchs who organized patrimonial regimes in association with a diversified collection of MNCs, especially from Asia and Europe.

The proxy wars in Central America had mixed results. In Nicaragua the Sandinista revolution defeated the US/Israeli-backed Somoza regime but immediately confronted a US-financed, armed and trained counter-revolutionary mercenary army (the 'Contras') based in Honduras. The US war destroyed many of the progressive economic projects, undermined the economy and eventually led to an electoral victory by the US-backed political client Violeta Chamorro. Two decades later the US proxies were defeated by a deradicalized Sandinista led political coalition.

In El Salvador, Guatemala and Honduras, the US proxy wars led to the consolidation of client regimes presiding over the destruction of the productive economy, and the flight of millions of war refugees to the United States. US imperial dominance eroded the bases for a productive labour market that spawned the growth of murderous drug gangs.

In summary, the US proxy wars succeeded, in most cases, in preventing the rise of nationalist-leftist regimes, but also led to the destruction of the economic and political bases of a stable and prosperous empire of neo-colonies.

US Imperialism in Latin America: Changing Strategies, External and Internal Contingencies, Shifting Priorities and Global Constraints

To understand the operations, agency and performance of US imperialism in Latin America, it is necessary to recognize the specific constellation of competing forces that shaped imperial state policies. Unlike the Middle East where the militarist-Zionist faction has established hegemony, in Latin America the MNCs have played a leading role in directing imperial state policy. In Latin America, the militarists played a lesser role, constrained by the power of the MNCs, the shifts in political power in Latin America from the right to the centre-left, and the impact of economic crises and the commodity boom.

In contrast to the Middle East, the Zionist power configuration has little influence over imperial state policy, as Israel's interests are focused on the Middle East and, with the possible exception of Argentina, Latin America is not a priority.

For over a century and a half, the US MNCs and banks dominated and dictated US imperial policy toward Latin America. The US armed forces and CIA were instruments of economic imperialism via direct intervention (invasions), proxy 'military coups' or a combination of both.

US imperial economic power in Latin America peaked between 1975–1999. Vassal states and client rulers were imposed via proxy military coups, direct military invasions (Dominican Republic, Panama and Grenada) and military-civilian controlled elections. The results were the dismantling of the welfare state and the imposition of neoliberal policies. The MNC-led imperial state and its international financial appendages (IMF, WB, IDB) privatized lucrative strategic economic sectors, dominated trade and projected a regional integration scheme that would codify US imperial dominance.

Imperial economic expansion in Latin America was not simply a result of the internal dynamics and operations of the MNCs, but depended on the receptivity of the 'host' country or more precisely the internal correlation of class forces in Latin America, which in turn revolved around the performance of the economy—its growth or susceptibility to crisis.

Latin America demonstrates that contingencies such as the demise of client regimes and collaborator classes can have a profound negative impact on the dynamics of imperialism, undermining the power of the imperial state and reversing the economic advance of the MNCs.

The advance of US economic imperialism during the 1975–2000 period was manifest in the adoption of neoliberal policies, the pillage of national resources, the increase of illicit debts and the overseas transfer of billions of dollars However, the concentration of wealth and property precipitated a deep socio-economic crises throughout the region which eventually led to the overthrow or ouster of the imperial collaborators in Ecuador, Bolivia, Venezuela, Argentina, Brazil, Uruguay, Paraguay and Nicaragua. Powerful anti-imperialist social movements especially in the countryside emerged in Brazil and the Andean countries. Urban unemployed workers' movements and public employees' unions in Argentina and Uruguay spearheaded electoral changes, bringing to power centre-left regimes which 're-negotiated' relations with the US imperial state.

US-based MNC influence in Latin America waned. They could not count on the full battery of military resources of the imperial state to intervene and re-impose neoliberal clients because of its military priorities elsewhere: the Middle East, South Asia and North Africa.

Unlike the past, the US MNCs in Latin America lacked two essential props of power: the full backing of the US armed forces and powerful civilian-military clients in Latin America.

The strategy of US-centred integration was rejected by the centre-left regimes. The imperial state turned to bilateral free trade agreements with Mexico, Chile, Colombia, Panama and Peru. As a result of the economic crises and collapse of most Latin American economies, neoliberalism, the dominant ideology of imperialism, was discredited. The advocates of neoliberalism were marginalized.

Changes in the world economy had a profound impact on US–Latin America trade and investment relations. The dynamic growth of China and the subsequent boom in demand and the rising prices of commodities, led to a sharp decline of US dominance of Latin American markets.

Latin American states diversified trade, sought and gained new overseas markets, especially in China. The increase in export revenues created greater capacity for self-financing. The IMF, WB and IDB, economic instruments for leveraging US financial impositions ('conditionality'), were sidelined.

The US imperial state faced Latin American regimes that embraced diverse economic options, markets and sources of financing. With powerful domestic popular support and unified civilian-military command, Latin America moved tentatively out of the US sphere of imperialist domination.

The imperial state and its MNCs, deeply influenced by their 'success' in the 1990s, responded to the decline of influence by proceeding by 'trial and error' in the face of the negative constraints of the 21st century. The MNCs backed policymakers in the imperial state continued to back the collapsing neoliberal regimes, losing all credibility in Latin America. The imperial state failed to accommodate changes—deepening popular and centre-left regime opposition to 'free markets' and the deregulation of banks. No large-scale economic aid programs, like President Kennedy's effort to counter the revolutionary appeal of the Cuban revolution by promoting social reforms via the 'Alliance for Progress,' were fashioned to win over the centre-left, probably because of budget constraints resulting from costly wars elsewhere.

The demise of the neoliberal regimes, the glue that held the different factions of the imperial state together, led to competing proposals of how to regain dominance. The 'militarist faction' resorted to and revived the military coup formula for restoration: coups were organized in Venezuela, Ecuador, Bolivia, Honduras and Paraguay, but all were defeated except for the latter two. The defeat of US proxies led to the consolidation of the independent, anti-imperialist centre-left regimes. Even the 'success' of the US coup in Honduras resulted in a major diplomatic defeat, as every Latin American government condemned it and the US role, further isolating Washington in the region.

The defeat of the militarist strategy strengthened the political and diplomatic factions of the imperial state. With positive overtures toward ostensibly 'center-left regimes,' this faction gained diplomatic leverage, retained military ties and deepened the expansion of the MNCs in Uruguay, Brazil, Chile and Peru. With the latter two countries the economic imperialist faction of the imperial state secured bilateral free trade agreements.

A third MNC–military faction, overlapping with the previous two, combined diplomatic-political accommodations toward Cuba, with an aggressive political destabilization strategy aimed at 'regime change' (via a coup d'état) in Venezuela (see Part 3).

The heterogeneity of imperial state factions and their competing orientations, reflects the complexity of interests engaged in empire building in Latin America and results in seemingly contradictory policies, a phenomenon less evident in the Middle East where the militarist-zionist power configuration dominates imperial policymaking. For example, the promotion of military bases and counter-insurgency operations in Colombia (a priority of the militarist faction) is accompanied by bilateral free market agreements and peace negotiations between the Santos regime and the FARC armed insurgency (a priority of the MNC faction).

Regaining imperial dominance in Argentina involves (i) promoting the electoral fortunes of the neoliberal governor of Buenos Aires Macri; (ii) backing the pro-imperial media conglomerate, Clarin, facing legislation breaking up its monopoly; (iii) exploiting the death of prosecutor and CIA-Mossad collaborator, Alberto Nisman to discredit the Kirchner-Fernandez regime; and (iv) backing New York speculators' (vulture) investment fund attempting to extract exorbitant interest payments and, with the aid of a dubious judicial ruling, blocking Argentina's access to financial markets.

Both the militarist and MNC factions of the imperial state converge in backing a multi-pronged electoral—and coup—approach, which seeks to restore a US-controlled neoliberal regime to power.

The contingencies that forestalled the recovery of imperial power over the past decade are now acting in reverse. The drop in commodity prices has weakened post neoliberal regimes in Venezuela, Argentina and Ecuador. The ebbing of anti-imperialist movements resulting from centre-left co-optation tactics has strengthened imperial state backed right-wing movements and street demonstrators. The decline in Chinese growth has weakened the Latin American market diversification strategies. The internal balance of class forces has shifted to the Right, toward US-backed political clients in Brazil, Argentina, Peru and Paraguay.

Theoretical Reflections on Empire Building in Latin America

US empire building in Latin America is a cyclical process, reflecting the structural shifts in political power, and the restructuring of the world economy—forces and factors which 'override' the imperial state and capital's drive to accumulate. Capital accumulation and expansion does not depend merely on the impersonal forces of 'the market'—because the social relations under which the 'market' functions, operate under the constraints of the class struggle.

The centrepiece of imperial state activities—namely the prolonged territorial wars in the Middle East—are absent in Latin America. The driving force of

US imperial state policy is the pursuit of resources (agro-mining), labour power (lowly paid autoworkers), and markets (size and purchasing power of 600 million consumers). The economic interests of the MNCs are the motives for imperial expansion.

Even as, from a geo-strategic vantage point, the Caribbean, Central America as well as South America are located most proximate to the US, economic not military objectives predominate. However, the militarist-Zionist faction in the imperial state, ignore these traditional economic motives and deliberately choose to act on other priorities—control over oil producing regions, destruction of Islamic nations or movements or simply to destroy anti-imperialist adversaries. The militarists-Zionist faction counted the 'benefits' to Israel, its Middle East military supremacy, more important than the US securing economic supremacy in Latin America. This is clearly the case if we were to measure imperial priorities by state resources expended in pursuit of political goals.

Even if we take the goal of 'national security,' interpreted in the broadest sense, of securing the safety of the territorial homeland of the empire, the US military assault of Islamic countries driven by accompanying Islamophobic ideology and the resulting mass killings and uprooting a millions of Islamic people, has led to 'blowback': reciprocal terrorism. US 'total wars' against civilians has provoked Islamic assaults against the citizens of the West.

Latin America countries targeted by economic imperialism are less belligerent than Middle Eastern countries targeted by US militarists. A cost/benefit analysis would demonstrate the totally 'irrational' nature of militarist strategy. However, if we take account of the specific composition and interests that motivate particularly imperial state policymakers, there is a kind of perverse 'rationality'. The militarists defend the rationality of costly and unending wars by citing the advantages of seizing the 'gateways to oil' and the Zionists cite their success in enhancing Israel's regional power.

Whereas Latin America, for over a century was a priority region of imperial economic conquest, by the 21st century it lost primacy to the Middle East.

The Demise of the USSR and China's Turn Towards Capitalism

The greatest impetus to successful US imperial expansion did not take place via proxy wars or military invasions. Rather, the US Empire achieved its greatest growth and conquest, with the aid of client political leaders, organizations and vassal states throughout the USSR, Eastern Europe, the Baltic States, the Balkans and the Caucuses. Long-term and large-scale US and EU political penetration and funding succeeded in overthrowing the hegemonic collectivist regimes in Russia and the USSR, and installing vassal states. They would soon serve NATO and be incorporated in the European Union. Bonn annexed East Germany and dominated the markets of Poland, the Czech Republic and other Central European states. American and London bankers collaborated with Russian-Israeli gangster-oligarchs in joint ventures plundering resources, industries, real estate and pension funds. The European Union exploited tens of millions of highly trained scientists, technicians and workers—by importing them or stripping them of their welfare benefits and labour rights and exploiting them as cheap labour reserves in their own country.

'Imperialism by invitation' hosted by the vassal Yeltsin regime, easily appropriated Russian wealth. The ex-Warsaw Pact military forces were incorporated into a foreign legion for US imperial wars in Afghanistan, Iraq and Syria. Their military installations were converted into military bases and missile sites encircling Russia.

The US imperial conquest of the East created a 'unipolar world' in which Washington decision-makers and strategists believed that, as the world's supreme power, they could intervene in every region with impunity.

The scope and depth of the US world empire was enhanced by China's embrace of capitalism and its ruler's invitation to US and EU MNCs to enter and exploit cheap Chinese labour. The global expansion of the US empire led to a sense of unlimited power, encouraging its rulers' to exercise power against any adversary or competitor.

In the 1990s the US expanded its military bases to the borders of Russia. US MNCs expanded into China and Indo-China. US-backed client regimes throughout Latin America dismantled the national economies, privatizing and denationalizing over five thousand lucrative strategic firms. Every sector was affected: natural resources, transport, telecommunications and finance.

The US proceeded throughout the 1990s to expand via political penetration and military force. George H.W. Bush launched a war against Iraq. Clinton bombed Yugoslavia and Germany and the EU joined the US in dividing Yugoslavia into 'mini states'.

The Pivotal Year 2000: The Pinnacle and Decline of Empire

The very rapid and extensive imperial expansion from 1989 to 1999, and the easy conquests and the accompanying plunder, created the conditions for the decline of the US empire.

The pillage and impoverishment of Russia led to the rise of a new leadership under President Putin intent on reconstructing the state and economy and ending vassalage.

The Chinese leadership harnessed its dependence on the West for capital investments and technology into instruments for creating a powerful export economy and the growth of a dynamic national public-private manufacturing complex. The imperial centres of finance that flourished under lax regulation crashed. The domestic foundations of empire were severely strained. The imperial war machine competed with the financial sector for federal budgetary expenditures and subsidies.

The easy growth of empire led to its over-extension. Multiple areas of conflict reflected world-wide resentment and hostility at the destruction wrought by bombings and invasions. Collaborative imperial client rulers were weakened. The worldwide empire exceeded the capacity of the US to successfully police its new vassal states. The colonial outposts demanded new infusions of troops, arms and funds at a time when countervailing domestic pressures were demanding retrenchment and retreat.

All the recent conquests—outside of Europe—were costly. The sense of invincibility and impunity led imperial planners to overestimate their capacity to expand, retain, control and contain the inevitable anti-imperialist resistance.

The crisis and collapse of the neoliberal vassal states in Latin America accelerated. Anti-imperialist uprisings spread from Venezuela (1999), to Argentina (2001), Ecuador (2000–2005) and Bolivia (2003–2005). Centre-left regimes emerged in Brazil, Uruguay and Honduras. Mass movements in rural regions and indigenous and mining communities gained momentum. Imperial plans formulated to secure US-centred integration were rejected. Instead, multiple regional pacts excluding the US proliferated: ALBA, UNASUR, CELAC. Latin America's domestic rebellion coincided with the economic rise of China. A prolonged commodity boom severely weakened US imperial supremacy. The US had few local allies in Latin America and over ambitious commitments to control the Middle East, South Asia and North Africa.

Washington lost its automatic majority in Latin America: its backing of coups in Honduras and Paraguay and its intervention in Venezuela (2002) and blockade of Cuba were repudiated by every regime, even by conservative allies.

Having easily established a global empire, Washington found it was not so easy to defend it. Imperial strategists in Washington viewed the Middle East wars through the prism of the Israeli military priorities, ignoring the global economic interests of the MNC.

Imperial military strategists overestimated the military capacity of vassals and clients, ill prepared by Washington to rule in countries with growing armed national resistance movements. Wars, invasions and military occupations were launched in multiple sites. Yemen, Somalia, Libya, Syria, and Pakistan were added to Afghanistan and Iraq. US imperial state expenditures far exceeded any transfer of wealth from the occupied countries.

A vast civilian–military–mercenary bureaucracy pillaged hundreds of billions of dollars from the US Treasury.

The centrality of wars of conquest destroyed the economic foundations and institutional infrastructure necessary for MNC entry and profit.

Once entrenched in strategic military conceptions of empire, the military-political leadership of the imperial state fashioned a global ideology to justify and motivate a policy of permanent and multiple warfare. The doctrine of the 'war on terror' justified war everywhere and nowhere. The doctrine was 'elastic'—adapted to every region of conflict and inviting new military engagements: Afghanistan, Libya, Iran and Lebanon were all designated as war zones.

The 'terror doctrine,' global in scope, provided a justification for multiple wars and the massive destruction (not exploitation) of societies and economic resources. Above all the 'war on terrorism' justified torture (Aba Gharib) concentration camps (Guantanamo), and civilian targets (via drones) anywhere. Troops were withdrawn and returned to Afghanistan and Iraq as the nationalist resistance advanced. Thousands of Special Forces in scores of countries were active, purveying death and mayhem. Moreover, the violent uprooting, degradation and stigmatization of entire Islamic peoples led to the spread of violence in the imperial centers of Paris, New York, London, Madrid and Copenhagen. The globalization of imperial state terror led to personal terror.

Imperial terror evoked domestic terror: the former on a massive, sustained scale encompassing entire civilizations and conducted and justified by elected political officials and military authorities. The latter by a cross section of 'internationalists' who directly identified with the victims of imperial state terror.

Contemporary Imperialism: Current and Future Perspectives

To understand the future of US imperialism it is important to sum up and evaluate the experience and policies of the past quarter of a century.

If we compare US empire building between 1990 and 2015 it is clearly in decline economically, politically and even militarily in most regions of the world, though the process of decline is not linear and probably not irreversible.

Despite talk in Washington of reconfiguring imperial priorities to take account of MNC economic interests, little has been accomplished. Obama's so-called 'pivot to Asia' has resulted in new military base agreements with Japan, Australia and the Philippines surrounding China and reflects an inability to fashion free trade agreements that exclude China. Meantime, the US has militarily restarted the war and re-entered Iraq and Afghanistan in addition to launching new wars in Syria and the Ukraine. It is clear that the primacy of the militarist faction is still the determinant factor in shaping imperial state policies.

The imperial military drive is most evident in the US intervention in support of the coup in the Ukraine and subsequent financing and arming of the Kiev junta. The imperial takeover of the Ukraine and plans to incorporate it into the EU and NATO, represents military aggression in its most blatant form: The expansion of US military bases and installations and military manoeuvres on Russia's borders and the US initiated economic sanctions, have severely damaged EU trade and investment with Russia. US empire building continues to prioritize military expansion even at the cost of Western imperial economic interests in Europe.

The US-EU bombing of Libya destroyed the burgeoning trade and investment agreements between imperial oil and gas MNCs and the Gadhafi regime. NATO air assaults destroyed the economy, society and political order, converting Libya into a territory overrun by warring clans, gangs, terrorists and armed thuggery.

Over the past half-century, the political leadership and strategies of the imperial state have changed dramatically. During the period between 1975 and 1990, the MNCs played a central role in defining the direction of imperial state policy: leveraging markets in Asia; negotiating market openings with China; promoting and backing neoliberal military and civilian regimes in Latin America; installing and financing pro-capitalist regimes in Russia, Eastern Europe, the Baltic and Balkan states. Even in the cases where the imperial state resorted to military intervention, Yugoslavia and Iraq, the bombings led to favourable economic opportunities for the US-based MNCs. The Bush Sr. regime promoted US oil interests via an oil-for-food agreement with Saddam Hussein in Iraq. Clinton promoted free market regimes in the mini-states resulting from the break-up of socialist Yugoslavia.

However, the imperial state's leadership and policies shifted dramatically during the late 1990s onward. President Clinton's imperial state was composed of long-standing MNC representatives, Wall Street bankers and newly ascending militarist-Zionist officials. The result was a hybrid policy in which the imperial state actively promoted MNC opportunities under neoliberal regimes in the ex-Communist countries of Europe and Latin America, and expanded MNC ties with China and Vietnam while launching destructive military interventions in Somalia, Yugoslavia and Iraq.

The correlation and balance of force within the imperialist state shifted dramatically in favour the militarist-Zionist faction with 9/11: the terrorist attack of dubious origins and false flag demolitions in New York and Washington served to entrench the militarists in control of a vastly expanded imperial state apparatus. As a consequence of 9/11 the militarist-Zionist faction of the imperial state subordinated the interests of the MNC to its strategy of total wars. This in turn led to the invasion, occupation and destruction of civilian infrastructure in Iraq and Afghanistan (instead of harnessing it to MNC expansion). The US colonial regime dismantled the Iraqi state (instead of re-ordering it to serve the MNCs). The assassination and forced out-migration of millions of skilled professionals, administrators, police and military officials crippled any economic recovery (instead of their incorporation as servants of the colonial state and MNC).

The militarist-Zionist ascendancy in the imperial state introduced major changes in policy, orientation, priorities and the modus operandi of US imperialism. The ideology of the 'global war on terror' replaced the MNC doctrine of promoting 'economic globalization'.

Perpetual wars vs. 'terrorists' were not confined to place and time: they replaced limited wars or interventions directed at opening markets or changing regimes which would implement neoliberal policies benefitting US MNCs.

The locus of imperial state activity shifted from exploiting economic opportunities, in Asia, Latin America and the ex-Communist countries of Eastern Europe to wars in the Middle East, South Asia and North Africa—targeting Muslim countries which opposed Israel's colonial expansion in Palestine, Syria, Lebanon and elsewhere.

The new militarist power configuration's conception of empire building required vast—trillion dollar—expenditures, without care or thought of returns to private capital. In contrast, under the hegemony of the MNC, the imperial state intervened to secure concessions of oil, gas and minerals in Latin America and the Middle East. The costs of military conquest were more than compensated by the returns to the MNCs. The militarist imperial state configuration pillaged the US Treasury to finance its occupations, financing a vast army of corrupt colonial collaborators, private mercenary 'military contractors' and soon to be millionaire, US military procurement (sic) officials.

Previously, MNC-directed overseas exploitation led to healthy returns to the US Treasury both in terms of direct tax payments and via the revenues generated from trade and the processing of raw materials.

Over the past decade and a half, the biggest and most stable returns to the MNC take place in regions and countries where the militarized imperial state is least involved: China, Latin America and Europe. The MNCs have profited least and have lost most in areas of greatest imperial state involvement.

The 'war zones' that extend from Libya, Somalia, Lebanon, Syria, Iraq, Ukraine, Iran and Afghanistan and Pakistan are the regions where imperial MNCs have suffered the biggest decline and exodus.

The main 'beneficiaries' of the current imperial state policies are the war contractors and the security-military-industrial complex in the US. Overseas the state beneficiaries include Israel and Saudi Arabia. In addition, Jordanian, Egyptian, Iraqi, Afghani and Pakistani client rulers have squirreled away tens of billions in offshore private bank accounts.

The 'non-state' beneficiaries include mercenary, proxy armies. In Syria, Iraq, Libya, Somalia and the Ukraine, tens of thousands of collaborators in self-styled 'nongovernmental' organizations—civil society—have also profited.

The Loss–benefit Calculus, or Empire Building under the Aegis of the Militarist-Zionist Imperial State

Sufficient time has passed over the past decade and a half of militarist-Zionist dominance of the imperial state to evaluate their performance.

The US and its Western European allies, especially Germany successfully expanded their empire in Eastern Europe, the Balkans and the Baltic regions without firing a shot. These countries were converted into EU vassal states. Their markets dominated and industries denationalized. Their armed forces were recruited as NATO mercenaries. West Germany annexed the East. Cheap highly qualified and educated labour, as immigrants and as a labour reserve, increased profits for EU and US MNCs. Russia was temporarily reduced to a vassal state between 1991 and 2001. Living standards plunged and welfare programs were reduced. Mortality rates increased. Class inequalities widened. Millionaires and billionaires seized public resources and joined with the imperial MNC in plundering the economy. Socialist and Communist leaders and parties were repressed or co-opted. In contrast, imperial military expansion of the 21st century was a costly failure. The 'war in Afghanistan' was costly in lives and expenditures and led to an ignominious retreat. What remained was a fragile puppet regime and an unreliable mercenary military. The US-Afghanistan war was the longest war in US history and one of the biggest failures. In the end the nationalist-Islamist resistance movements—the so-called 'Taliban' and allied ethno-religious and nationalist anti-imperialist resistance groups—dominate the countryside, repeatedly penetrate and attack urban centres and prepare to take power.

The Iraq war and the imperial state's invasion and decade long occupation decimated the economy. The occupation fomented ethno-religious warfare. The secular Ba'thist officers and military professionals joined with Islamist-nationalists and subsequently formed a powerful resistance movement (ISIS), which defeated the imperial backed Shia mercenary army during the second decade of the war. The imperial state was condemned to re-enter and engage directly in a prolonged war. The cost of war spiralled to over a trillion dollars. Oil exploitation was hampered and the US Treasury poured tens of billions to sustain a 'war without end'.

The US imperial state and the EU, along with Saudi Arabia and Turkey financed armed Islamic mercenary militias to invade Syria and overthrow the secular, nationalist, anti-Zionist Bashar Assad regime. The imperial war opened the door for the expansion of the Islamic–Ba'thist forces—ISIS—into Syria. The Kurds and other armed groups seized territory, fragmenting the country. After nearly five years of warfare and rising military costs the US and EU MNCS have been cut off from the Syrian market.

US support for Israeli aggression against Lebanon has led to the growth in power of the anti-imperialist Hezbollah armed resistance. Lebanon, Syria and Iran now represent a serious alternative to the US, EU, Saudi Arabia, Israeli axis.

The US sanctions policy toward Iran has failed to undermine the nationalist regime and has totally undercut the economic opportunities of all the major US and EU oil and gas MNCS as well as US manufacturing exporters. China has replaced them.

The US-EU invasion of Libya led to the destruction of the economy and the flight of billions in MNC investments and the disruption of exports.

The US imperial states' seizure of power via a proxy coup in Kiev provoked a powerful anti-imperialist rebellion led by armed militia in the East (Donetsk and Luhansk) and the decimation of the Ukraine economy.

To summarize, the military-Zionist takeover of the imperial state has led to prolonged, unwinnable costly wars that have undermined markets and investment sites for US MNCS. Imperial militarism has undermined the imperial economic presence and provoked long-term, growing anti-imperialist resistance movements, as well as chaotic, unstable and unviable countries out of imperial control.

Economic imperialism has continued to profit in parts of Europe, Asia, Latin America and Africa despite the imperial wars and economic sanctions pursued by the highly militarized imperial state elsewhere.

However, the US militarists' seizure of power in the Ukraine and the sanctions against Russia have eroded the EU's profitable trade and investments in Russia. The Ukraine under IMF-EU-US tutelage has become a heavily indebted and broken economy run by kleptocrats who are totally dependent on foreign loans and military intervention.

Because the militarized imperial state prioritizes conflict and sanctions with Russia, Iran and Syria, it has failed to deepen and expand its economic ties with Asia, Latin America and Africa. The political and economic conquest of East Europe and parts of the USSR has lost significance. The perpetual, lost wars in the Middle East, North Africa and the Caucuses have weakened the imperial state's capacity for empire building in Asia and Latin America.

The outflow of wealth, the domestic cost of perpetual wars has eroded the electoral foundations of empire building. Only a fundamental change in the composition of the imperial state and a reorientation of priorities toward centering on economic expansion can alter the current decline of empire. The danger is that as the militarist Zionist imperialist state pursues losing wars, it may escalate and raise the ante, and move toward a major nuclear confrontation: an empire amidst nuclear ashes!

CHAPTER 8

Networks of Empire and Realignments of World Power

Imperial states build networks that link economic, military and political activities into a coherent mutually reinforcing system. This role is largely performed by the various institutions of the imperial state. Thus imperial action is not always directly economic, as military action in one country or region is necessary to open or protect economic zones. Nor are all military actions decided by economic interests if the leading sector of the imperial state is decidedly militarist.

Moreover, the sequence of imperial action may vary according to the particular conditions necessary for empire building. Thus, state aid may buy collaborators; military intervention may secure client regimes followed later by private investors. In other circumstances, the entry of private corporations may precede state intervention.

In either private or state economic- or military-led penetration, in furtherance of empire building, the strategic purpose is to exploit the special economic and geopolitical features of the targeted country to create empire-centred networks. In the post-Eurocentric colonial world, the privileged position of the US in its empire-centred policies, treaties, trade and military agreements is disguised and justified by an ideological gloss, which varies with time and circumstances. In the war to break-up Yugoslavia and establish client regimes, as in Kosovo, imperial ideology utilized humanitarian rhetoric. In the genocidal wars in the Middle East, anti-terrorism and anti-Islamic ideology is central. Against China, democratic and human rights rhetoric predominates. In Latin America, receding imperial power relies on democratic and anti-authoritarian rhetoric aimed at the democratically elected Chávez government.

The effectiveness of imperial ideology is in direct relation to the capacity of empire to promote viable and dynamic development alternatives to their targeted countries. By that criteria imperial ideology has had little persuasive power among target populations. The Islamophobic and anti-terrorist rhetoric has made no impact on the people of the Middle East and alienated the Islamic world. Latin America's lucrative trade relations with the Chavist Maduro regime and the decline of the US economy has undermined Washington's ideological campaign to isolate Venezuela. The US human rights campaign against China has been totally ignored in the EU, Africa and Latin America, and by the

500 biggest US MNCs (and even by the US Treasury busy selling treasury bonds to China to finance the ballooning US budget deficit).

The weakening influence of imperial propaganda and the declining economic leverage of Washington, means that the US imperial networks built over the past half century are being eroded or at least subject to centrifugal forces. Former fully integrated networks in Asia are now merely military bases as the economies secure greater autonomy and orient toward China and beyond. In other words the imperial networks are now being transformed into limited operations' outposts, rather than centres for imperial economic plunder.

Imperial Networks: The Crucial Role of Collaborators

Empire-building is essentially a process of penetrating a country or region, establishing a privileged position and retaining control in order to secure (i) lucrative resources, markets and cheap labour; (ii) establish a military platform to expand into adjoining countries and regions; (iii) military bases to establish a choke-hold over strategic roads or waterways to deny or limit access of competitors or adversaries; and (iv) intelligence and clandestine operations against adversaries and competitors.

History has demonstrated that the lowest cost in sustaining imperial domination in the long term is by developing local collaborators, whether in the form of political, economic and/or military leaders operating from client regimes. Overt politico-military imperial rule results in costly wars and disruption, especially among a broad array of classes adversely affected by the imperial presence.

Formation of collaborator rulers and classes results from diverse short and long term imperial policies ranging from direct military, electoral and extra-parliamentary activities to middle-to-long term recruitment, training and orientation of promising young leaders via propaganda and educational programs, cultural-financial inducements, promises of political and economic backing on assuming political office and through substantial clandestine financial backing.

The most basic appeal by imperial policy-makers to the 'new ruling class' in emerging client states is the opportunity to participate in an economic system tied to the imperial centers, in which local elites share economic wealth with their imperial benefactors. To secure mass support, the collaborator classes obfuscate the new forms of imperial subservience and economic exploitation by emphasizing political independence, personal freedom, economic opportunity and private consumerism.

The mechanisms for the transfer of power to an emerging client state combine imperial propaganda, financing of mass organizations and electoral

parties, as well as violent coups or 'popular uprisings'. Authoritarian bureau-
cratically ossified regimes relying on police controls to limit or oppose imperial expansion are 'soft targets'. Selective human rights campaigns become the
most effective organizational weapon to recruit activists and promote leaders
for the imperial-centred new political order. Once the power transfer takes
place, the former members of the political, economic and cultural elite are
banned, repressed, arrested and jailed. A new homogenous political culture of
competing parties embracing the imperial centred world order emerges. The
first order of business beyond the political purge is the privatization and
handover of the commanding heights of the economy to imperial enterprises.
The client regimes proceed to provide soldiers to engage as paid mercenaries
in imperial wars and to transfer military bases to imperial forces as platforms
of intervention. The entire 'independence' charade is accompanied by the
massive dismantling of public social welfare programs (pensions, free health
and education), labour codes and full employment policies. Promotion of a
highly polarized class structure is the ultimate consequence of client rule. The
imperial-centred economies of the client regimes, as a replica of any common-
place satrap state, is justified (or legitimated) in the name of an electoral system dubbed democratic—which is in fact a political system dominated by new
capitalist elites and their heavily funded mass media.

Imperial centred regimes run by collaborating elites spanning the Baltic
States, Central and Eastern Europe to the Balkans are the most striking example of imperial expansion in the 20th century. The breakup and takeover of
the Soviet Union and the Eastern bloc and its incorporation into the US
led NATO alliance and the European Union resulted in imperial hubris.
Washington made premature declarations of a unipolar world while Western
Europe proceeded to plunder public resources, ranging from factories to real
estate, exploiting cheap labour, overseas and via immigration, drawing on a
formidable 'reserve army' to undermine living standards of unionized labour
in the West.

The unity of purpose of European and US imperial regimes allowed for the
peaceful joint takeover of the wealth of the new regions by private monopolies. The imperial states initially subsidized the new client regimes with large-
scale transfers and loans on condition that they allowed imperial firms to
seize resources, real estate, land, factories, service sectors, media outlets etc.
Heavily indebted states went from a sharp crisis in the initial period to 'spec-
tacular' growth to profound and chronic social crises with double-digit unemployment in the 20-year period of client building. While worker protests
emerged as wages deteriorated, unemployment soared and welfare provi-
sions were cut, destitution spread. However, the 'new middle class' embedded

in the political and media apparatuses and in joint economic ventures are sufficiently funded by imperial financial institutions to protect their dominance.

The dynamic of imperial expansion in East, Central and Southern Europe however did not provide the impetus for strategic advance, because of the ascendancy of highly volatile financial capital and a powerful militarist caste in the Euro-American political centres. In important respects military and political expansion was no longer harnessed to economic conquest. The reverse was true: economic plunder and political dominance served as instruments for projecting military power.

Imperial Sequences: From War for Exploitation to Exploitation for War

The relations between imperial military policies and economic interests are complex and changing over time and historical context. In some circumstances, an imperial regime will invest heavily in military personnel and augment monetary expenditures to overthrow an anti-imperialist ruler and establish a client regime far beyond any state or private economic return. For example, US wars in Iraq and Afghanistan, proxy wars in Somalia and Yemen have not resulted in greater profits for US MNCs nor have they enhanced private exploitation of raw materials, labour or markets. At best, imperial wars have provided profits for mercenary contractors, construction companies and related 'war industries' profiting through transfers from the US treasury and the exploitation of US taxpayers, mostly wage and salary earners.

In many cases, especially after the Second World War, the emerging US imperial state lavished a multi-billion dollar loan and aid program for Western Europe. The Marshall Plan forestalled anti-capitalist social upheavals and restored capitalist political dominance. This allowed for the emergence of NATO (a military alliance led and dominated by the US). Subsequently, US MNCs invested in and traded with Western Europe reaping lucrative profits, once the imperial state created favourable political and economic conditions. In other words, imperial state politico-military intervention preceded the rise and expansion of US multinational capital. A myopic short-term analysis of the initial post-war activity would downplay the importance of private US economic interests as the driving force of US policy. Extending the time period to the following two decades, the interplay between initial high cost state military and economic expenditures with later private high return gains provides a perfect example of how the process of imperial power operates.

The role of the imperial state as an instrument for opening, protecting and expanding private market, labour and resource exploitation corresponds to a time in which both the state and the dominant classes were primarily motivated by industrial empire building.

US-directed military intervention and coups in Iran (1953), Guatemala (1954), Chile (1973), the Dominican Republic (1965) were linked to specific imperial economic interests and corporations. For example, US and English oil corporations sought to reverse the nationalization of oil in Iran. The US, United Fruit Company opposed the agrarian reform policies in Guatemala. The major US copper and telecommunication companies supported and called for the US-backed coup in Chile.

In contrast, current US military interventions and wars in the Middle East, South Asia and the Horn of Africa are not promoted by US multi-nationals. The imperial policies are promoted by militarists and Zionists embedded in the state, mass media and powerful 'civil' organizations. The same imperial methods (coups and wars) serve different imperial rulers and interests.

Clients, Allies and Puppet Regimes

Imperial networks involve securing a variety of complementary economic, military and political 'resource bases' that are both part of the imperial system and retain varying degrees of political and economic autonomy.

In the dynamic earlier stages of US Empire building, roughly from the 1950s to the 1970s, US-based MNCs and the economy as a whole dominated the world economy. Its allies in Europe and Asia were highly dependent on US markets, financing and development. US military hegemony was reflected in a series of regional military pacts that secured almost instant support for US regional wars, military coups and the construction of military bases and naval ports on their territory. Many countries in the developing world were forced into an international division of labour that served the interests of capital and the US Empire.

Western Europe was a military outpost, industrial partner and ideological collaborator. Asia, primarily Japan and South Korea served as 'frontline military outposts', as well as industrial partners. Indonesia, Malaysia, the Philippines were essentially client regimes which provided raw materials as well as military bases. Singapore and Hong Kong were financial and commercial entrepots. Pakistan was a client military regime serving as a frontline pressure on China. Saudi Arabia, Iran and the Gulf mini-states, ruled by client authoritarian regimes, provided oil and military bases. Egypt and Jordan and Israel anchored imperial interests in the Middle East. Beirut served as a financial centre for US, European and Middle East bankers. Africa and Latin America, including client and nationalist-populist regimes, were a source of raw materials as well as markets for finished goods and cheap labour.

The prolonged US-Vietnam war and Washington's subsequent defeat eroded the power of the empire. Western Europe, Japan and South Korea's industrial expansion challenged US industrial primacy. Latin America's pursuit of nationalist, import-substitution policies forced US investment toward overseas manufacturing. In the Middle East nationalist movements toppled US clients in Iran and Iraq and undermined military outposts. Revolutions in Angola, Namibia, Mozambique, Algeria, Nicaragua and elsewhere curtailed Euro-American 'open ended' access to raw materials, at least temporarily.

The decline of the US Empire was temporarily arrested by the collapse of Communism in the Soviet Union and Eastern Europe and the establishment of client regimes throughout the region. Likewise, the upsurge of imperial-centred client regimes in Latin America between the mid 1970s to the end of the 1990s gave the appearance of an imperialist recovery. The 1990s, however, were not the beginning of a repeat of the early 1950s imperial take-off: it was the last hurrah before a slow but steady irreversible decline. The entire imperial political apparatus, so successful in its clandestine operations in subverting the Soviet and Eastern European regimes, played a marginal role when it came to capitalizing on the economic opportunities that ensued. Germany and other EU countries led the way in the takeover of lucrative privatized enterprises. Russian-Israeli oligarchs (seven of the top eight) seized and pillaged privatized strategic industries, banks and natural resources. The principal US beneficiaries were the banks and Wall Street firms that laundered billions of illicit earnings and collected lucrative fees from mergers, acquisitions, stock listings and other less than transparent activities. In other words, the collapse of Soviet collectivism strengthened the parasitical financial sector of the US Empire. Worse still, the assumption of a 'unipolar world' fostered by US ideologues, played into the hands of the militarists, who now assumed that former constraints on US military assaults on nationalists and Soviet allies had disappeared. As a result, military intervention became the principle driving force in US empire building, leading to the first Iraq war, the Yugoslav and Somali invasion and the expansion of US military bases throughout the former Soviet bloc and Eastern Europe.

At the very pinnacle of US global-political and military power during the 1990s, with all the major Latin American regimes enveloped in an empire-centred neoliberal time warp, the seeds of decay and decline set in. The economic crises of the late 1990s, led to major uprisings and electoral defeats of practically all US clients in Latin America, signalling the decline of US imperial domination. China's extraordinary dynamic and cumulative growth displaced US manufacturing capital and weakened US leverage over rulers in Asia, Africa and Latin America. The vast transfer of US state resources to overseas imperial adventures, military bases and the shoring up of clients and allies led to domestic decline.

The US empire, passively facing economic competitors displacing the US in vital markets and engaged in prolonged and unending wars which drained the treasury, attracted a cohort of mediocre policymakers who lacked a coherent strategy for rectifying policies and reconstructing the state to serve productive activity capable of 'retaking markets'. Instead the policies of open-ended and unsustainable wars played into the hands of a special sub-group (sui generis) of militarists, American Zionists. They capitalized on their infiltration of strategic positions in the state, enhanced their influence in the mass media and a vast network of organized 'pressure groups' to reinforce US subordination to Israel's drive for Middle East supremacy.

The result was an 'unbalancing' of the US imperial apparatus: military action was unhinged from economic empire building. A highly influential upper caste of Zionist-militarists harnessed US military power to an economically marginal state (Israel), in perpetual hostility toward the 1.5 billion Muslim world. Equally damaging, American Zionist ideologues and policymakers promoted repressive institutions and legislation and Islamophobic ideological propaganda designed to terrorize the US population. Equally important Islamophobic ideology served to justify permanent war in South Asia and the Middle East and the exorbitant military budgets, at a time of sharply deteriorating domestic socio-economic conditions. Hundreds of billions of dollars were spent unproductively as 'Homeland Security', which strived in every way to recruit, train, frame and arrest Afro-American Muslim men as 'terrorists'. Thousands of secret agencies with hundreds of thousands of national, state and local officials spied on US citizens who at some point may have sought to speak or act to rectify or reform the militarist-financial-Zionist centered imperialist policies.

By the end of the first decade of the 21st century, the US empire could only destroy adversaries (Iraq, Pakistan, and Afghanistan) provoke military tensions (Korean peninsula, China Sea) and undermine relations with potentially lucrative trading partners (Iran, Venezuela). Galloping authoritarianism fused with fifth column Zionist militarism to foment Islamophobic ideology. The convergence of authoritarian mediocrities, upwardly mobile knaves and fifth column tribal loyalists in the Obama regime precluded any foreseeable reversal of imperial decay.

China's growing global economic network and dynamic advance in cutting edge applied technology in everything from alternative energy to high-speed trains, stands in contrast to the Zionist-militarist infested empire of the US.

The US demands on client Pakistan rulers to empty their treasury in support of US Islamic wars in Afghanistan and Pakistan, stands in contrast to the US$30 billion dollar Chinese investments in infrastructure, energy and electrical power and multi-billion dollar increases in trade.

Military subsidies to Israel in the order of three billion dollars stand in contrast to China's multi-billion dollar investments in Iranian oil and trade agreements. US funding of wars against Islamic countries in Central and South Asia stands in contrast to Turkey's expanding economic trade and investment agreements in the same region. China has replaced the US as the key trading partner in leading South American countries, while the US unequal 'free trade' agreement (NAFTA) impoverished Mexico. Trade between the European Union and China exceeds that with the US.

In Africa, the US subsidizes wars in Somalia and the Horn of Africa, while China signs on to multi-billion dollar investment and trade agreements, building up African infrastructure in exchange for access to raw materials. There is no question that the economic future of Africa is increasingly linked to China.

The US Empire, in contrast, is in a deadly embrace with an insignificant colonial militarist state (Israel), failed states in Yemen and Somalia, corrupt stagnant client regimes in Jordan and Egypt and the decadent rent collecting absolutist petrol-states of Saudi Arabia and the Gulf. All form part of an unproductive atavistic coalition bent on retaining power via military supremacy. Yet Empires of the 21st century are built on the bases of productive economies with global networks linked to dynamic trading partners.

Recognizing the economic primacy and market opportunities linked to becoming part of the Chinese global network, former or existing US clients and even puppet rulers have begun to edge away from submission to US mandates. Fundamental shifts in economic relations and political alignments have occurred throughout Latin America. Brazil, Venezuela, Bolivia and other countries supported and continue to support Iran's non-military nuclear program in defiance of Zionist-led Washington aggression. Several countries have defied Israel-US policymakers by recognizing Palestine as a state. Trade with China surpasses trade with the US in the biggest countries in the region.

Puppet regimes in Iraq, Afghanistan and Pakistan have signed major economic agreements with China, Iran and Turkey even while the US pours billions to bolster its military position. Turkey an erstwhile military client of the US-NATO command broadens its own quest for capitalist hegemony by expanding economic ties with Iran, Central Asia and the Arab-Muslim world, challenging US-Israeli military hegemony.

The US Empire still retains major clients and nearly a thousand military bases around the world. As client and puppet regimes decline, Washington increases the role and scope of extra-territorial death squad operations from

50 to 80 countries. The growing independence of regimes in the developing world is especially fuelled by an economic calculus: China offers greater economic returns and less political-military interference than the US.

Washington's imperial network is increasingly based on military ties with allies: Australia, Japan, South Korea, Taiwan in the Far East and Oceana; the European Union in the West; and a smattering of Central and South American states in the South. Even here, the military allies are no longer economic dependencies: Australia and New Zealand's principle export markets are in Asia (China). EU-China trade is growing exponentially. Japan, South Korea and Taiwan are increasingly tied by trade and investment with China...as is Pakistan and India.

Equally important, new regional networks that exclude the US have been formed in Latin America and Asia, creating the potential for new economic blocs. In other words, the US imperial economic network constructed after World War II and amplified by the collapse of the USSR is in the process of decay, even as the military bases and treaties remain as a formidable 'platform' for new military interventions.

What is clear is that the military, political and ideological gains in network-building by the US around the world with the collapse of the USSR and the post-Soviet wars are not sustainable. On the contrary, the overdevelopment of the ideological-military-security apparatus raised economic expectations and depleted economic resources resulting in the incapacity to exploit economic opportunities or consolidate economic networks. US-funded 'popular uprisings' in the Ukraine led to client regimes incapable of promoting growth. In the case of Georgia, the regime engaged in an adventurous war with Russia resulting in trade and territorial losses. It is a matter of time before existing client regimes in Egypt, Jordan, Saudi Arabia, the Philippines and Mexico will face major upheavals, due to the precarious bases of rule by corrupt, stagnant and repressive rulers.

The process of decay of the US Empire is both cause and consequence of the challenge by rising economic powers establishing alternative centres of growth and development. Changes within countries at the periphery of the empire and growing indebtedness and trade deficits at the 'centre' of the empire are eroding the empire. The US ruling governing class, in both its financial and militarist elements, show neither will nor interest in confronting the causes of decay. Instead, each mutually supports the other: the financial sector lowers taxes deepening the public debt and plunders the treasury. The military caste drains the treasury in pursuit of wars and military outposts and increases the trade deficit by undermining commercial and investment undertakings.

CHAPTER 9

Paradoxes of Anti-Imperialism and Class Struggle

The complexities of the new political relations in Latin America require that we break down what previously was the unified components of anti-imperialist politics. For example in the past, anti-imperialist regimes pursued policies which opposed US military aggression and intervention in Latin America and throughout the third world; opposed foreign investment especially in extractive sectors; and, not infrequently, expropriated or nationalized strategic sectors; opposed joint military exercises and training missions; supported nationalist liberation movements and extended political-material support; diversified trade and investment to other economic regions and countries; developed regional political organizations which opposed imperialism and formed regional economic organizations which excluded the US.

Today, few if any of the anti-imperialist countries fit these criteria. Moreover, some of the countries 'favoured' by Washington fit all the criteria of an imperial collaborator. For example, among the most prominent 'anti-imperialist regimes' in Latin America today, Bolivia and Ecuador are big promoters and supporters of a development model that relies on foreign multi-national corporations exploiting mining and energy sectors. Moreover both regimes, in pursuit of extractive capital accumulation have dispossessed local indigenous and peasant communities (e.g., the Tipnis reserve in Bolivia).

In line with the 'double discourse' of these contemporary 'anti-imperialists', the Bolivian Vice President chaired a meeting in Cochabamba by a prominent anti-imperialist academic critic, David Harvey, to expound on the issue of 'capital accumulation by dispossession'. Needless to say, Harvey ignored, or chose to overlook, the pervasive extractive practices of his generous hosts.

On the other side of the ledger, several Latin American regimes which are in favour with Washington and have embraced the Trans-Pacific Alliance namely Peru and Chile, have diversified their trade away from the US and have turned to China, Washington's leading global competitor.

The lines separating the critics and backers of Washington, the nationalists from the neoliberals are not as clear as in the past. There is a great deal of overlap, especially with regard to the extractive model of capitalist development, the presence and dependence on foreign multi-national capital and the pursuit of orthodox fiscal policies.

The sharpest distinction between the anti-imperialist and neoliberal regimes revolves around foreign policy, but even here, there is some overlap. Bolivia,

Ecuador, Venezuela, Cuba and to a lesser degree Brazil and Argentina condemn the so-called 'US war on terror', its pretext for launching wars and military intervention in the Middle East, Africa and South Asia. Washington's favoured regimes, Colombia, Mexico, Peru, Paraguay and its Central American clients, support US global militarism. Colombia offers troops or maintains a discreet silence. Yet in Latin America, even Washington's favoured regimes support exclusive Latin American organizations, Mercosur, ALBA, CELAC; opposed (temporarily) the US-backed coup in Honduras; reject the US blockade of Cuba and interference in Venezuelan politics. Even Colombia, which has allowed seven US military bases, has signed off on several military understandings and economic agreements with Venezuela—even as the US heightens its hostility to the Maduro government in Caracas.

The theoretical point is that in the present conjuncture we need to work with a revised conception of what constitutes a pro and anti-imperialist political framework. We will be looking at the specific economic relations and linkages, the divergences between specific public pronouncements on foreign policy issues and the long term, large-scale economic strategies. At the 'extremes', for example Mexico and Venezuela, the differences are significant.

Mexico is the most favoured imperial client in both foreign and economic policy. It supports NAFTA (integration with the US); its security forces are subject to US oversight; it has the lowest minimum wage in Latin America (even below Honduras); it is privatizing the strategic petrol sector firm PEMEX; it is a major 'labour reserve' for cheap manufacturing workers (especially in the auto industry); it has the lowest effective tax rate; it has joined the US war on drugs and war on terror by militarizing its domestic society. Few countries in Latin America can match Mexico's submission to Washington and few regimes would want to!

In contrast, Venezuela is the US's bête noir: Washington has been engaged in permanent war with the democratic governments of Chávez and Maduro because they oppose the US wars in the Middle East, Asia and Africa. They nationalized select enterprises; financed large-scale long-term social welfare programs that reduced unemployment, poverty and inequality. They imposed controls on financial transactions (rather weak and ineffective). They offer generous aid programs to Caribbean and Central American countries, enticing them out of the US orbit. Caracas has ended US military training and indoctrination programs and encouraged the growth of nationalist consciousness among officers. Venezuela has increased economic ties with US adversaries (Iran and Russia) and competitors (China).

The rest of Latin America falls somewhat in between these two polar opposites, overlapping with each or developing their own combinations of pro and anti-imperialist policies. This makes it difficult to generalize and create 'typologies', as many of the contrasts and similarities overlap.

However, there are two good reasons to make the effort. First of all, with all the complexities, specific politico-economic configurations are evolving which are determining the correlation of forces in the Hemisphere and over time will decide whether the region will take an independent role or fall back under US hegemony.

Secondly, and equally important, the 'external relations' or international relations of the regimes are playing out in the context of a new set of class relations and social conflicts, which do not necessarily correlate with the degree of pro- or anti-imperialism of the regimes. For example both the Bolivian and Ecuadorean regimes, which are considered leading anti-imperialists, have repressed, co-opted or denied legitimacy to class organizations.

For both these reasons we will now turn to classifying the pro-imperial and anti-imperial regimes, in order to then proceed to analyze how these regimes face up to the emerging class and social conflicts.

Classifying Pro- and Anti-Imperialist Regimes

The key to the classification of Latin American countries is the scope and depth of land grants that regimes have made to large foreign and domestic multinational corporations. Over the past two decades Latin America has experienced re-colonization by invitation: government grants of millions of acres of territory under the quasi-exclusive jurisdiction of giant mining and plantation consortiums. These land grants are accompanied by mineral exploitation and water rights, license to contaminate and the free use of the state to evict local inhabitants, to repress rebellious communities and to construct transport grids centered in the colonial land grant. The phrase 'capital accumulation via dispossession' is too narrow and vague. The concept 'recolonization' captures more accurately the large scale long term transfer of sovereign wealth, natural resources and special 'colonial' laws and regulations, that exempt these huge holdings from what previously passed for 'national sovereignty'. In other words, when we speak of imperialist and anti-imperialist regimes, we are really writing about the scope and depth of recolonization (populist rhetoric not withstanding).

What we have in contemporary Latin America is a new combination of seemingly contradictory features: greater diversification of international markets, the emergence of an affluent 'national bourgeoisie' and the granting and recolonization of vast sectors of territory and resources by imperial capital.

This is clearly the case with a cluster of states that have forsaken regulatory controls, denationalized key mining sectors and adopted a Big Push strategy directed to the 'extractive sector'. This is clearly reflected in the accentuated colonial character of their trade relations: large-scale and long-term exports of raw materials and imports of finished goods (machinery, intermediary and consumer goods).

The Colonial Extractive Regimes

The leading colonial-extractive regimes are found in Mexico, Colombia, Peru, Paraguay and Central America. This cluster conforms to the all-around criteria for a pro-imperial regime: integration into the US-centred geopolitical order, as well as containing vast colonial agro-mineral enclaves.

Mexico under President Enrique Péna Nieto, Colombia under Presidents Uribe and Santos and Peru under President Ollanta Humala have granted millions of acres to giant mining corporations and savagely repressed and dispossessed communities, farmers and local enterprises to 'make room' for the colonial mining operations. These regimes compete to lower labour costs—with Mexico heading the list with the lowest minimum wage, the most repressive anti-trade union practices and the weakest regulations of environmental contamination.

Peru under Humala, like Nieto and Santos, has worked closely with US 'anti-terrorist', 'anti-narcotics' military forces to savage any popular insurgency and any economic activity which conflicts with the 'Gran Mineria'. In the context of growing resistance by the communities that are negatively affected by the operations of extractive capital (the big mining companies) the Humala regime in 2013 allowed into the country a contingent of 125 soldiers, masking and justifying this imperialist intervention in terms of the war against drug-trafficking. In March 2015 the US announced its decision to increase its contingent of troops to 3,200 by next September.

The troika of Santos, Peña Nieto and Humala have moved decisively to privatize major resource industries and opening up the extractive sector to foreign investors and multinational corporations, allowing them to pillage the country's resources at minimal cost (next to no royalties and an exceedingly low tax regime) and great profit (on this see the studies in Veltmeyer & Petras, 2014). This cluster of neocolonial regimes are solid supporters of the Trans-Pacific Partnership and have bilateral free trade agreements with the US and in practical terms have downgraded Latin American integration.

The class struggle in 'the pro-imperialist cluster' is evidenced at the sectoral and regional levels, varying in intensity and consistency over time and place. In both Peru and Colombia, intense struggles have involved displaced peasants and to a lesser degree miners and the adjoining labourforce. In Colombia large-scale marches by the rural poor have crisscrossed the country, demanding the return of their land, a greater allocation of state aid (a reallocation from agro-mining). Under Santos selective assassinations have replaced the massacres of the previous Uribe regime. In Peru, large-scale community rebellions have confronted the Humala regime, which has done a complete about face from social-reformer to free market advocate. Civic strikes, community and region-wide protests have confronted military occupations directed at facilitating massive foreign mining colonization and enrichment. These pro-imperial regimes, especially Peru under Humala, faced with massive opposition, have embraced a policy of 'inclusion', combining the extractive colonial regime to 'trickle down economics'—allocating a fraction of the mining tax toward social welfare.

The Eclectic Cluster: Colonial Economies and Anti-Imperialist Foreign Policy

There is no sharp break between the extractive colonial economies of the pro-imperial cluster and the moderate 'anti-imperialist' grouping. In fact in some cases the distinction hardly can be made. The moderate anti-imperialists include Brazil, Argentina, Uruguay, and Chile.

Chile and Uruguay have embraced free trade models, depend heavily on mining and agro-exports and have pursued free trade agreements, Chile more than Uruguay. Yet there are some key differences with the imperial cluster. Neither Chile, Uruguay, nor Brazil or Argentina support and collaborate with US military and counter-insurgency forces in policing their country as is the case with Colombia (seven US bases) Peru and Mexico. Nor have they actively contributed to overseas occupations, with the notorious exception of Haiti.

What is pre-eminently clear however is that this grouping of pragmatic neo-liberal or post-neoliberal and moderate anti-imperialist regimes have not pri-oritized their relation with Washington over their regional associations (with the exception of Chile). They have diversified their trade and investment part-ners and in some key instances have taken positions strongly opposed to Washington. In particular the countries have multiple relations with Cuba, Venezuela, Iran and other US adversaries. Their ties to China are expanding at the expense of Washington. Their policies oppose 'US centred' integration schemes. All the countries have opposed the US judicial process favouring the

New York speculative hedge fund and support Argentina's offer to settle on the terms of the original bondholders.

However, this grouping of moderate post-neoliberal regimes at no point has ever considered a 'rupture' with imperialism—a sharp break in relations or an adversarial political alliance. Its brand of anti-imperialism is more a gradual, incremental shift of economic ties, a firm opposition to US interventions and military coups. They favour a growing regional identity and a weakening of engagement with highly militarized programs such as the 'antiterrorist', 'antidrug' crusades which place their security services and military under US tutelage. The highly militarized global direction of US imperial policy has contributed to the weakening of ties with the moderate grouping, whose prime concern is driven by an economic developmentalist agenda—namely greater trade, increased investments and wider markets.

This 'moderate group' of post-neoliberal neocolonial regimes has adapted to the rise of large-scale national and foreign private agro-mineral elites to power. They have played a major role, with greater or lesser success, in coordinating their accommodations with the entry of large-scale foreign multinationals. Their 'nationalism' or 'anti-imperialism' is mostly directed at managing these mix of enterprises, regulating the operations of both and securing taxes to subsidize moderate welfare programs, under the rubric of 'inclusive development'.

The key issues for Washington are the lack of automatic submission on foreign policy, the presence of a national option with regard to access to resources and the lack of support for US centred hemispheric integration. It appears that Washington's frame of reference in dealing with the moderate group is still embedded in the 1980s and 90s when debt leverage secured compliance with the Washington Consensus; when neoliberal regimes engaged in wholesale privatization and denationalization of entire economic sectors; when the Latin American regimes were embedded in the imperial state structure.

The moderate countries have moved to a new type of relation with the US in which relationships and agreements are negotiated, taking into account national capitalist interests, diverse extractive export markets, regional economic ties and residual, but occasionally important, nationalist and democratic pressures from leaders with a radical past.

Most of the moderate anti-imperialist leaders in an earlier period were active in revolutionary or radical social and national liberation movements. Brazilian President Dilma Rousseff, President Bachelet in Chile, President Mujica in Uruguay, President Ceren in El Salvador, all were engaged in revolutionary anti-capitalist struggles. They have broken decisively with their revolutionary past and embraced electoral politics but still retain the legacy of popular commitments, of being 'on the Left'. This allows them to secure the backing of plebeian electoral sectors. While their past has not in any way influenced their pursuit of foreign capital and their promotion of agro-mineral extractive economic growth, their past experience reminds them that they need a "social dimension" and anti-imperial symbolic action to retain strategic mass support.

The Anti-Imperial Quartet: Venezuela, Cuba, Bolivia and Ecuador

The centrepiece of US imperial hostility focuses on four countries, which have consistently opposed US efforts to re-assert dominance in the region. While, in themselves, the four are not major powers, they exert a direct and especially indirect impact on the rest of the continent especially among the 'moderate group'. Moreover, even in this anti-imperial grouping, there are important departures and inconsistencies especially in the realm of policy to foreign direct investment agreements.

The four countries that form the quartet are in different degrees in opposition to imperialism. They also share a common platform of support for a greater degree of regional integration, opposition to US military interventions and economic sanctions, and an ideology which proclaims some variants of 'socialism'— whether '21st century socialism' (Ecuador), Bolivarian Socialism (Venezuela), Socialist humanism (Cuba), or 'communitarian socialism' (Bolivia).

All four countries have faced and defeated recent US-sponsored subversion and coups in recent years: Cuba uncovered a USAID financed plot to recruit agents (2009–11). Venezuela defeated a coup (2002), a lockout (2003), a violent destabilization campaign (2014). Ecuador defeated an abortive police uprising (2009). Ecuador's President Correa partially defaulted on dubiously incurred foreign debt. Chávez 'renationalized' the oil and other industries, transferring oil revenues from overseas operations to domestic welfare programs. Bolivia claimed to have 'nationalized' its oil and gas industry, when in fact it raised royalty payments and state ownership shares. Cuba has operated a planned collectivist economy up to now.

If we go beyond the common political and ideological anti-imperialist practices of the quartet, to examine the dynamics of economic policy and the structure of ownership of strategic economic sectors, the notion of anti-imperialism becomes very fuzzy and elusive.

Bolivia is a case in point. Evo Morales' ardent political attacks on imperial wars needs to be balanced by his welcoming embrace of foreign multi-national corporations in every sector of the strategic mining sector: iron, gold, petrol, zinc, lithium, etc.

Similarly, while condemning US imperialism, terminating the US military base agreement in Manta and denouncing Texaco's pollution of its oil site, Ecuador has signed off on multiple oil agreements with Chinese and other foreign multi-nationals. It has signed off on an IMF loan and retains the dollarization of the economy.

Venezuela, which has consistently challenged US dominance in the Caribbean, Central America and elsewhere with aid programs, still depends on the US oil market for most of its exports and US food imports for most of its foodstuffs. In addition, the great bulk of its non-oil economy is directly controlled by domestic and foreign capitalists.

Cuba's relationship to imperialism is a more complex and changing phenomenon. For nearly a half-century Cuba was in the forefront of global anti-imperialist struggles in Latin America, Africa and Asia backing their ideology with revolutionary volunteers, material and more support.

In recent decades, however, Cuba has shifted toward domestic priorities while retaining international solidarity in the areas of health and education. In line with its attempt to overcome bureaucratic bottlenecks and economic stagnation, the Cuban government has adopted a new economic strategy based on attracting foreign investment and gradually liberalizing the economy.

The problems facing the collectivist economy are real; the needs for investments, markets and technology are great. But so are the political consequences resulting from adapting to the needs of foreign capital as far as the idea of sustaining an international anti-imperialist policy. The accommodation with foreign multinational capital in Cuba means that criticism, let alone opposition elsewhere will be diluted.

Anti-Imperialism, Yesterday and Today

The notion of anti-imperialism that emerged in the early 20th century and reached its peak in the last half of the 20th century, combining political (anti-colonialism) and economic (anti-foreign capital control) policies, has been 'redefined' in the 21st century.

Today, the practice of the 'anti-imperialist quartet', combines powerful opposition to military and political imperial expansion and collaborative association with the major foreign agro-mining multinationals. While denouncing the most extreme forms of US centred integration proposals and favouring regional integration and diversified trade agreements, the quartet has pursued a colonial style development strategy, emphasizing the export of primary commodities and the import of finished goods. And 'anti-neoliberalism', the battle-flag of the quartet, revolves around a more equitable distribution of the revenues from...free trade!

Thus the differences between the 'radical' and 'moderate' anti-imperialist regimes are greatly diluted when we consider the realm of international economic relations and policies. And the differences between the moderate nucleus and the pro-imperialists in the realm of political alignments become blurred.

The blurring lines and overlap have two effects. One involves weakening the alignment of the pro-imperialists regimes with Washington especially on economic issues. The second involves weakening the anti-imperialists, especially, but not exclusively, the 'moderates' support for anti-imperialist struggles. There is a tendency to converge and redefine 'anti-imperialism' in political terms and to line-up with the pro-imperialists with the economic demands for greater trade, investment and growth. This is the framework in which we now turn to examine how the contemporary 'anti-imperialism' relates to the class struggle.

Class Struggle and Anti-Imperialism in the 21st Century

The nature and scope of the class struggle has changed dramatically over the course of the 21st century. The revolutionary struggles characterized by large-scale worker occupation of factories as part of a political offensive have virtually disappeared. The general strike as a weapon to block anti-labour legislation, austerity programs, welfare cuts and the onset of authoritarian regimes has become a rarity.

The decline of traditional industrial workers centred mass direct action is not wholly the result of diminished militancy. Part of the reason is that 'times have changed' with the onset of centre-left 'progressive' regimes. In the aftermath of earlier popular upheavals during the previous decade, industrial workers have secured incremental, steady and persistent wage increases and access to tripartite negotiations.

Secondly, with the shift to primarization of the economy, the manufacturing sector has ceased to be the dynamic centre of the development process. It has partially given way to the agro-mineral export sector. Hence it no longer is numerically or qualitatively in a position to leverage power.

Thirdly, the centre-left regimes in particular, have fostered mass consumer borrowing via easy credit terms, turning workers toward individual consumption over collective struggles for social consumption.

However, the diminution of the role of the industrial working class does not mean class struggle has been eliminated. Moreover, new class forces and 'working peoples' movements have burst upon the scene, engaging in new forms of class, national and ethnic struggles against the new model of extractive capital and its backers, including in many cases the 'anti-imperialist' regimes.

This new class struggle, or more accurately popular social struggles, more frequently than not revolves around economic relations; more specifically, the dispossession of land, the uprooting of communities, the colonization of land and resources by large-scale multi-national corporations and the destruction and contamination of water, air, crops and fish.

Major conflicts involve direct confrontations with the state—and pit the popular classes, including peasants, workers, local artisans, small business-people, against the local and national repressive apparatus.

Unlike early 'economistic' struggles between workers and capital, the struggles today are directly political; popular demands are directed against state policies, development agencies and economic strategies.

The shift of the epicentre of class struggle has evolved over time, but has come to the fore over the past decade. The historical change is necessary to understand the current configuration of class forces.

In contemporary Latin America, we can identify four types of class struggles: the moderate, the militant, the radical-urban and struggles with armed direct action.

Moderate Class Struggle

Moderate class-social struggle largely involves little mass involvement and direct action. It is largely a process of elite negotiations between labour union officials, employers and the Labour Ministry. It operates largely within the wage and salary framework (guidelines) established by the Finance Ministry.

This type of institutionalized class struggle paradoxically is a result of earlier militant class struggles in which regime change (the rise of the centre-left) resulted in a 'historical' compromise in which labour was recognized as a 'legitimate' interlocutor, and wage and salary raises were granted in exchange for renouncing anti-capitalist struggles and challenges for state power. The regime's subsequent shift to extractive capital and neocolonial land grants has not evoked any sustained struggle from the organized urban working class, encased in the tri-partite framework.

Militant Class Struggle

The struggles over extractive capital involves new classes and social movements. This second type of social struggle involves militant mass direct action by classes and communities and takes place in and around the centres of extractive capital. The large-scale colonization by invitation of land and minerals by multi-national corporations, aided and abetted by military and paramilitary forces, has provoked major confrontations throughout Latin America.

The protagonists of this militant form of class struggle involve provincial, semi-rural and rural community based organizations with ethnic, class and ecological driven agendas.

Radical Urban Class Struggle

The third type of social struggle revolves around mass urban based movements, demanding a massive reallocation of economic resources from corporate subsidies and tax exonerations to social spending on education, health, public transport and housing, increases in public social service employee salaries and the minimum wage.

Armed Struggle and Direct Action

The fourth type of social struggle includes armed rural struggle as in the case of the Colombian guerrillas, land occupations as in the case of the Rural Landless Workers movement in Brazil (MST) and the selective occupation of factories in Venezuela. This form of class conflict is on the decline. The Colombian guerrillas are negotiating a peace accord. The MST land occupations have diminished. The Venezuelan labour movement is too fragmented and economistic to move toward a general offensive featuring factory occupations.

Types of Class Struggle According to Country

Latin America exhibits all four types of class struggle, but in varying degrees of prominence. No single form of class conflict exists independently of other types. However, we can identify the most prominent and dynamic forms that are most closely linked to the possibility of bringing about substantive social change or structural transformation, and that are linked to the dynamics of extractive capital and extractive imperialism. We identify countries where one or another type of struggle predominates and then proceed to analyze the relationship between 'anti-imperialist countries' and types of class struggle in the context of the growth of the extractive capital model.

Institutional Class Struggle

The major urban trade unions, in Brazil, Argentina, Uruguay, Bolivia, Chile, Venezuela and Mexico are by and large engaged in collective bargaining mediated by the state, over wages, salaries, pensions, etc. The behaviour of the trade unions is dictated by an ideological affinity with the regimes in power (Centre-Left) in the case of Brazil, Argentina, Uruguay, Venezuela and Bolivia. In other countries, repressive action by the state (Mexico, Paraguay) enforces conformity. Struggles are limited in scope, duration and frequency. More often than not the trade unions' do not question, let alone challenge, the extractive imperial economic model. In most cases the trade unions are not engaged with other popular movements involved in more consequential forms of class action in the agro-mineral sector or even in urban mass actions demanding changes in state budgets.

Mass Direct Action against Extractive Capital

Mass direct action against extractive capital is most intense and widespread in regions and sectors associated with the dynamic expansion of agro-mineral extraction. With few exceptions, the greater the scope and expansion of extractive capitalist exploitation, the more likely there will occur large scale clashes, not only between capital and the popular classes, but with the state.

Peru, Ecuador, Colombia, Mexico, Bolivia, Argentina, Paraguay and Brazil have all been sites of conflicts between expanding extractive capital and the local communities, farmers, peasants, popular and civic organizations. Provincial-wide strikes, road and transport blockages, occupations of work sites have led to the state intervening and military repression: the killing, wounding and arrest of numerous protestors.

The radicalism and militancy of the popular movements is a direct result of the material stakes that are involved. In the first instance, local producers, whether farmers or artisan miners and households, are dispossessed, uprooted and abandoned. Theirs is a struggle for the survival of a 'way of life'. Unlike other forms of struggle, urban or trade union, theirs is not over an incremental gain or loss in salary or wages. Secondly, the struggle is over the basic necessities of everyday life: clean air, unpolluted water, uncontaminated food, health and mortality. Mining and agro-chemical export economic activity absorbs irrigation water, pollutes drinking water, fills the air with deadly fumes. Toxic chemicals, pesticides and herbicides are sprayed constantly, undermining the local economy and making the region unliveable. Thirdly, local cultural and community customs and practices are eroded as large-scale mining organizations draw the riff-raff of the world-prostitutes, drug dealers, smugglers. In addition, corporate-centred diversions erode class-community solidarity.

The extreme and pervasive erosion of social and personal relations, the radical uprooting and deterioration of everyday life provokes wide-spread and sustained militant social action which is directed at the state which promotes extractive capital as well as the foreign and national owners. These struggles are political as well as economic and social, unlike the trade union 'peso and centavos' centred demands.

Mass Urban Struggles over Social Expenditures

During the World Cup extravaganza in Brazil, multi-million person mass demonstrations occurred demanding a massive shift in state priorities toward education, health and public transport. In Chile for the better part of 2011–14, hundreds of thousands of students demanded free, public, quality higher education with the backing of community groups and teachers' unions.

In Venezuela mass urban protests organized by right-wing parties and violent social movements, backed by Washington, attacked the national populist government, exploiting popular grievance against shortages of consumer goods, induced by corporate hoarding and contraband gangs.

Leftist trade unions engaged in counter-protests, as well as strikes over wages and in a few cases for a greater role in managing public enterprises. More significantly hundreds of elected community councils have emerged and have formed parallel administrations, challenging local municipal governments on the left and right. The demands for 'popular power' include greater security and control of the distribution of consumer goods and prices.

In Argentina the mass urban struggles of the unemployed that led to successive regime changes in 2001–02 have practically disappeared, as has the factory occupation movement. Dynamic growth led to a sharp reduction of unemployment and pension and wage increases. As a result the axis of social struggle has turned to the growth of movements protesting the depredations of extractive capital—in particular agro-toxic exploitation led by Monsanto. This 'struggle', however, has little resonance in the large urban centres and among the trade unions,

Armed Struggle, Land Occupations and Revolutionary Transformation

The only regime changes through extra parliamentary means have been engineered or attempted by us-backed military-oligarchical elites. In Honduras a us-backed junta overthrew the elected centre-left Zelaya government. In Paraguay an oligarchical palace coup ousted the elected President Fernando Lugo. Unsuccessful and aborted us-backed coups took place in Venezuela 2002, 2003 and 2014; Bolivia in 2009; and Ecuador in 2010.

In contrast, social movement backed leftist parties pursued and secured power via the electoral process throughout the continent. In the course of which they played down class struggle and harnessed the movements, trade unions and political activists to their electoral machinery. As a result the advent of the Centre-Left to power was accompanied by the decline of class struggle. The opening of the electoral route eliminated the revolutionary road to class power. The armed struggle movements in Latin America declined or demobilized. Revolutionary mass uprisings have led to changes and popular demobilizations.

The remaining centre of armed popular action is Colombia, where the guerrilla movements (FARC, ELN) are currently in negotiations with the Santos regime over the socio-political and economic reforms that should accompany their incorporation to electoral and mass politics.

Nevertheless, land occupation movements in Honduras, Brazil, Bolivia, Paraguay, Colombia, persist even as their scope and intensity varies between countries and time frames. Today 'land occupations' are tactic to block the expansion of extractive, agro-toxic—export corporations and a vehicle to pressure for land reform, repossession of land and a key element in a strategy for 'food security' based on non-GM crops.

With the exception of the 'institutionalized class struggle', the other three types of class struggle clash with the dominant extractive imperialist development model pursued by both pro-imperial and anti-imperial regimes.

Class Struggle in the Form of Anti-Imperialism and 'Free Trade'

The key to the growth of extractive imperialism has been the abilities of the regimes to contain, fragment, co-opt or repress the class struggle. The reason is because extractive capital concentrates wealth, enriches the multinational corporations, pillages wealth, reproduces a 'colonial style' trade relation and pollutes the environment.

Paradoxically, the most successful extractive regimes, in terms of growth, stability and in containing the class struggle and attracting and retaining extractive capital, are the Centre-Left regimes. 'Anti-imperialism' has been a useful ideological weapon in securing legitimacy even as the regimes hand over vast territories for foreign capitalist exploitation.

Secondly, the incorporation of social movement and trade union leaders and former guerrilla militants to the centre-left regimes creates a political cushion, a layer of savvy, well-connected quasi-functionaries who set the boundaries for class struggle and adjudication of grievances. Moreover, the centre-left use their "anti-imperialist" posture to disqualify class struggle activists as 'agents of foreign powers'. The Centre-Left regimes then feel justified in repressing or jailing class struggle practitioners as part of their mission of defending the 'nation', 'change' or the 'Revolution'.

Pro-imperialist regimes, like Peru, Mexico and Colombia rely to a greater extent on physical repression, less on co-optation or more likely a combination of both. Large-scale grants of land are accompanied by regional or national militarization. For the pro-imperialist right, anti-drug and anti-terrorist campaigns serve to justify their defense of the extractive capitalist model.

The anti-imperialist regimes speak of extractive capital with 'social inclusion'—the transfer of a fraction of extractive revenues to poverty-reduction—not to well-paying jobs in industry or to reducing pollution or increasing spending on health, education and welfare, and certainly not financing any consequential land reform or increase in workers management of natural resource exploitation.

In sharp contrast to the past, contemporary anti-imperialism is also profoundly hostile to the politics of class struggle. The key to the success of their extractive model is class collaboration: between the centre-left progressive regime, the multinational corporations and the leaders of the co-opted class organizations.

Conclusion: Wither the Class Struggle?

With reference to the contemporary dynamics of the class struggle and the anti-imperialist struggle, it is evident that the forces of resistance are directed against the operational agencies of extractive capital and the imperial state, but there are clear signs that the emerging regional struggles can expand beyond the extractive sector. For example, the urban popular struggles over state expenditures, although anchored in a different set of concerns and demands, pursues the same enemy: a state which allocates most resources to infrastructure designed to facilitate extractive revenues over and above the deteriorating socioeconomic conditions of the urban middle and working class. Secondly, the struggles against the extractive sector have secured important victories against Monsanto in Argentina and the mining and oil companies in Peru, Ecuador and Mexico. These are partial and limited gains, but demonstrate that the 'extractive model' is vulnerable and susceptible to challenge by unified mass based community movements.

Moreover, the entire structure of the extractive imperial model is based on vulnerable foundations. The rapid growth and rise in revenues is based in large part on world demand and high commodity prices.

China's growth is slowing. The European Union is in recession. The US has not demonstrated any capacity to return as the 'locomotor' of the world economy. If and when the commodity mega boom collapses, the capacity of the regimes to contain the class struggle by co-opting the urban trade unions and social movement leaders will wither. The current alliance between 'anti-imperialists' and global extractive capital will splinter.

If and when that occurs the real anti-imperialist struggle combating the imperial firms as well as the state will once again converge with the class struggle. In the meantime, the epicenter of class struggle will be found in mass movements, not in guerrilla detachments; in the agro-mineral regions and not in the urban factories; in the struggles over allocations of state budgets and the quality of life and not merely in wages and salaries.

The specific extractive character of imperialism suggests that the previous undifferentiated view of 'imperialism' and 'anti-imperialism' is no longer relevant: the distinctions between progressive and reactionary regimes need to be reconceptualized.

PART 3

The Venezuela Pivot of US Imperialism

CHAPTER 10

The United States and Venezuela: Decades of Defeats and Destabilization

US policy toward Venezuela is a microcosm of its broader strategy in regard to Latin America. The aim of this strategy is to reverse the regional trend towards the construction of an independent foreign policy and to restore US dominance; curtail the diversification of trading and investment partners and re-centre economic relations to the US; replace regional integration pacts with US-centred economic integration schemes; and privatize firms that have been partly or wholly nationalized.

The resort to military coups in Venezuela is a strategy designed to impose a client regime. This is a replay of US strategy during the 1964–1983 period. In those two decades US strategists successfully collaborated with business-military elites to overthrow nationalist and socialist governments, privatize public enterprises and reverse social, labour and welfare policies. The client regimes implemented neoliberal policies and supported US-centred 'integration'. The entire spectrum of representative institutions, political parties, trade unions and civil society organizations were banned and replaced by imperial funded NGOs, state controlled parties and trade unions. With this perspective in mind the US has returned to all out 'regime change' in Venezuela as the first step to a continent-wide transformation to reassert political, economic and social dominance.

Washington's resort to political violence, all out media warfare, economic sabotage and military coups in Venezuela is an attempt to discover the effectiveness of these tactics under favourable conditions, including a deepening economic recession, double digit inflation, declining living standards and weakening political support, as a dress rehearsal for other countries in the region

Washington's earlier resort to a 'regime change' strategy in Venezuela, Bolivia, Argentina and Ecuador failed because objective circumstances were unfavourable. Between 2003 to 2012 the national-populist or centre-left regimes were increasing political support, their economies were growing, incomes and consumption were improving and pro-US regimes and clients had earlier collapsed under the weight of a systemic crises. Moreover, the negative consequences of military coups were fresh in peoples' minds. Today Washington's strategists believe that Venezuela is the easiest and most important target because of its structural vulnerabilities and because Caracas is the linchpin to Latin American integration and welfare populism.

According to Washington's domino theory, Cuba will be more susceptible to pressure if it is cut-off from Venezuela's subsidized oil-for-medical services agreement. Ecuador and Bolivia will be vulnerable. Regional integration will be diluted or replaced by US directed trade agreements. Argentina's drift to the right will be accelerated. The US military presence will be enlarged beyond Colombia, Peru, Paraguay and Central America. Radical anti-imperialist ideology will be replaced by a revised form of 'pan-Americanism', a euphemism for imperial primacy.

The concentrated and prolonged US war against Venezuela and the resort to extremist tactics and groups can only be accounted for by what US strategists perceive as the large-scale (continent-wide) long-term interests at stake.

In this chapter we proceed by discussing and analyzing the US fifteen-year war (2000–2015) against Venezuela, now reaching a climax. We then turn to an examination of the past and current strengths and weaknesses of Venezuela's democratic, anti-imperialist government.

Prolonged Political Warfare: Multiple Forms of Attack in Changing Political Conjunctures

The war waged by the US against Venezuela started shortly after President Chávez's election in 1999. His convoking of a constitutional assembly and referendum and the subsequent inclusion of a strong component of popular participatory and nationalist clauses 'rang bells' in Washington. The presence of a large contingent of former guerrillas, Marxists and Leftists in the Chávez electoral campaign and regime, was the signal for Washington to develop a strategy of regrouping traditional business and political clients to pressure and limit changes.

Subsequent to 9/11 Washington launched its global military offensive, projecting power via the so-called 'war on terror'. Washington's quest to reassert dominance in the Americas included demands that Venezuela fall into line and back Washington's global military offensive. President Chávez refused and set an example of independent politics for the nationalist-populist movements and emerging centre-left regimes in Latin America. President Chávez told President Bush 'you don't fight terror with terror'.

In response, by November 2001 Washington strategists shifted from a policy of pressure to contain change to a strategy of all-out warfare to overthrow the Chávez regime via a business-military coup (April 2002).

The US backed coup was defeated in less than 72 hours and Chávez was restored to power by an alliance of loyalist military forces backed by a spontaneous million person march led by thousands of supports from the popular or working-class neighbourhoods and barrios, the social base of the grassroots revolutionary collectives that would come to make up the most organized element of *chavismo*. Washington lost important 'assets' among the military and business elite, who fled into exile or were jailed.

From December 2002 to February 2003, The White House backed an executive lockout in the strategic oil industry, supported by corrupt trade union officials aligned with Washington and the AFL-CIO. After three months the lockout was defeated through an alliance of loyalist trade unionists, mass organizations and overseas petrol producing countries. The US lost strategic assets in the oil industry as over 15,000 executives, managers and workers were fired and replaced by nationalist loyalists. The oil industry was renationalized—its earnings were put at the service of social welfare.

Having lost assets essential to violent warfare, Washington promoted a strategy of electoral politics—organizing a referendum in 2004, which was won by Chávez and a boycott of the 2005 congressional elections, which failed and led to an overwhelming majority for the pro-Chávez forces.

Having failed to secure regime change via internal violent and electoral warfare, Washington, having suffered a serious loss of internal assets, turned outside by organizing paramilitary death squads and the Colombian military to engage in cross border conflicts in alliance with the far right regime of Alvaro Uribe. Colombia's military incursions led Venezuela to break economic ties, costing influential Colombian agro-business exporters and manufacturers' losses exceeding eight billion dollars. Uribe backed off and signed a non-aggression accord with Chávez, undermining the US 'proxy war' strategy.

Washington revised its tactics, returning to electoral and street fighting tactics. Between 2008 and 2012 Washington channelled millions of dollars to finance electoral party politicians, NGOs, mass media outlets (newspapers, television and radio) and direct action saboteurs of public energy, electricity and power stations.

The US 'internal' political offensive had limited success—a coalition of warring right-wing political groups elected a minority of officials thus regaining an institutional presence. A Chávez-backed overtly socialist referendum was defeated (by less than one percent). NGOs gained influence in the universities and in some popular neighbourhoods exploiting the corruption and ineptness of local Chávez elected officials. But the US strategy failed to dislodge or weaken the Chávez led regime for several reasons. Venezuela's economy was riding the prolonged commodity boom. Oil prices were soaring above US$100 a barrel, financing free health, education, housing, fuel and food subsidy programs, undercutting the so-called 'grassroots' agitation of US-funded NGOs.

Government subsidies of imports and lax regulation of dollar reserves secured support even among the capitalists and loosened their support for the violent opposition. Sectors of the middle class voted for Chávez as a ticket to the consumer society. Secondly, President Chávez's charismatic appeal, promotion and support of popular neighbourhood groups counter-acted the ill effects of corrupt and inept local 'Chavista' officials who otherwise played into the hands of US-backed opposition. Thirdly, US intervention in Venezuela alienated not only the centre-left, but the entire political spectrum in Latin America, isolating Washington. This was especially evident by the universal condemnation of the US-backed military coup in Honduras in 2009. Fourthly, the US could not counter Venezuela's subsidized oil sales to Caribbean and Central American regimes. Petrocaribe strengthened Venezuela and weakened US dominance in Washington's 'backyard'.

The entire electoral strategy of the US depended on fomenting an economic crises—and given the favourable world prices for oil on the world market, it failed. As a result Washington depended on non-market strategies to disrupt the socioeconomic links between mass consumers and the Chávez government.

Washington encouraged sabotage of the power and electrical grid. It encouraged hoarding and price gouging by commercial capitalists (supermarket owners). It encouraged smugglers to purchase thousands of tons of subsidized consumer goods and sell them across the border in Colombia. In other words, the US combined its electoral strategy with violent sabotage and illegal economic disruption.

This strategy was intensified with the onset of the economic crises following the financial crash of 2009, the decline of commodity prices and the death of President Hugo Chávez. The US and its mass media megaphones went all-out to defend the protagonists and practitioners of illegal violent actions—branding arrested saboteurs, assassins, street fighters, and assailants of public institutions as 'political prisoners'. Washington and its media branded the government, as 'authoritarian' for protecting the constitution. It accused the independent judiciary as biased. The police and military were labelled as 'repressive' for arresting fire bombers of schools, transport and clinics. No violent crime or criminal behaviour by opposition politicos was exempt from Washington's scrofulous screeds about defending 'human rights'.

The crisis and collapse of oil prices greatly enhanced the opportunities for the US and its Venezuelan collaborator's campaign to weaken the government. Venezuela's dependence on President Chávez, as the singular transformative figure, suffered a serious blow with his death. Personalistic leadership weakened organic mass organization.

The US relaunched a multi-pronged offensive to undermine and overthrow the newly elected Nicolas Maduro regime. Washington, at first, promoted the *via electoral* as the route to regime change, funding opposition leader Henrique Capriles.

After Capriles' electoral defeat, Washington resorted to an intense post-electoral propaganda campaign to de-legitimize the voting outcome. It promoted street violence and sabotage of the electrical grid. For over a year the Obama regime refused to recognize the electoral outcome, accepted and recognized throughout Latin America and the world. In the subsequent congressional, gubernatorial and municipal elections the US backed candidates suffered resounding defeats. President Nicolas Maduro's United Socialist Party of Venezuela won three quarters of the governorships and retained a solid two-thirds majority in Congress.

Beginning in 2013 the US escalated its 'extra-parliamentary' offensive— massive hoarding of consumer goods by wholesale distributors and retail supermarkets led to acute shortages, long lines, long waits and empty shelves.

Hoarding, black market speculation of the currency, wholesale smuggling of shipments of consumer goods across the border to Colombia (facilitated by opposition officials governing in border-states and corrupt National Guard commanders) exacerbated shortages.

US strategists sought to drive a political wedge between the consumer driven middle and lower classes and the Maduro government. Over time they succeeded in fomenting discontent among the lower middle class and directing it against the government and not at the big business elite and US financed opposition politicians, NGOs and parties.

In February 2014 emboldened by growing discontent the US moved rapidly toward a decisive confrontation. Washington backed the most violent extra parliamentary opposition. Led by Leopoldo López, an ultra-rightist who openly called for a coup and launched a nationwide assault on public buildings, authorities and pro-democracy activists. As a result 43 people were killed and 870 injured—mostly government supporters and military and police officials—and hundreds of millions of dollars of damage was inflicted on schools, hospitals and state supermarkets.

After two months, the uprising was finally put down and the street barricades were dismantled—as even right-wing business operators suffered losses as their revenues diminished and there was no chance for victory.

Washington proclaimed the jailed terrorists leaders as 'political prisoners', a line parroted by al the mass media and the bogus Human Rights Watch. The Obama regime sought to secure the release of its armed thugs to prepare for the next round of violent confrontation.

Washington accelerated the pace of planning, organizing and executing the next coup throughout 2014. Taking advantage of the Maduro regime's lax or non-existent enforcement of laws forbidding 'foreign funding of political organizations', the US via NED and its 'front groups' poured tens of millions, into NGOs, political parties, leaders and active and retired military officials willing and able to pursue 'regime change' by means of a coup d'état.

Exactly one year following the violent uprising of 2014, on February 14, 2015, the US backed a civilian-military coup. The coup was thwarted by military intelligence and denunciations by lower level loyalist soldiers.

Two power grabs in a year is a clear indication that Washington is accelerating its move to establish a client regime. But what makes these policies especially dangerous, is not simply their proximity, but the context in which they occur and the recruits who Washington is targeting. Unlike the coup of 2002, which occurred at a time of an improving economy, the most recent failed coup (see Chapter 12 for a analysis of its political dynamics) took place in the context of declining economic indicators—declining incomes, a devaluation which further reduced purchasing power, rising inflation (62 percent), and plummeting oil prices.

Moreover, the US has once again gained converts in the military, as was the case in the 2002 coup but not in 2014. Three generals, three colonels, nine lieutenants and a captain signed on to the coup and it can be surmised that they were in contact with others. The deteriorating loyalties in the military are not simply a product of US bribery. It is also a reflection of the socioeconomic decline of sectors of the middle class to which middle level officers belong by family ties and social identification.

Subsequent to the earlier coup (that of 2002) then President Chávez called for the formation of popular militias, National Reserve and a rural defense force to 'complement' the armed forces. Some 300,000 militia volunteers were registered. But as in the case of many radical ideas little came of it.

As the US moves to activate its 'military option', Venezuela must consider activating and linking these militias to mass popular community based organizations, trade unions and peasant movements. The US has developed a strategic concept for seizing power by proxy. A war of attrition built upon exploiting the social consequences of the fall of oil revenues, shortages of basic commodities and the growing fissures in the military and state institutions.

In 2015 Washington has embraced the 2002 strategy of combining multiple forms of attack including economic destabilization, electoral politics, sabotage and military penetration. All are directed toward a military-civilian coalition seizing power.

Facing the US Offensive: Strengths and Weaknesses of the Maduro Government

The basic strength of the Chavista government of President Maduro is the legacy of nearly 15 years of progressive legislation, including rising incomes, grass roots community based democracy, the affirmation of racial, class and national dignity and independence. Despite the real hardships of the past three years, forty percent of the electorate, mostly the urban and rural poor, remains as a solid core of support of the democratic process, the President and his efforts to reverse the decline and return the country to prosperity.

Up to now the Maduro government has successfully rebuffed and defeated the offensive by US proxies. President Maduro won electorally, and more recently has pacified the coup-makers by adopting firmer security measures and more technically efficient intelligence. Equally important he has demanded that the US reduce its embassy operatives from 100 to 17, equal to Venezuela's staff in Washington. Many embassy personnel were engaged in meetings with Venezuelan organizers of violent activity and in efforts to subvert military officials.

Yet these security measures and administrative improvements, as important and necessary as they are, reflect short-range solutions. The deeper and more fundamental issues relate to the structural weakness of the Venezuelan economy and state.

First and foremost, Venezuela cannot continue running on a petrol based 'rentier economy' especially one that still depends on the US market. Venezuela's 'consumer socialism' totally depends on oil revenues and high oil prices to finance the importation of foodstuffs and other essential commodities. A strategy of 'national defense' against the imperial offensive requires a far higher level of 'self-sufficiency', a greater degree of local production and decentralized control.

Secondly, next to US intervention and destabilization, the greatest threat to the democratic regime is the government's executive, managerial and elected officials who have misallocated billions in investment funds, failed to effectively carry out programs and who largely improvise according to day to day considerations. In this context it is essential that Maduro advance the strategic priorities ensuring basic popular interests.

The Chávez and the Maduro governments outlined general guidelines that were passed off as a strategic plan. But neither financial resources, nor state personnel were systematically ordered to implement them. Instead the government responded or better still reacted, defensively, to the immediate threats of the opposition induced shortages and oil revenue shortfalls. They chose the easy route of securing loans from China by mortgaging future oil exports. They also took out commercial loans—borrowed at the highest rates in the world (18 percent)!

The post commodity boom requires a decisive break with the petrol economy...continuing costly debt financing staves off the day of reckoning, which is fast approaching.

US military coups and political warfare are with us and will not fade away even as Washington loses battles. The jailing of individual plotters is not enough. They are expendable...Washington can buy others.

The Maduro government faces a national emergency which requires a society-wide mobilization to launch a war-economy capable of producing and delivering class specific commodities to meet popular needs.

The February 12, 2015 coup, dubbed Plan Jericho was funded by the US NGO the National Endowment for Democracy and its subsidiaries, the International Republican Institute and the National Democratic Institute and Freedom House. The coup organizers led by former Venezuelan Congresswomen Corina Machado, (a White House invitee) was designated to head up the post-coup dictatorship.

As a matter of survival the Maduro government must clamp down and prosecute all self-styled 'NGO' which are recipients of overseas funding and serve as conduits for US-backed coups and destabilization activity.

No doubt the Obama regime will seek to protect its proxy financing and howl about 'growing authoritarianism'. That is predictable. But the Venezuelan governments' duty is to protect the constitutional order, and defend the security of its citizens. It must move decisively to prosecute not only the recipients of US funds but the entire US political network, organizations and collaborators as terrorists.

Venezuela can take a page out of the US legal code that provides for five-year prison sentences for 'nationals' who receive overseas funds and fail to register as foreign agents. More to the point, the Obama regime has prosecuted organized groups suspected of conspiring to commit violent acts to lifetime prison sentences. It has justified extra judicial assassinations (via drones) of US 'terrorist suspects'.

President Maduro need not go to the extremes of the Obama regime. But he should recognize that the policy of 'denunciation, arrest and release' is totally out of line with international norms regarding the fight against terrorism in Venezuela.

What the US has in mind is not merely a 'palace coup' in which the democratic incumbents are ousted and replaced by US clients. Washington wants to go far beyond a change in personnel, beyond a friendly regime amenable to providing unconditional backing to the US foreign policy agenda.

A coup and post-coup regime would only be the first step toward a systematic and comprehensive reversal of the socioeconomic and political transformations of the past 16 years! Heading the list of steps to be taken will be the crushing of the mass popular community organizations that will oppose the coup. This will be accompanied by a mass purge, of all representative institutions, the constitutionalist armed forces, police and nationalist officials in charge of the oil industry and other public enterprises. All the major public welfare programs in education, health, housing and low cost retail food outlets, will be dismantled or suffer major budget cuts. The oil industry and dozens of other publically owned enterprises and banks will be privatized and denationalized. And US-based MNCs will be the main beneficiaries. The agrarian land reform will be reversed: recipients will be evicted and the land returned to the landed oligarchs.

Given how many of the Venezuelan working class and rural poor will be adversely affected and given the combative spirit which permeates popular culture, the implementation of the US backed neoliberal agenda will require prolonged large-scale repression. This means, tens of thousands of killings, arrests and incarceration.

The US coup-masters and their Venezuelan proxies will unleash all their pent-up hostility against what they will deem the blood purge necessary to punish, in Henry Kissinger's infamous phrase, 'an irresponsible people' who dare to affirm their dignity and independence.

The US backing of violence in the run-up to the February 2015 coup undoubtedly will be escalated in the run-up to the inevitable next coup. Contemporary US imperial wars in Iraq, Afghanistan, Syria and Libya and past US backed bloody military coups installing neoliberal regimes in Brazil, Chile, Argentina, Bolivia and Uruguay a few decades past, demonstrate that Washington places no limits on how many tens of thousands of lives are destroyed, how many millions are uprooted, if it is 'necessary' to secure imperial dominance.

There is no doubt that the Venezuelan economy is on shaky foundations; that officials have yet to devise and implement a coherent strategy to exit the crises. But it is of decisive importance to remember that even in these times of intensifying imperial warfare, basic freedoms and social justice inform the framework of government and popular representation. Now is the time, and time is running short, for the Maduro government to mobilize all the mass organizations, popular militias and loyal military officials to administer a decisive political defeat to the US proxies and then to proceed forward to socializing the economy. It must take the opportunity of turning the US orchestrated offensives into a historic defeat. It must convert the drive to restore neoliberal privilege into the graveyard of rentier capitalism.

Summary and Epilogue: A Review of the Dynamics of
the US-Venezuela Relation

Unlike past political confrontations between US imperial regimes and left-wing Latin American governments, in the case of Venezuela the US has suffered numerous major defeats with regard to domestic and foreign policy, over the past 15 years.

In 2001 the US demanded Venezuela support its 'war on terrorism', its global quest for domination via war. President Chávez refused to back it, arguing successfully that *you cannot fight terror with terror*, and winning support worldwide.

In April 12, 2002, the US organized and backed a military-business coup that was defeated by a mass uprising backed by constitutionalist armed forces. The US lost key assets in the military, trade union bureaucracy and business sector.

In the period from December 2002 to February 2003 the US backed a CEO—directed lockout designed to shutdown the oil industry and overthrow the Chávez government that was defeated, as workers and engineers took charge and overseas oil partners supplied petroleum. The US lost assets in the oil industry.

In 2004, a referendum to oust Chávez, funded by the US and organized by NED-funded NGOs was defeated. US electoral assets were demoralized.

In 2006 a US backed boycott of Congressional elections was defeated. The electorate turned out in force. US congressional assets lost their institutional power base and influence. Chávez is re-elected for a second time. The US-backed candidate is badly beaten.

In 2007 a US-backed coalition managed to squeak out a one percent margin of victory in defeating constitutional amendments designed to socialize the economy.

In 2009 President Chávez wins a referendum on constitutional amendments including the abolition of term limits.

In 2012 Chávez wins re-election for the fourth time defeating a US-financed opposition candidate.

In 2013 Chávez's selected candidate Maduro wins the Presidency defeating Obama's anointed candidate. Pro-Chávez parties win resounding congressional majorities in all elections between 1999 and 2010.

Repeated electoral defeats convinced Washington's political strategists to rely on violent, unconstitutional roads to power.

The anti-capitalist domestic social reforms and ideology were one of two key motivating factors in Washington's prolonged political war against Venezuela. Equally important was Chávez and Maduro's foreign policy which included

Venezuela's leading role in opposing US centred regional integration organizations like ALCA, regional political organizations like the OAS and its military missions.

Venezuela promoted Latin American centred integration organizations that excluded the US. They included Petro-Caribe, a Venezuela-sponsored trade and investment organization that benefited Caribbean and Central America countries, and UNASUR (Union of South American Nations), a regional political organization that displaced the US-dominated OAS and included 33 Latin American and Caribbean states.

Venezuela joined MERCOSUR, a 'free trade' organization, which included Brazil, Argentina, Uruguay and Paraguay.

Venezuela's leading role in promoting five organizations promoting Latin American and Caribbean integration—excluding the US and Canada—was seen as a mortal threat to Washington's political dominance of Latin American politics and markets.

Venezuela's political and economic ties with Cuba undermined the US economic blockade and reinforced Cuba's links with and support by the rest of Latin America.

Venezuela opposed the US-backed coup against Haiti's reformist President Jean-Bertrand Aristide.

Its opposition to the US invasions of Afghanistan, Iraq, Syria and (later) Libya and its increased investment and trade ties with Iran in opposition to US sanctions, set US plans of a global empire on a collision course with Venezuela's embrace of a global anti-imperialist policy.

US failure to secure passage of a US centred Latin American Free Trade Treaty and incapacity to secure across the board support in Latin America for its Middle East wars and Iran sanctions was largely the result of Venezuelan foreign policy.

It would not be an exaggeration to say that Venezuela's foreign policy successes in countering US imperialist policies, especially with regard to Latin American integration, are the main reason that Washington has persisted in its effort to overthrow the Venezuelan government.

The US escalation of its global military interventions under Obama and its increasing belligerency toward the multiplication of independent Latin American regional organizations, coincides with the intensification of its violent destabilization campaign in Venezuela.

Faced with the growth of Latin American trade and investment ties with China—with $250 billion in the pipeline over the next ten years—pioneered by Venezuela, Washington fears the loss of the 600 million Latin American consumer market.

The current US political offensive against Venezuela is a reaction to over 15 years of political defeats including failed coups, resounding electoral defeats, the loss of strategic political assets and above all decisive setbacks in its attempts to impose US centred integration schemes.

More than ever, US imperial strategists today are going all-out to subvert Venezuela's anti-imperialist government, because they sense with the decline of oil revenue and export earnings, double-digit inflation and consumer shortages, they can divide and subvert sectors of the armed forces, mobilize violent street mobs via their mercenary street fighters, secure the backing of elected opposition officials and seize power. What is at stake in the US—Venezuelan conflict is the future of Latin American independence and the US Empire.

The Chávez Factor in US Imperialism

During his lifetime Venezuela's President Hugo Chávez was the world's leading secular, democratically elected political leader who consistently and publicly opposed imperialist wars in the Middle East, attacked extraterritorial intervention and US and EU complicity in kidnapping and torture in diverse theatres of the global class war. Venezuela at the time played the major role in sharply reducing the price of oil for the poorest countries in the Caribbean region and Central America, thus substantially aiding them in their balance of payments, without attaching any 'strings' to this vital assistance. Chávez was on the cutting edge of efforts toward greater Latin American integration—despite opposition from the US and several regional regimes, who have opted for bilateral free trade agreements with the US. Of even greater significance, Chávez was the only elected president to reverse a US-backed military coup (in 48 hours) and defeat a (US-backed) bosses' lockout, and return the economy to double-digit growth over the subsequent four years (Weisbrot, Mark & Sandoval, 2008). He was the only elected leader in the history of Latin America to successfully win eleven straight electoral contests against US-financed political parties and almost the entire private mass media over a nine-year period. Finally, Chávez was the only leader in the last half-century who came within a whisker of having a popular referendum for a 'socialist transformation' approved, a particularly surprising result in a country in which fewer than 30 percent of the workforce is made up of peasants and factory workers.

Although the gains made under Chávez's presidency have been seriously eroded in recent years with Maduro as President, Chávez significantly reduced long-term deeply entrenched poverty faster than any regime in the region,[1] demonstrating that a nationalist-welfare regime can be more effective in ending endemic social ills than its neoliberal counterparts. However, this achievement was equalled by other centre-left or popular nationalist regimes formed in the new millennium under conditions of widespread rejection of neoliberalism as an economic model, the resurgence of 'inclusionary state activism'

---

1 Venezuela's poverty rate was cut in half from 2003, at the height of the bosses' lockout, to 2007—from 54 to 27 percent. And extreme poverty was reduced from 43 percent in 1996 to nine percent in 2007, while unemployment was cut from 17 percent in 1998 to seven percent in 2007 (Weisbrot, Mark & Sandoval, 2008). The economy has created jobs at a rate nearly three times that of the US during its most recent economic expansion.

under the aegis of a post-Washington Consensus on the need for a more inclusive form of national development, and a (re)turn towards extractivism as a development strategy (see Part 1 above).

Under Chávez's presidency accessible healthcare for the poor was dramatically expanded, with the number of primary care physicians in the public sector increasing from 1,628 in 1998 to 19,571 by early 2007. About 40 percent of the population had access to subsidized food, while access to education, especially higher education, was greatly expanded for poor families. Real (i.e. inflation adjusted) social spending per person over this period increased by over 300 percent (Weisbrot & Sandoval, 2008).

Chávez's policies refuted the notion that the competitive demands of 'globalization' (deep and extensive insertion in the world market) are incompatible with social welfare policies. His government demonstrated that links to the world market are compatible with the construction of a more developed welfare state under a popular and democratically elected government that nationalized enterprises in key sectors of the economy and put it on the path towards the 'socialism of the 20th century'. However, the considerable accomplishments of the Chávez government were overlooked by liberal and social democratic academics in Venezuela and their colleagues in the US and Europe, who preferred to focus on and emphasize the institutional and policy weaknesses, failing to take into account the world-historic significance of the changes taking place in the context of a hostile, aggressively militarist-driven empire—changes that have been partly undermined by subsequent actions taken against Venezuela under the Maduro government.

Advances and Limitations of Economic Policy in Venezuela

Venezuela has made tremendous advances in the economy since the failed coup of April 11, 2002 and the employers' lockout of December 2002–February 2003, which led to a 24 percent decline in the GDP (Weisbrot, 2008: 10). Under Chávez' leadership and with favourable terms of trade, Venezuela's economy grew by over ten percent during Chávez's last five last years, decreasing poverty levels from over 50 to under 28 percent, surpassing any country in the world in terms of the rate of poverty-reduction. In contrast to the past, the economy accumulated over $35 billion dollars in foreign exchange reserves despite a vast increase in social spending and totally freed itself of dependence on the onerous terms imposed by the self-styled 'international banks' (IMF, World Bank and Inter-American Development Bank) by paying off its debt (Weisbrot, 2008: 10).

The government nationalized strategic enterprises in the oil and gas industries, steel, cement, food production and distribution, telecommunications and electricity industries. It passed new excess profits taxes, doubling its revenues. It signed new petroleum and gas joint ventures with over a dozen European, Asian and Latin American multinationals giving the Venezuelan state majority control. It expropriated several million acres of uncultivated farmland from speculators and absentee owners and an additional 32 under-producing plantations.[2] The importance of these structural changes cannot be understated. In the first place they increased the capacity of the government to make or influence strategic decisions regarding investment, pricing and marketing. The increase in state ownership increased the flow of revenues and profits into the federal treasury, enhancing financing of productive investments, social programs and downstream processing plants and services. And the government began to slowly diversify its petroleum markets from a hostile adversary (the US) to trade and investment with countries like China, Brazil, Iran and Russia, thus reducing Venezuela's vulnerability to arbitrary economic boycotts.

The government started a project to diversify the economy and become food self-sufficient in staples like milk, meat, vegetables and poultry.[3] Equally important, investments were made in processing raw petroleum into value-added products like fertilizers and plastics. New refineries were scheduled to substitute dependence on US based operations and to add value to their exports. Over 2.5 billion Strong Bolivars, the new Venezuelan currency (over US $1 billion dollars) were allocated in the form of incentives, credit and subsidies to promote the increase in agricultural production and processing (*Vea*, February 25, 2008: p. 2). Investments in new lines of production linked to social programs, including new enterprises manufacturing 15,000 prefabricated houses per year, were introduced.[4]

But Venezuela was much concerned with, if not deeply affected by, inflation, especially in regard to imported food. Inflation escalated over the last three years of Chávez's presidency, rising from 14 percent in 2005 to 22 percent in 2007, threatening to undermine the gains in living standards made over the previous five years (Weisbrot, 2008). In any case, attempts by government officials to control inflation and impose price controls had a very limited effect as investors pulled out their capital or reduced their investments, big food producers cut back on production, food distributors decreased shipments and

---

2 Interview with peasant leaders of the Frente Nacional Campesino Ezquiel Zamora in Caracas, February 27, 2008. *Boston Globe,* April 11, 2008.

3 Interview with President Chávez, Caracas, March 2, 2008.

4 Interview with President Chávez, March 2, 2008.

hoarded essential goods that retail sellers traded on the black market—all according to an orchestrated plan to destabilize the economy and bring down the government (see Chapter 10).

Inflation and the resultant negative impact was one of the principal reasons for popular abstention during the December 2007 referendum and the cause of popular discontent today in Venezuela.[5] And of course both the far right and the ultra-left (especially in some neighbourhoods and trade unions) have been exploiting this discontent.

Inflation is one of the principal reasons for the decline of the popularity of various regimes on the Left, Centre and Right throughout history in Europe, as well as in Latin America. In large part this is because the great majority of workers in Venezuela as in Mexico and other countries in the region are 'self-employed', working 'on their own account' on the streets, and have no organization or indexed wages or income to keep up with the rise in prices. In Venezuela, even the major industries, like petroleum, steel and aluminum, have 'sub-contracted' most of their workers who lack any power to negotiate for wage increases tied to inflation. In this mixed economy, government subsidies and promotional incentives to industrial and agricultural capitalists to promote productivity have led to increased profits without commensurate increases in wage income.

During the period from February to April 2008, the state intervened directly in the productive process through the takeover of unproductive companies and farms. New worker and peasant demands include 'opening the books' of the profitable firms and farms in pursuit of wage and collective bargaining negotiations, re-opening closed firms and investments in new public enterprises. Chávez's advisors recognized that the problem of production (supply) would continue to lead to too many Bolivars chasing too few consumer goods—inflation, discontent and political vulnerability—unless the nationalization process was accelerated and public ownership extended, hence the actions taken in 2008 to nationalize economic enterprises in the steel and cement industries.

---

5   Few issues are as critical to the poor and as ignored by the political Left as inflation. It was the issue that in 1994 catapulted Cardoso to state power in Brazil and eroded the significant electoral advantage held by Lula over Cardoso in the months leading up to the election. It would take Lula two more runs at the presidency before he and his advisors wised up to the importance of inflation, recognizing that it is not just a right-wing issue but very much a working class (and also middle class) issue. On the *political* significance of inflation in the current context of export primarization and runaway inflation in the price of gasoline, cooking fuel and foodstuffs see Petras (2008).

But in advancing the Bolivarian road to socialism the regime had to deal with its own incompetent and reactionary officials. For example, prior to the nation-alization of the major steel multinational SIDOR, the Minister of Labour, an incompetent and inexperienced functionary with no prior relation to labour, sided with the company and approved the repressive measures of the Governor of the state of Bolivar in calling out the National Guard to break the strike. Throughout 2007–2008, the management of SIDOR refused to negotiate in good faith with the unions, which provoked strikes in January, February and March 2008. The intransigence of the steel bosses increased the militancy of the workers and led to Chávez's intervention. In defense of his order to nation-alize, Chávez cited the positive role of the steel workers in opposing the coup, the 'slave-like' work conditions and the export strategies, which denied the domestic construction industry the steel it needed for high-priority homebuild-ing. He called on the nationalized industry to be run by 'workers councils' in an efficient and productive manner—advancing a strictly socialist form of orga-nizing production (*Reuters News Service,* April 9, 2008; BBC *News,* April 2, 2008).

Government repression of strikes provoked regional union solidarity and worker-led marches against the National Guard and calls for the resignation of the ineffective Labour Minister. After Chávez nationalized steel, trade unions from major industrial sectors met to coordinate support for the President and press for further moves in the direction of public ownership and socialism. As for the National Guard, it is part of the state apparatus but it is by no means clear whether its power can be called upon or exercised by the government itself. The brutality and excess use of force ordered by the General in charge of the National Guard was indicative of a profoundly anti-working class, pro-big business bias of the Guard officers, a dangerous threat to the Chávez-Maduro government.[6]

However, by confronting the problem of inflation and the overvalued, strong Venezuelan Bolivar Chávez is dealing with an issue that is real and deeply felt by most workers—showing that he has learned the hard lessons of the Left in the 1980s, that viewed inflation as a right-wing issue. Failure by the government to deal with the structural roots of inflation makes it vulnerable to demagogic appeals by the Right and the sectarian ultra-left and its principal beneficiary: US imperialism.

By the beginning of 2008, public spending, which is not always efficiently invested or entirely free of corruption, reduced unemployment 8.5 percent, the lowest in decades. However, a government goal of 5.5 percent seems overly

---

6   "La grave represión de los trabajadores siderúgicos," *Argenpress,* March 24, 2008.

optimistic, especially in light of the fallout from the US recession and decline in European demand.

The big challenge to Chávez' economic policy in 2008, a year of important state and local elections in November, was to ensure that the inevitable mid-year increase in public spending was directed toward productive investments and not to populist short-term programs, which could ignite another wave of inflation. As expected as the elections approached the capitalist class once again resorted to 'planned shortages', distribution blockages, as well as other politically induced economic problems in order to blame and discredit the government. Thus, unless the government reduces its reliance on the private sector for investments, employment, production, finance and distribution, it will be forced into taking costly and improvised measures to avoid electoral losses and popular abstention. The indivisible ties between private business control over strategic economic decisions and its paramount interest in pursuing political measures designed to undermine the Chávez government, meant that the government remained under constant threat unless it managed to take control of the commanding heights of the economy. And indeed in recognition of those structural factors Chávez announced plans to nationalize strategic sectors. The government in this sense appeared to have become somewhat pro-active, anticipating shocks from the economic elite and displacing them from power. Unfortunately the government continued to depend on the private sector, forcing it to continue to be 'reactive', improvising responses to economic attacks during and after the fact and suffering the negative political consequences.

Politics: The Chavistas Strike Back

During the latter half of 2007, in the run-up to the referendum, and early 2008, the right-wing offensive (aided by the ultra-left) took hold and put the government on the defensive. Early March 2008, the pro-Chávez forces regrouped and launched a new political party—The Venezuelan United Socialist Party (PSUV) at a national convention in Maracaibo. In response to the defeat of the referendum, President Chávez called on his supporters to engage in a '3-R Campaign': Review, Rectify and Re-launch. This initiative led to the election of new party leaders, a decline in old guard paternalistic bosses in the leadership of the PSUV, a rejection of sectarianism toward other pro-Chávez parties and a revitalization of grassroots activism.[7] The party was intended to oversee the

---

7 "Partido Socialista Unido de Venezuela: Herramiento de Masas in Gestión," *Rebelión,* March 25, 2008.

mobilization of the Chávez supporters and to educate and organize potential working and lower middle class constituents. The party was mandated to evaluate, criticize and correct the implementation of policies by local officials and engage the mass social movements in common struggle. Unfortunately the party failed to organize local popular power to counteract corrupt Chávez-affiliated as well as opposition policymakers, press local demands and initiatives, counter right-wing infiltration of neighbourhoods by Colombian and local terrorists and turn out the vote at election time.

For the PSUV to succeed as a political organization it needed to take power away from the local clientelistic political machines built around some of the state, regional and municipal level Chavista officials. It needed to overcome the tendency to appoint leaders and candidates from above and to deepen rank and file control over decisions and leaders.[8] Even during the founding congress of the PSUV several delegations criticized the process of electing the national leadership—for neglecting popular representation and overloading it with much criticized political officials.[9]

Active communal councils under democratic control have been effective in giving voice and representation to a large number of urban and poor neighbourhoods. They have secured popular loyalty and support wherever they have delivered needed services and led struggles against incompetent or recalcitrant Chavista officials.

Violence, crime and personal insecurity are major issues for most poor and lower middle class supporters of the Chávez regime and the police are viewed as ineffective reducing crime and securing their neighbourhoods and as, at times, complicit with the gangsters.[20] Proposals by the government for greater cooperation between neighbourhood committees and the police in identifying criminals have had little effect. This is in part because police have shown little interest in developing on-the-ground, day-by-day relations in the poorer barrios, which they tend to view as 'criminal breeding grounds'.

Armed gangs controlling the poor neighbourhoods commit most of the crime. Local residents fear retaliation if they cooperate or worse, they think that the police are complicit with the criminals. Even more seriously reports from reliable intelligence sources have identified large-scale infiltration of Colombian death squad narcotraffickers who combine drugs peddling and right-wing organizing, posing a double threat to local and national security. While the government has taken notice of the general problem of individual insecurity and the specific problem of narcopolitical infiltration, no national

---

8 Ibid.
9 Interview in Caracas with PSUV delegates, March 1, 2008.

plan of action has yet been put into practice, apart from periodic routine round-ups of low-level common criminals.[10]

Venezuela could learn from the example of Cuba, which has had successful crime fighting and anti-terrorist programs for decades organized around a tight network of local 'committees to defend the revolution' and backed by a politically trained rapid action internal security force and an efficient judiciary. Individual security and political freedom depends on the collective knowledge of crime groups' infiltration and the courage of local committees and individuals. Their cooperation requires trust in the integrity, respect and political loyalty of the internal security forces. Their intelligence, evidence collection and testimony depend on the protection of local citizens by the internal security forces against gangster retaliation.

A new type of 'police official' needs to be created who does not view the neighbourhood and its committees as hostile territory; they must live and identify with the people they are paid to protect. To be effective at the local level, the Chávez government must display exemplary behaviour at the national level: It must prosecute and jail criminals and not grant amnesty or give light sentences to coup-makers and economic saboteurs, as Chávez did in early 2008. The failure of the current Attorney General to pursue the murderers of her predecessor, Attorney General Danilo Anderson, was not only a shameful act, it set an example of incompetent and feeble law enforcement which does not create confidence in the will of the state to fight political assassins.[11]

'Popular power' will only become meaningful to the masses when they feel secure enough to walk their streets without assaults and intimidation, when the gangs no longer break into homes and local stores, and when armed narcotraffickers no longer flaunt the law. In Venezuela, the struggle against the oligarchs, George Bush and Colombia's Uribe begins with a community-based war against local criminals, including a comprehensive tactical and strategic sweep of known criminal gangs followed by exemplary punishment for those convicted of terrorizing the residents. This is one way to make the government respected at the grassroots level and to reassert and make operative the term popular sovereignty. In every barrio it was not only the right-wing US-funded NGOs that challenge Chávez's authority, but the armed criminal elements, increasingly linked with reactionary political groups. To successfully

---

10   Interview with Minister of the Interior Ramon Rodriguez Chacun, *La Jornada*, March 31, 2008.

11   Interview with Communal Councils, February 29, 2008. According to a poll by the respected polling group, Barometro, in early April 2008, 66.5% of Venezuelans approved Chávez presidency.

confront the external threats, it was incumbent on the government to defeat the gangsters and narcotraffickers that represent a real obstacle to mass mobilization in time of a national emergency such as a new coup attempt, which, as it turned out, was made in February 2015 when economic conditions had deteriorated to the point of creating what the US and the Right-wing opposition deemed to be opportune for a successful assault on the regime.

Failures by some middle level Chávez officials to ensure security and resolve local problems eroded popular support for political incumbents. The majority of local residents, popular leaders and activists still voiced support for President Chávez and later, to a lesser extent, President Maduro even as they were critical of the people around them—'his advisers' and 'the opportunists'.[12] Under the circumstances, without fundamental changes in candidates and policies it was inevitable that the opposition would and did increase their representation in state and municipal governments.

Social and Cultural Advances and Contradictions

Under the leadership of President Chávez, Venezuela made unprecedented social and cultural changes benefiting the broad majority of the urban and rural poor, and working and lower middle classes. Nine new Bolivarian universities and dozens of technical schools were established with over 200,000 students.[13] Over 2.5 million books, pamphlets and journals were published by the new state-financed publishing houses, including novels, technical books, poetry, history, social research, natural sciences, medical and scientific texts.[14] Two major television studios and communitarian-based TV stations provided international, national and local news coverage that challenges opposition and US-based (CNN) anti-government propaganda. A major news daily, *Vea*, and several monthly and weekly magazines debated and promoted pro-Chávez policies.[15]

Several government-funded 'social missions', composed of tens of thousands of young volunteers, reduced urban and (to a lesser degree) rural illiteracy, extended health coverage, while increasing local participation and organization

---

12 Commentaries from Communal Council delegates and peasant activists in Caracas, 'Popular Power Meeting' at the Ministry of Culture and Popular Power. February 29, 2008.

13 Interview with Carmen Boqueron, Ministry of Culture, February 25, 2008.

14 Interview with Miguel Marquez, President, Editorial El Perro y la Rana, State Publishing House, March 5, 2008.

15 See *La Plena Voz, Memórias, Política Exterior y Soberania*, among other magazines.

in the urban 'ranchos' or shantytowns.[16] Major cultural events, including musi-
cal, theatre and dance groups regularly performed in working class neighbourhoods. The Ministry of Culture and Popular Power initiated a vast number of
overseas and local programs involving the Caribbean and Latin American countries.[17] Sports programs, with the aid of Cuban trainers, received large-scale government funding for physical infrastructure (gymnasiums, playing fields,
uniforms and professional trainers) and have vastly increased the number of
athletes among the urban poor. Major funding to defend and promote indigenous and Afro-Venezuelan culture has been in the works and some movement
to 'affirmative action' was envisioned, though cultural representation in fields
other than sports, music and dance is still quite limited. There is no question
that Venezuela has undergone a 'Cultural Revolution'—reconstructing and
recovering its popular, historical and nationalist roots buried in the frivolous
and imitative artefacts of a century of culturally colonized oligarchs and their
middle class followers.

The emergence of the autonomous pro-Chávez communal councils, linked
to the Ministry of Culture and Popular Power, was probably the most effective
counter-hegemonic movement instigated by the government under Chávez's
leadership. It is also the cell of a new potential popular decentralized socialist
state based on workers control over the workplace and community control
over local development.[18] The political and social activities of party activists
and leaders of the PSUV partially succeed in creating a new class consciousness in so far as they involved the masses in solving their own practical problems and assumed local responsibility for their actions. Chavista cadres, with a
paternalistic mind-and action-set, create patron-client consciousness vulnerable to quick switches to oligarchic-client relations. The key contradiction in
the cultural reformation is in the 'middle class' Chavista configuration that

---

16   These 'misiones sociales', a key feature of the Bolivarian Revolution, have been estab-
      lished in diverse areas: in the launching of a major literacy campaign (Misión Robinson),
      launched on July 1, 2003, on the basis of Cuba's 'Yo, Sí Puedo' system and extensive direct
      support from Cuba in the form of teachers; health (Misión Barrio Adentro), launched on
      December 14, 2003, although with Cuban support in the form of thousands of health pro-
      fessionals; and food enterprise development and provision to the poor in the barrios
      (Misión MERCAL, January 2004). On these 'misiones' and their contribution to moving
      Venezuela towards socialism see Sánchez (2005). As for the extraordinary contribution of
      Cuba's internationalism towards social development in Venezuela since 2003, see Saney
      (2008).

17   Interview with Carmen Boquerón, February 26, 2008.

18   These programs were severely tested after 2011 with the collapse of oil prices.

carries over its paternal orientation in implementing its class consciousness-raising programs to the popular classes.

There is a great need for recruitment and education of young local cadres from the barrios, who speak the language of the people and have the class bonds to integrate the masses into a nationalist and socialist cultural-social program. The government's cultural and popular power movement is a formidable force but it faces tenacious opposition from the virulent and disreputable mass media aligned with the oligarchy. As the Venezuelan process moves toward egalitarian socialist values, it faces the more subtle but more insidious opposition of middle class students, professors and professionals who in the name of 'liberal democracy' and 'pluralism' seek to destroy cultural class solidarity. In other words, we have a struggle between the progressive minority from the middle class in the government against the majority of reactionary liberal middle class individuals embedded in academic institutions and in the community-based NGOs. Only by gaining the support of the people outside the middle class, i.e. the radical and exploited popular classes, can the cultural reformists in the Culture Ministry create a dominant popular hegemony.

Popular versus Reactionary Middle Class Movements

To discuss the highly polarized social confrontation between the pro-Chávez popular movements and the US-backed oligarch-supported middle class movements, it is important to contextualize the social, political and economic relations that preceded the ascendancy of the Chávez government. The US has been and remains the principal point of reference for Venezuela's oligarchy and the middle class. US-Venezuelan relations were based on US hegemony in all spheres—from oil to consumerism, from sports to lifestyle, from bank accounts to marriage partners. The role models and life styles of the Venezuelan middle class were found in the upscale Miami suburbs, shopping malls, condos and financial services. The affluent classes were upper class consumers; they never possessed a national entrepreneurial vocation.

The oil contracts between US and European firms and the PDVSA were among the most lucrative and favourable joint ventures in the world. They included negligible tax and royalty payments and long term contracts to exploit one of the biggest petroleum sites in the world (the Orinoco 'tar belt'). The entire executive leadership of what was formally described as a 'state enterprise' was heavily engaged in dubious overseas investments with heavy overhead costs, which disguised what was really executive pillage and extensive

cost overruns, that is, massive sustained corruption.[19] From the senior oil executives, the pillaged oil wealth flowed to the upper middle class, lawyers, con-
sultants, publicists, media and conglomerate directors, a small army of upscale
boutique retailers, real estate speculators and their political retainers and their
entourage among middle level employees, accountants, military officials,
police chiefs and subsidized academic advisers. All of these 'beneficiaries' of
the oil pillage banked their money in US banks, especially in Miami, or invested
it in US banks, bonds and real estate. In a word, Venezuela was a model case of
a rentier-bureaucratic ruling class profoundly integrated into the US circuits of
petroleum-investment-finance. Systematically, culturally and ideologically
they saw themselves as subordinate players in the US 'free trade-free market'
scheme of things. Chávez's assertions of sovereignty and his policies re-
nationalizing Venezuelan resources were seen as direct threats to the upper-
middle class' essential ties to the US, and to their visions of a 'Miami' life style.

This deep subordinated integration and the colonized middle class values
and interests that accompanied it, were deeply shaken by the crash in the
Venezuelan economy throughout the 1980s and 1990s. Emigration and relative
impoverishment of a wide swath of pubic employees, professionals and previously better-paid workers seemed to 'radicalize' them or create widespread
malaise. The profound downward mobility of the impoverished working class
and lower-middle class, as well as professionals, led to the discredit of the
endemically corrupt leaders of the two major political parties, mass urban
riots, strikes and public support for an aborted Chávez-led military uprising
(1992). These events led to his subsequent election (1998) and the approval of
the referendum authorizing the writing of a new, more profoundly democratic
constitution. Yet the middle class rebellion and even protest vote in favour of
Chávez was not accompanied by any change in political ideology or basic values. They saw Chávez as a stepladder to overcome their diminished status, and
paradoxically, to refinance their 'Miami' life-style, and gain access to the US
consumer market.

Time and circumstance demonstrated that when push came to shove, in
November 2001–April 2002, when the US collaborated and was complicit
in the short-lived but failed coup, the bulk of the middle class backed the
US-Venezuelan elite.[20] The US-backed coup was a direct response to President

---

19   As of the first nationalization in 1976 under President Carlos Andres Perez, the funda-
      mental question was 'nationalization for whom?'. In the 1970s to the re-privatizations, the
      answer was the wealthy elites (Petras, Morley & Smith, 1977).

20   Eva Golinger's detailed documentary study based on files secured from the US Government
      through the Freedom of Information Act provides ample evidence of US intervention.

Chávez' refusal to support the White House-Zionist orchestrated 'War on Terror'. Chávez declared: 'You don't fight terror with terror' in answer to President Bush's post-September 11, 2001 call to arms against Afghanistan. This affirmed Chávez' principled defense of the rights of self-determination and his unwavering stand against colonial wars. US Undersecretary of State for Political Affairs, Mark Grossman personally led an unsuccessful mission to Caracas in the fall of 2001 to pressure Chávez to back down.[21] Chávez was the only president in the world prepared to stand up to the new militarist Bush doctrine and thus was designated an enemy. Even worse, from the point of view of the Bush Administration, Chávez' nationalist policies represented an alternative in Latin America at a time (2000–2003) when mass insurrections, popular uprisings and the collapse of pro-US client rulers (Argentina, Ecuador and Bolivia) were constant front-page news.

In the run up to the April 2002 coup, the policies of the Chávez government were extremely friendly to what are reputed to be 'middle class' values and interests—in terms of democratic freedoms, incremental socioeconomic reforms, orthodox fiscal policies and respect for foreign and national property holdings and capitalist labour relations. There were no objective material reasons for the middle classes or even the economic oligarchy to support the coup except for the fact that their status, consumerist dreams, life style and economic investments were closely linked with the United States. In a word, the US exercised near complete hegemony over the Venezuelan upper and middle classes. As a result, its policies and its global interests became identified as 'the interests' of the wealthy Venezuelans. Venezuelan elite identification with US policy was so strong that it compelled them to back a violent coup against their own democratically elected government. The Caracas ruling class supported the imposition of an ephemeral US-backed dictatorial political regime and an agenda, which, if fully implemented, would have reduced their access to oil revenues, and the trade and socioeconomic benefits they had enjoyed under Chávez. The brief coup-determined junta proposed to withdraw from OPEC, weakening Venezuela's bargaining position with the US and EU, expel over 20,000 Cuban physicians, nurses, dentists and other health workers who were providing services to over two-million low-income Venezuelans without receiving any reciprocal compensation from Washington.

The economic elite and the middle class's second attempt to overthrow Chávez began in December 2002 with a bosses and oil executive lockout. This lasted until February 2003 and cost over US $10-billion dollars in lost revenues, wages, salaries and profits (Weisbrot & Sandoval, 2008).

---

21   Interview with Venezuelan Presidential adviser, Paris, November 2001.

Many Venezuelan businessmen and women committed economic suicide in their zeal to destroy Chávez; unable to meet loan and rent payments, they went bankrupt. Over 15,000 executives and professionals at the PDVSA, who actively promoted the strike and, in a fit of elite 'Luddite' folly, sabotaged the entire computerized oil production process, were fired. The principal pro-US and long time CIA-funded trade union confederation suffered a double defeat for their participation in the attempted coup and lockout, becoming an empty bureaucratic shell. The upper and middle classes ultimately became political and social losers in their failed attempts to recover their 'privileged status' and retain their 'special relation' with the US. While the privileged classes saw themselves as 'downwardly mobile' (an image which did not correspond with the reality of their new wealth especially during the commodity boom of 2004–2008), their frustrations and resentments festered and produced grotesque fantasies of their being ruled by a 'brutal communist dictator'. In fact, under the Chávez presidency (after 2003), they have enjoyed a rising standard of living, a mixed economy, bountiful consumer imports and were constantly entertained by the most creatively hysterical, rabidly anti-government private media in the entire hemisphere. The media propaganda fed their delusions of oppression. The hard-core privileged middle-class minority came out of their violent struggle against Chávez depleted of their military allies. Many of their leaders from the business associations and moribund trade union apparatus were briefly imprisoned, in exile or out of a job.

On the other hand, the pro-Chávez mass supporters who took to the streets in their millions and restored him to the Presidency, and the workers who played a major role in putting the oil industry back in production and the factories back to work, provided the basis for the creation of new mass popular movements. Chávez never forgot their support during the emergency. One of the reasons he cited for nationalizing the steel industry was the support of the steel workers in smashing the bosses' lockout and keeping the factories in operation.

Venezuela is one of the few countries where both the Left and the Right have built mass social movements with the capacity to mobilize large numbers of people. It is also the country where these movements have passed through intense cyclical volatility. The tendency has been for organizations to emerge out of mass struggle with great promise and then fade after a 'great event' only to be replaced by another organized 'movement', which, in turn, retains some activists but fails to consolidate its mass base. In effect what has been occurring is largely sequential movements based on pre-existing class commitments that respond in moments of national crises and then return to everyday 'local activities' around family survival, consumer spending, home and neighbourhood improvements. While this ebb-and-flow cycle of mobilization is common enough, what is striking in Venezuela is the degree of engagement and withdrawal: the mass outpouring and the limited number of continuing activists.

Looking at the big picture over the decade of Chávez rule there is no question that civil society was denser, and more varied and expressive in its actions than during any other government in the last sixty years. Starting from the popular democratic restoration movement that ousted the short-lived military-civilian junta and returned Chávez to power, local community based movements proliferated throughout the ranchos (slums) of the big cities, especially in Caracas.

With the bosses lockout and actual sabotage, the factory and oil field workers and a loyal minority of technicians took the lead in the restoration of production and defeating the US-backed executive elite. The direct action committees became the nuclei for the formation of communal councils, the launching of a new labour confederation (UNT), and new 'electoral battalions', which decisively defeated a referendum to oust Chávez. From these 'defensive organizations' sprang the idea (from the government) to organize production cooperatives and self-governing neighbourhood councils to bypass established regional and local officials. Peasant organizing grew and successfully pressured for the implementation of the land reform law of 2001. As the Left organized, the Right also turned to its 'normal institutional base'—FEDECAMARAS (the big business association), the cattle and large landowner organizations, the retailers and private professionals in the Chambers of Commerce and toward neighbourhood organizations in the up-scale barrios of Altimar and elsewhere.

After suffering several demoralizing defeats, the Right increasingly turned its attention toward US funding and training from NGOs, like SUMATE, to penetrate lower class barrios and exploit discontent and frustrations among the middle class university students whose street demonstrations became detonators of wider conflicts (Golinger, 2006).[22]

The Chavistas consolidated their organizational presence with health clinics, subsidized food stores and coops and educational programs. The Right consolidated its hold over the major prestigious universities and private high schools. Both competed in trying to gain the allegiance of important sectors of the less politicized, sometimes religious low-income informal workers and higher paid unionized workers—both focused on immediate income issues.

---

22   Golinger provides extensive documentation of US financing of the self-styled NGOs through USAID and NED (National Endowment for Democracy), a government conduit for destabilizing regimes critical of the US.

The Chavistas secured nearly 50 percent of the vote among the voters in a radical referendum spelling out a transition to socialism, losing by one percent. The right wing capitalized on the abstention of three million, mostly pro-Chávez, voters to defeat the referendum. For a more detailed analysis see Petras (2007).

The right-wing, via violence and sustained disinvestment in the country, has polarized Venezuela despite nearly double-digit sustained growth over a five-year period. This basic contradiction reflects the fact that the 'socialist project' of the government takes place in the socioeconomic framework in which big capitalists continue to control key sectors of the banking, financing, distribution, manufacturing, transport and service enterprises against the gas-oil-telecom, electricity, steel, cement and social service sectors of the government. In April 2008, Chávez launched a major offensive to reverse this adverse correlation of economic power in favour of the working classes by expropriating 27 sugar plantations, food distribution networks, meat packing chains, as well as the major cement and steel complexes.

In 2008 Chávez recognized that the populace mobilized 'from below' was stymied by 'commands' issued by the economic elite 'from above'. Whether it is food distribution or production, job creation or informal/contingent employment, funding small farmers or speculative landlords trading in bonds or financing oil derivative plants—all of these strategic economic decisions which affect class relations, class organization, class struggle and class consciousness were in the hands of the mortal enemies of the Chávez government and its mass base. By directly attacking these crucial areas affecting everyday life, Chávez was revitalizing and sustaining mass popular organization. Otherwise to remain subject to elite economic sabotage and disinvestment is to demoralize and alienate the popular classes from their natural gravitation to the Chávez government.

US-Venezuela Relations under Chávez

More than in most current Latin American societies, the Venezuelan ruling and middle classes have demonstrated a willingness to sacrifice their immediate economic interests, current remunerative opportunities, lucrative profits and income in pursuit of the high risk political interests of the US. How else can one explain their backing of the US-orchestrated coup of April 2002 at a time when Chávez was following fairly orthodox fiscal and monetary policies, and had adopted a strict constitutionalist approach to institutional reform? How else can one explain engaging in an executive and bosses two-month lockout of industry and oil production, leading to the loss of billions in private revenues, profits and salaries and ultimately the bankruptcy of hundreds of private firms and the firing of over 15,000 well-paid senior and middle level oil executives?

The shadow of the US hegemon over the Venezuelan elite and middle class has a strong component of ideological-psychological self-delusion: a deep, almost pathological identification with the powerful, superior white producer-consumer society and state and a profound hostility and disparagement of 'deep Venezuela'—the Afro-Indian-mestizo masses.

Typifying Theodor Adorno's 'authoritarian personality', the Venezuelan elite and its middle class imitators are at the feet and bidding of those idealized North Americans above and at the throat of those perceived as degraded dark-skinned, poor Venezuelans below. This hypothesis of the colonial mentality can explain the pathological behaviour of Venezuelan professionals who, like its doctors and academics, eagerly seek prestigious post-graduate training in the US while disparaging the 'poor quality' of new neighbourhood clinics for the poor where none had existed before and the new open admission policies of the Bolivarian universities—open to the once marginalized masses.

The deep integration—through consumption, investments and vicarious identification—of the Venezuelan upper and middle classes with the US elite forms the bedrock of Washington's campaign to destabilize and overthrow the Chávez government and destroy the constitutional order. Formal and informal psychosocial ties are strengthened by the parasitical and rentierist economic links based on the monthly/yearly consumer pilgrimages to Miami. Real estate investments and illegal financial transfers and transactions with US financial institutions, as well as the lucrative illegal profit sharing between the former executives of PDVSA and US oil majors provide the material basis for pro-imperialist policies.

US policy makers have a 'natural collaborator class' within Venezuela willing and able to become the active transmission belt of US policy and to serve US interests. As such, it is correct to refer to these Venezuelans as 'vassal classes'.

After the abject failures of Washington's vassal classes to directly seize power through a violent putsch and after having nearly self-destructed in a failed attempt to rule or ruin via the bosses' lockout, the US State Department oriented them toward a war of attrition. This involves intensified propaganda and perpetual harassment campaigns designed to erode the influence of the Chávez government over its mass popular base.

Imperial academic advisers, media experts and ideologues have proposed several lines of ideological-political warfare, duly adapted and incorporated by the Venezuelan 'vassal classes'. This exercise in so-called 'soft-power' (propaganda and social organizing) is meant to create optimal conditions for the eventual use of 'hard power': military intervention, coup d'état, terror, sabotage, regional war or, more likely, some combination of these tactics.[23] The predominance of 'soft power' at one point in time does not preclude selective exercises of 'hard power' such as the recent Colombian cross-border military attack on Venezuela's ally Ecuador in March 2008. Soft power is not an end in itself; it is a means of accumulating forces and building the capacity to launch a violent frontal assault on the Venezuelan government's 'weakest moment'.

The Imperial-Vassal 'Soft Power' Campaign: Drugs, Human Rights and Terrorism

In the period between 2007–2008, the US and the Venezuelan elite attempted to discredit the Venezuelan government through the publication and dissemination of a report fabricated to paint Venezuela as a 'narco-centre'. A DEA (US Drug Enforcement Agency) report named Venezuela as a 'major transport point' and ignored the fact that, under Washington's key client in Latin America President Alvaro Uribe, Colombia is the major producer, processor and exporter of cocaine, is beyond bizarre. Blatant omissions are of little importance to the US State Department and the private Venezuelan mass media. The fact that Venezuela is successfully intercepting massive amounts of drugs from Colombia is of no importance. For US academic apologists of empire, lies at the service of destabilizing Chávez are a virtuous exercise in 'soft power'.[24]

The US, its vassal classes and the Washington-financed human rights groups have disseminated false charges of human rights abuses under Chávez, while ignoring US and Israeli Middle East genocidal practices and the Colombian government's long-standing campaigns of killing scores of trade unionists and hundreds of peasants each year. Washington's attempt to label Venezuela as a supporter of 'terrorists' was resoundingly rejected by a United Nation's report issued in April 2008.[25] There is no evidence of systematic state sponsored

---

23 The phrase 'soft power' is credited to Harvard political science professor and long time US presidential adviser, Joseph Nye, who offers his expertise on empire management and the uses of imperial power (Nye, 2004).

24 Venezuelan drug interdiction has captured 360 tons of drugs between 2000–2007, according to the National Anti-Drug Office, January 2008.

25 On the Colombian State's mass terror, see the annual reports of the International Labour Organization, *Via Campesino*, Human Rights Watch and Amnesty International.

human rights violations in Venezuela. There are significant human rights abuses by the opposition-backed big landowners, murdering over 200 landless rural workers. There are workplace abuses by numerous FEDECAMARAS-affiliated private employers.[26] It is precisely in response to capitalist violations of workers rights that Chávez decided to nationalize the steel plants. No doubt Washington will fail to properly 'acknowledge' these human rights advances on the part of Chávez.

The point of the 'human rights' charges is to reverse roles: Venezuela, the victim of US and vassal class' coups and assassinations is labeled a human rights abuser while the real executioners are portrayed as 'victims'. This is, of course, a common propaganda technique used by aggressor regimes and classes to justify the unilateral exercise of brutality and repression.

In line with its global militarist-imperialist ideology Washington and its Venezuelan vassals have charged the Venezuelan government with aiding and abetting 'terrorists', namely the FARC insurgency in Colombia. Neither the Bush or Uribe regimes have presented evidence of material aid to the FARC. As mentioned above, a UN review of the Washington-Uribe charges against the Chávez government rejected every allegation. This fabrication is used to camouflage the fact that US Special Forces and the Colombian armed forces have been infiltrating armed paramilitary forces into Venezuela's poor neighbourhoods to establish footholds and block future barrio mobilizations defending Chávez.

The Hard Power Campaign: Economic Boycotts, Low Intensity Warfare and Colombia

Complementing the propaganda campaign, Washington instrumentalized a major oil producer (Exxon-Mobil) to reject a negotiated compensation settlement, which would have left the US oil giant with lucrative minority shares in one of the world's biggest oil fields (the Orinoco oil fields). All the other European oil companies signed on to the new public-private oil contracts.[27]

When Exxon-Mobil demanded compensation PDVSA made a generous offer, which was abruptly rejected. When PDVSA agreed to overseas arbitration,

---

26   Interview with peasant leaders from the *Frente Nacional Campesino Ezequiel Zamora*, February 27, 2008.

27   Throughout the dispute between Exxon-Mobil and the PDVSA, the European press sided with their more conciliatory multinationals while the *Washington Post*, NY *Times* and *Wall Street Journal* engaged in vituperative attacks on Venezuela.

Exxon-Mobil abruptly secured court orders in the US, Amsterdam and Great Britain 'freezing' PDVSA overseas assets. A London court quickly threw out Exxon-Mobil's case. As with other countries' experiences, such as Cuba in 1960, Chile in 1971–73 and Iran in 1953, the oil majors act as a political instrument of US foreign policy rather than as economic institutions respecting national sovereignty. In this case, Washington has used Exxon-Mobil as an instrument of psychological warfare to heighten tensions and provide their local vassals with an 'incident' that they can manufacture into fear propaganda. The Venezuelan private media cite the threat of a US oil boycott and evoke a scenario of a collapsing economy causing starvation; they attribute this fantastic scene to the Chávez government's 'provocation'. By evoking this illusion of US power and Venezuelan impotence, they obfuscate the fact that the new oil contracts will add billions of dollars to the Venezuelan Treasury, which will benefit all Venezuelans.

US military strategy options were severely limited by its prolonged and open-ended wars in Iraq and Afghanistan and its military build-up threatening Iran. As a result, US military strategy toward Venezuela involved a US $6 billion dollar military build-up of Colombia over the last eight years, including arms, training, combat advisers, Special Forces, mercenaries and logistics. US advisers encourage Colombian armed forces to engage in cross-frontier operations including the kidnapping of Venezuelan citizens, armed assaults and paramilitary infiltration capped by the bombing in Ecuador of a campsite of a FARC negotiating team preparing a prisoner release. The US dual purpose of these low intensity military pressures was to probe Venezuela's response, its capacity for military mobilization, and to test the loyalties and allegiances of leading intelligence officials and officers in the Venezuelan military. The US was involved in the infiltration of paramilitary and military operatives into Venezuela, exploiting the easy entrance through the border state of Zulia, the only state governed by the opposition, led by Governor Rosales.

The third component of the military strategy was 'to integrate' Venezuela's armed forces into a 'regional military command' proposed by Brazilian President Lula da Silva and endorsed by US Secretary of State Condoleezza Rice.[28] Within that framework, Washington could use its friendly and client generals to pressure Venezuela to accept US military-political hegemony disguised as 'regional' initiatives. Unfortunately for Washington, Brazil ruled out a US presence, at least for now.

The US military strategy toward Venezuela was dependent on the Colombian Army's defeat or containment of the guerrillas and the re-conquest of the vast

---

28   While Condoleezza Rice gave her backing to the 'Regional Command', Lula immediately informed her that the US was not part of it.

rural areas under insurgent control. This was designed to clear the way for Colombia's army to attack Venezuela. A military attack would depend crucially on a sharp political deterioration within Venezuela, based on the opposition gaining control of key states and municipal offices in the up-coming November elections. From advances in institutional positions Washington's vassals could undermine the popular national social, economic and neighbourhood programs.

Only when the 'internal circumstances' of polarized disorder can create sufficient insecurity and undermine everyday production, consumption and transport can the US planners consider moving toward large-scale public confrontation and preparations for a military attack. The US military strategists envision the final phase of an air offensive-Special Forces intervention only when they can be assured of a large-scale Colombian intervention, an internal politico-military uprising and vacillating executive officials unwilling to exercise emergency powers and mass military mobilization. The US strategists require these stringent conditions because the current regime in Washington is politically isolated and discredited, the economy is in a deepening recession, and the budget deficit is ballooning especially its military expenditures in Iraq and Afghanistan. Only marginal extremists in the White House envision a direct military assault in the immediate future. But that could change to the degree that their vassals succeed in sowing domestic chaos and disorder.

Vulnerability, Opportunities and Challenges

Notwithstanding the steps and strides made by Chávez in the path towards the 'socialism of the 21st century' Venezuela was vulnerable to attack on several fronts. This was largely the result of several internal contradictions as well as problems related to the machinations of the right-wing opposition and actions taken by the imperialist state. As for internal contradictions a number of them can be located in the state, social economy and national security sectors. In the sphere of politics for example, the basic issue is one of democratic representation, articulation and implementation of popular interests by elected and administrative officials. Often one heard among the Chavista masses in public and private discussions that 'We support President Chávez and his policies but...' and then follows a litany of criticism of local mayors, ministry officials, governors and Chávez's 'bad advisers'.[29] Some of the elected officials were

---

29   The testimony of a militant female peasant leader at a meeting organized by the Ministry of Popular Power was very demonstrative: 'We support President Chávez; we defend President Chávez; but he has to replace those incompetent officials in the ministry who

running their campaign on the bases of traditional liberal clientele politics that reward the few electoral faithful at the expense of the many. The key is to democratize the nomination process and not simply assume that the incumbent in office—no matter how incompetent or unpopular—should run for office again. Clearly the PSUV has to break free from the personality-based electoral politics and establish independent criteria, which respond to popular evaluations of incumbents and party candidates. Communal councils need to be empowered to evaluate, report and have a voice in judging inefficient ministries and administrative agencies which fail to provide adequate services. While we noticed improvements in the punctuality and preparation of more agency officials, there were still too many highly placed functionaries who failed to keep appointments, comply with their professional responsibilities or inform themselves about the subject matter of their ministries.[30] The dead hand of the reactionary past was present in the practices, personnel and paralysis of the existing administrative structures, and worst of all influences some of the new Chavista appointments.

The tactic of creating new parallel agencies to overcome existing obstructionist bureaucracies did not work because in many cases the new administrators were ill prepared (arrive late or miss appointments, derelict in rectifying problems, fail to meet commitments, etc.). Nothing irritates the Chavista masses more than to deal with officials who cannot fulfill their commitments in a reasonable time frame. This is the general source of mass discontent, political alienation and government vulnerability. In part the issue is one of incompetent personnel and, for the most part, the solution is structural: empowering popular power organizations to chastise and oust ineffective and corrupt officials.

In the economic sphere there is a need for a serious rethinking of the entire strategy in several areas. In place of massive and largely wasted funding of small-scale cooperatives to be run by the poor with little or no productive, managerial or even basic bookkeeping skills, investment funds should have been channelled into modern middle and large scale factories that combine skilled managers and workers as well as unskilled workers, producing goods which have high demand in the domestic (and future foreign) markets. The new public enterprise building 15,000 prefabricated houses is an example.

---

fail to provide us with credit so we can buy seed and fertilizer in time to plant our crops' (Ministry of Popular Power, February 27, 2008).

30   Of course, this problem of bureaucratic incompetence is not a problem peculiar to the administration of communal councils. It is deeply embedded in Venezuela's political culture and will not be easily fixed without a major overhaul of the entire bureaucratic and political apparatus.

The second area of economic vulnerability is agriculture in that the Agriculture Ministry had been a major failure in the development of food production (exemplified by the massive food imports), distribution networks and above all in accelerating the agrarian reform program. If any ministry cost Chávez the referendum it was the Agriculture Ministry, which over nine years failed to raise production, productivity and the availability of food. Past policies of controlling or de-controlling prices, of subsidies and credits to the major big producers were an abysmal failure. The reason is obvious: The big land-owner recipients of the government's generous agricultural credits and grants are not investing in agricultural production, in raising cattle, purchasing new seeds, new machinery, new dairy animals. They transferred government funding into real estate, Government bonds, banking and speculative investment funds or overseas. This illegal misallocation of government finance is evident in the gap between the high levels of government finance to the self-styled agricultural 'producers' and the meagre (or even negative) growth of production and productivity on the large estates.[31]

In April 2008, President Chávez recognized that fundamental changes in the use and ownership of productive land was the only way to control the use of government credit, loans and investment to ensure that the funds would actually go into raising food and not purchasing or investing in new luxury apartments or real estate complexes or buying Argentine bonds. In March and April 2008, Chávez, with the backing of the major peasant movements and workers in the food processing industry, expropriated 27 plantations, a meat processing chain, a dairy producer and a major food distributor. The challenge was to ensure that competent managers are appointed and resourceful worker-peasant councils are elected to ensure efficient operations, new investments and equitable rewards. What was abundantly clear is that Chávez recognized that capitalist ownership even with government subsidies was incompatible with meeting the consumer needs of the Venezuelan people.

Thirdly, inflation erodes popular consumer power, fomenting wage demands by the unionized workers in the export sector while eroding wages and income for contingent and informal workers. The government announced a decline in

---

31   The anti-production behaviour of the big landowners and cattle barons has been the practice for decades. Back in the mid-1970s, President Carlos Andres Perez also pumped hundreds of millions into 'making Venezuela food self-sufficient' in a program he called 'ploughing the oil wealth into agriculture' with the same miserable results as the present. The reason is clear. Many of the big landlords are the same people. The lessons from the past are very clear: As long as the present government tries to develop agriculture through the existing landowners it is doomed to repeat the failures of the past.

the rate of inflation in January–February 2008 (21 percent), a positive indication that urgent attention was being paid to the issue. But that trend was
reversed and by 2015 inflation was running to the high 60s. The outrageous
rates of profit in both consumer and capital goods industries increased the
circulation of excess money, while the lack of investment in raising productivity and production weakened supply. The inflationary spiral was embedded in
the structure of ownership of the major capitalist enterprises, and no amount
of regulation of profit margins would result in increased productivity. Chávez
moved into 2008 to accelerate the socialist transformation through the nationalization of strategic industries.

The key is to invest large sums of public capital in a vast array of competitive
public enterprises run with an entrepreneurial vision under worker-engineer
control. Relying on 'incentives' to private capitalists in order to increase productivity ran afoul in most instances because of their rentierist rather than
entrepreneurial behaviour. When the government yielded to one set of business complaints by offering incentives it only resulted in a series of new excuses,
blaming 'pricing', 'insecurity', 'inflation', and 'imports' for the lack of investment.
Clearly counting on public-private cooperation was a failed policy.

The basis of the psychological malaise of business can be boiled down to
one issue: They would not invest or produce even in order to profit if it meant
supporting the Chávez regime and strengthening mass support by means of
rising employment and workers' income (Interview with an oil executive from
British Petroleum, Caracas, March 6, 2008).[32] They preferred to merely maintain their enterprises and raise prices in order to increase their profits.

In the social sphere, the government faced the problem of increasing political
consciousness and above all encouraging the organizing of its mass supporters
into cohesive, disciplined and class-conscious organizations. The government's
socialist project depended on mass social organizations capable of advancing
on the economic elite and cleaning the neighbourhoods of right-wing thugs,
gangsters and paramilitary agents of the Venezuelan oligarchs and the Uribe
regime.

The peasant movement, Ezequiel Zamora, established the kind of political-
educational cadre schools necessary to advance the agrarian reform. By pressuring the Agrarian Reform Institute, by occupying uncultivated land, by
resisting landlord gunmen from Colombia, this emerging movement provides
a small-scale model of social action that the government should promote and
multiply on a national scale.

---

32   They preferred to merely maintain their enterprises and raise prices in order to increase
      profits.

The principal obstacle was the counter-revolutionary role of the National Guard, led by General Arnaldo Carreño. He directed a raid on the peasant training and educational school with attack helicopters and 200 soldiers, arrested and beat educators and students, and wrecked the institute. No official action against the military officers responsible for this heinous action was taken.[33] Apart from the reactionary and counter-revolutionary nature of this assault on one of the most progressive Chavista movements, it was indicative of the presence of a military sector committed to the big landlords and most likely aligned to the Colombian-US military 'golpistas'.

Labour legislation still lagged. The new progressive social security law was tied up in Congress and/or buried by the dead hands of the Administration. Contingent (non-contracted, insecure) workers still predominated in key industries such as oil, steel, aluminum, and manufacturing. With oil at over US$100 a barrel both the pro-Chávez and the plethora of competing tendencies and self-proclaimed 'class unions'—fragmented into a half dozen or more factions, each attacking the other and incapable of organizing the vast majority of unorganized formal and informal workers. The result has been the relative immobilization of important sectors of the working class faced with big national challenges, such as the 12/2 Referendum, the Colombian-US military threats and the struggle to extend the agrarian reform, public enterprises and social security.

The government's relative neglect of the organized and unorganized manufacturing workers changed dramatically for the better, beginning in the first half of 2008. Chávez' forceful intervention in the steel (Techint Sidor), cement (CEMEX), meatpacking and sugar industries led to massive outpouring of worker support. A certain dialectic unfolded, in which militant worker conflicts and strikes against intransigent, 'irresponsible and disrespectful' employers led Chávez to intervene on their behalf, which in turn activated the spread and depth of worker and trade union support for his policies.[34]

---

33   'El Frente Nacional Campesino Ezequiel Zamora es atacado por militares' (March 22, 2008 report from the FNCEZ).

34   An interesting and revealing episode along these lines regards the Mexican-owned CEMEX, whose Venezuelan affiliate was expropriated (with compensation) mid-August before in the context of a project to nationalize the sector. In the following week, on August 21, 2008, Chávez characterized as 'irresponsible' and 'disrespectful' the owners and managers of CEMEX, in the following terms: 'The vegetation is completely covered with dust because CEMEX did not invest in the technology to eliminate it', and this because of that 'capitalist evil' ('maldición capitalista')—more profit. To these owners and managers, he adds, 'it does not matter if they contaminate people, the beach, vegetation, animals, everything' all in the process of 'pillaging the country's riches'.

This dialectic of reinforced mutual support led to meetings of inter-sector union leaders and militants from the transport, metallurgic, food processing and related industries. In response to increased trade union organized support, Chávez raised the prospect of nationalizing banks and the rest of the food production and distribution chain. Much would depend upon the unification and mobilization of the trade union leaders and their capacity to overcome their sectarian and personalist divisions and turn toward organizing the unorganized contingent and informal workers.

The sectarianism of the ultra-leftist sects and their supporters among a few trade union bureaucrats led them to see Chávez and his government and trade union supporters as 'the main enemy' leading them to strike for exorbitant pay increases. They organized street blockades to provoke 'repression' and then call for 'worker solidarity'. Most of the time they had little success as most workers ignored their calls for 'solidarity'. The unification of pro-Chávez union leaders around the current nationalizations and the growth of a powerful unified workers' trade union movement isolated the sects and limited their role. A unified working class movement could accelerate the struggle for social transformation of industry. It would strengthen the national defense of the transformative process in times of danger.

National Security Threats

The multi-country surveys reveal that most people in almost all countries think the US is the biggest threat to world peace. This is especially the case in Venezuela, a Caribbean country which has already been subject to two US-backed and orchestrated coup attempts, a employers and executives lockout of the vital petroleum industry, a US-financed recall-referendum, an international campaign to block the sale of defensive weapons and spare parts accompanied by a massive sustained military build-up of Colombia, its surrogate in the region.

The violent efforts of the US to overthrow President Chávez have a long and ugly pedigree in the Caribbean and Central America. Over the past half century the US directly invaded or attacked Guatemala, Panama, Cuba, the Dominican Republic, Grenada, Nicaragua and El Salvador; it organized death squads and counter-revolutionary surrogate armies in Guatemala, El Salvador, Nicaragua and Honduras, which murdered nearly 300,000 people (Petras & Morley, 1995).

The US assault against Venezuela includes many of the strategies applied in its previous murderous interventions. As in Guatemala, it continued to bribe, cajole and subvert individuals in the Venezuelan military and among National Guard officers. The plan was to use Venezuelan military officials to organize a coup, collaborate with Colombian cross border infiltrators and to encourage defections to the pro-US opposition. As in Central America, US operatives organized death-squad killers to infiltrate the Venezuelan countryside to attack peasant movements pursuing land reform and to consolidate support among big landowners.

As it did in Nicaragua, the US combined support for the systematic sabotage of the economy by the business elite to foment discontent while financing opposition electoral campaigns to exploit the unstable economic circumstances. Like its economic blockade of Cuba, the US organized a de facto arms and parts embargo as well as an international 'freeze' on Venezuela's PDVSA overseas assets through international court processes initiated by Exxon-Mobil. Colombia's cross-border bombing of Ecuador is as much a 'test' of Venezuela's preparedness as it is an overt aggression against Ecuador's President Correa's nationalist government's cancellation of the strategic US military base in Manta (Ecuador).

Chávez took several measures to counter the US-Colombian-Venezuelan Fifth Column threats to national security. Following the coup Chávez ousted several hundred military officers involved in the overthrow and promoted officers loyal to the constitution. Unfortunately, the new group included several pro-US and anti-Leftist officers open to CIA bribes, one of whom even became the Minister of Defense before he was 'retired' and became a virulent spokesperson against Chávez's transformative referendum.[35] Worse still, Chávez amnestied the military and civilian coup-makers and economic 'lockout' saboteurs after they had served only a small fraction of their sentences with oil at over US$100 a barrel to the utter shock and dismay of the mass of popular forces that shouldered the burden of their violent coup and economic sabotage and who were not consulted.

Venezuela purchased some light weapons (100,000 rifles and machine guns) and a dozen submarines from Russia and helicopters from Brazil to counter Colombia's six billion dollar light and heavy arms build-up. Clearly that was a step forward, but it was still inadequate given the massive arms deficit between the two countries. Venezuela needs to rapidly build up its ground to air defenses, modernize its fighter jets and naval fleet, upgrade its airborne battalions and vastly improve its ground forces capacity to engage in jungle and

---

35 General Baduel was always a virulent anti-communist who is said to have received a seven-figure payoff and threats of exposure of unseemly personal revelations if he didn't 'turn' against Chávez.

ground fighting. Colombia's army, after 45 years of counter-insurgency, has the training and experience lacking in Venezuela. Chávez took positive steps toward organizing a mass popular militia with oil at over $100 a barrel but the advances had a very mixed record, as training and enlistment lagged far below expectations for lack of political organization and military leadership.

While Chávez took important steps to strengthen border defenses the same cannot be said about internal defenses. In particular, several generals in the National Guard had been more aggressively dislodging peasant land occupiers than in hunting down and arresting landlord-financed gunmen who had murdered 200 peasant activists and land reform beneficiaries. Extensive interviews with peasant leaders and activists indicated active collaboration between high military officers and right-wing cattle barons, calling into question the political loyalties of rural based Guard garrisons.

There was an urgent need to accelerate the expropriation of the big estates and to arm and train peasant militias to counteract the complicity of the National Guard or negligence in the face of landlord-sponsored violence. There were thousands of peasants ready and willing to enlist in militias because they have a direct stake in defending their families, comrades and their land from the ongoing paramilitary attacks.

The most immediate threat to internal security took the form of a blend between a mass of hardened Venezuelan criminal gangs and narco-paramilitary infiltrators from Colombia, which terrorized the populace in low-income neighbourhoods. Police investigations, arrests and government prosecution were inadequate, incompetent, and corrupt and occasionally point to complicity. The infamous broad daylight assassination of the respected Attorney General Danilo Anderson remained unsolved, while the Attorney General buried the investigation and, even more importantly, buried the investigation into the economic elite networks planning future coups that Anderson was carrying out at the time of his murder.

Anderson was the chief investigator of the forces behind the April 2002 failed coup, the economic sabotage and a series of political assassinations. Venezuelans close to the case state that Anderson had compiled extensive documentation and testimony implicating top opposition political, economic and media figures and some influential figures in the Chávez administration. With his death the investigations came to an end, no new arrests were made and those already arrested were subsequently granted amnesties. And some of Anderson's top suspects are now operating in strategic sectors of the economy. There are two hypotheses: either sheer incompetence within the office of the new Attorney General, the Ministry of Justice and related agencies of government, derailed the investigation; or there was political complicity on the part of high officials to prevent undermining the present socialization strategy. In either case the weakness of law enforcement, especially with regard to a dangerous capitalist class operating an extensive network supporting the violent overthrow of the elected government, opened the door to a re-play of a coup d'état. Indeed the amnesty of the elite coup-makers and economic saboteurs and the case of Danilo Anderson weighed on the minds of militant Venezuelans who saw it as an example of the continued impunity for the elite.

Factory and anti-crime 'neighbourhood watches' and defense militias are of the utmost importance given the rising internal and external national security threats and crime wave. With the greater cooperation of communal councils, sweeps of local gangs is a top priority. Neighbourhood police and militia stations must saturate the poor communities. Large-scale lighting should be established to make streets and sidewalks of the ranchos safer. The war against drug traffic must delve into their bourgeois collaborators, bankers and real estate operators who launder money and use illegal funds to finance opposition activities. Petty and youth delinquents should be sentenced to vocational training programs and supervised rural and community service. Large-scale illegal financial transactions must be prosecuted by the confiscation of bank accounts and property. National and internal security is the *sine quo non* of maintaining any political order dedicated to transforming the socioeconomic system.

On April 9, 2008 Chávez took a major step toward reducing crime, strengthening community-police relations and improving the security of the people by passing a National Police Law through presidential law decree. Under the new law, a new national revolutionary police of the people will be established 'demolishing the old repressive police model with education, conscience, social organization and prevention'. He contrasted the past capitalist police who abused the poor with the new communal police who will be close to the citizens and dialogue oriented. To that end the newly formed communal councils were encouraged to join and help select a new type of police based on rigorous selection process and on their willingness to live and work with the neighbourhood. The PSUV and the communal councils were designed to become the backbone of creating the new political solidarity with the newly trained police from the communities. Chávez' recognition of the security issue in all its political and personal dimensions and his pursuit of democratic and egalitarian approach highlighted his commitment to both maintaining law and order and advance the revolutionary process (Suggett, 2008). Unfortunately the program failed to materialize as the bureaucracy blocked implementation and crime rates resurged especially with the growth of contraband and black market activities.

Advances towards Socialist Transformation

Despite the US's military threats, its administrative weaknesses and political institutional limitations at the time of Chávez's passing Venezuela had a number of advantageous economic, political and social conditions for a socialist transformation—the most favourable conjuncture in its history. Economically, Venezuela's economy was booming at nine percent growth, with oil at over $100 a barrel world prices for exports were at record levels, it had immense energy reserves—US$35 billion dollars in foreign exchange reserves—and it is was in the process of diversifying its overseas markets, although much too slow for its own security (Weisbrot & Sandoval, 2008). With the introduction in April 2008 of an excess profit tax which will take 50 percent of all revenues over US$70 dollars a barrel and an additional 60 percent of all revenues over US$100 a barrel, several billion dollars in additional income swelled the funds for financing the nationalization of all strategic sectors of the economy.

Venezuela has benefitted from a multi-polar economic world eager to purchase and invest in the country. Venezuela is in the best possible condition to upgrade the petroleum industry and manufacture dozens of downstream petrochemical products from plastics to fertilizers—if public investment is efficiently and rationally planned and implemented. Venezuela has over a million productive landless workers and small farmers ready and willing to put the vast tracts of oligarch-owned under-utilized lands to work and put Venezuela on the road to food self-sufficiency—if not an agro-exporting country. Millions more hardworking Colombian refugee-peasants are eager to work the land along side their Venezuelan counterparts. There is no shortage of fertile land, farmers or investment capital. What is needed is the political will to organize expropriations, cultivation and distribution.

Politically, Chávez provided a dynamic leadership backed by legislative and executive power, capable of mobilizing the vast majority of the urban and rural poor, organized and unorganized workers and youth. The majority of the military and the new academy graduates backed the government's programs and resisted the bribes and enticements of US agents. New Bolivarian-socialist military instructors and curricula and the expulsion of US military 'missions' will strengthen the democratic link between the military and the popular government.

The intelligence and counter-intelligence services have detected some subversive plots but remain the weakest link both in terms of information collecting, direct action against US-Colombian infiltration, detecting new coup plans and providing detailed documentation to expose US-Colombian assassination teams. Clearly housecleaning of dubious and incompetent elements in the intelligence agencies is in order. New training and recruitment processes are proceeding, rather slowly and have to demonstrate competence.

At the time of Chávez's passing he and the regime retained the support of over 65 percent of the electorate and nearly 50 percent of the people were in favour of an overtly socialist agenda in the referendum of December 2, 2007. If the communal councils were to take off, and the militias gain substance and organization and if the PSUV develops mass roots and the popular nationalization accelerates, the government could consolidate its mass support into a formidable organized force to secure a huge majority in a new referendum and to counter the US-backed counter-revolution.

Needless to say, with the right-wing machinations of the bourgeoisie and the concerted efforts of the US government to take advantage of Chávez's passing favourable conditions for this 'development' evaporated in a new correlation of force in the class struggle. A change in these conditions to some extent will depend on the current government's deepening and extending its social-economic transformation—increasing new public housing from 40,000 to 100,000 a year; reducing the informal labour sector to single digits and encouraging the trade unions to organize the 80 percent of the unorganized labour-force into class unions with the help of new labour legislation.

Despite the availability of mass social support, declining export earnings are eroding the positive social changes, weakening, the objective basis for the successful organization of a powerful pro-socialist, pro-Chávez movement today.

The challenge is the subjective factor: The shortages of well trained cadres, political education linked to local organizing, the elaboration of a socialist political-ideological framework and the elimination of personality-based liberal patronage officials in leading administrative and party offices. Within the mass Chavista base the struggle for a socialist consciousness remains the central challenge in Venezuela today.

Obama's Imperialist Offensive against Venezuela

Venezuela today leads the anti-imperialist struggle in Latin America. This struggle, in the current form of the Bolivarian Revolution, according to President Maduro, can be traced back twenty-six years (February 27–28, 1989) to the popular rebellion against the neoliberal policies of the Carlos Andrés Pérez government that produced the *Caracazo*—the massacre by government security forces of at least 3,000 protesters. 'This was,' he noted (in a telephone conversation with the governor of the state Aragua), 'the beginning of the Bolivarian Revolution to escape the mistreatment [of the people], the pillaging and neocolonialism, [and] the false democracy' [of the republic] (El Jorope, 2/28/2015). Venezuela, he noted—in a televised broadcast at the time—under the leadership of Hugo Chávez was the first country in the region to say 'no' to the concerted effort of imperialist forces to convert the countries in the region into 'colonies of the IMF' and to reject 'savage capitalism and neoliberalism'.

Maduro in this televised broadcast also alluded to the form that the anti-imperialist struggle would take under Chávez's leadership, that of the Bolivarian Revolution, or, as he had it: 'the miracle of the socialist revolution' and the *misiones*—the social programs of the government's the national executive.

The course of this open-ended and ongoing revolutionary process has been anything but smooth and far from consolidated—and indeed is currently in jeopardy, assailed as it is by forces of opposition from both within and outside the country. The aim of this chapter is to elucidate some of the political dynamics of this revolutionary process and the efforts of the US imperialist state to derail it.

First, we outline some of the critical features of Chávez's political project to bring about by means of the Bolivarian Revolution what he described as 'the socialism of the 21st century', the antidote to both capitalism in its neoliberal form and US imperialism. Our main focus here is on the strategic response of the US to Chávez's political project, and the political dynamics of class struggle associated with it.

Second, we trace out the changes in the correlation of force in the class and anti-imperialist struggle subsequent to Chávez's death and the transition towards the Madero regime. Our main concern here is to establish the diverse forms taken by the class struggle and US imperialism in this conjuncture, and the conditions of a failed attempted coup against a democratically elected regime.

Chávez and the Anti-Imperialist Struggle

The Chávez years witnessed the thwarting of US efforts to restore client regimes in Latin America and the growth of anti-imperialist movements in the region. However, Colombia—containing seven US military bases—remained the lynchpin of US foreign policy in the region, and principal adversary of Chávez's anti-imperialist struggle.

The anti-imperialist struggle from the 1950s to the 1970s predominantly took the form of armed movements of national liberation, which combined anti-imperialist struggles with movements for revolutionary change in the direction of socialism. In the new century under Chávez's leadership the anti-imperialist struggle took the form of the Bolivarian revolution, which involved mobilizing the resistance against imperialist exploitation, made tangible with two projects: (i) building a movement towards the socialism of the 21st century; and (ii) pushing for Latin America's integration, which has taken various forms including UNASUR, CELA and ALBA, conceived and led by Hugo Chávez and excluding Washington.

Needless to say both projects converted Chávez into US enemy number one in the region. In response Venezuela mobilized its power to deepen its commitment to Latin American centred trade and diplomatic blocs.

With the defeat of US efforts to oust Chávez in 2002, considerable advances were made to further the Chávez' project to socialize the economy and develop a comprehensive welfare state. In turning the society towards socialism the government proposed to nationalize production, placing decisions in the hands of elected community councils; join the PWC in progressive extractivism using oil resources to reduce poverty; and promoting ALBA as a counterweight to the US-dominated OAS.

The approach adopted by Chávez to bring about 21st century socialism was what might be termed 'progressive extractivism', or even the 'new developmentalism' based on a post-Washington Consensus on the need for a inclusive development, an approach focused on reducing poverty through the use of oil rents and promoting forms of social ownership. This strategy, considered by some economists as the 'new developmentalism', points to the need to bring the state back into the development process and increase social expenditures as a more inclusive form of economic growth. This strategy of 'progressive extractivism' was also pursued in Bolivia and Ecuador (Gudynas, 2010; Veltmeyer & Petras, 2014). In Venezuela, however, the government went much further, moving beyond the institutional pillars of the new developmentalism by redistributing the proceeds, socializing the means of production and purporting to put the economy in the hands of the workers. This approach took the form of nationalizing enterprises as a first step. The second step would involve instituting communal councils where decisions as to production and marketing would be made at the local level–development from below, it could be argued.

Maduro and US Imperialism

Over the past few years Venezuela has been in a state of permanent and worsening crisis, reflected in conditions of hyperinflation, economic stagnation and scarcities of basic consumer goods. Although the crisis has been exacerbated by policy measures (such as devaluation) that the government was forced to take in dealing with a serious external imbalance, the major reason for the crises was the fall in the world price for oil, the source of 95 percent of the country's export and fiscal revenues for financing its social programs. Equally important the crisis has resulted from a concerted strategy of economic and political destabilization engineered by the US imperial state. Acting through local supermarket owners and distributers organizing large-scale hoarding, Washington created a scarcity of products needed to meet the basic needs of the population. This has resulted in increased prices, resulting in hyperinflation that has eroded the living standards of the population and undermined the poverty reduction impacts of the government's progressive social policies. The economic crisis created conditions for two coups, including the failed attempt in February, 2015 (see the discussion below).

The crisis is also a result of serious imbalances in the economy, to some extent provoked by the destabilizing efforts of the US but also because of structural contradictions in the economic model, including the reliance on extractivism and oil rents. Up to 95 percent of exports takes the form of oil, exposing Venezuela to what has been described as a 'resource curse', distorting the exchange rate and placing enormous pressures on non petroleum exporters. When the world price of oil fell, the problems inherent in extractivism as a development strategy became evident. The US took advantage of this vulnerability by pressuring Saudi Arabia not to cut back and indeed to increase production placing enormous pressures on the economies of the US's main enemies: Russia, Iran and Venezuela. Oil price manipulation became a weapon in the Venezuelan class war.

The US Strategy Versus Maduro

The US has escalated its efforts to overthrow of the government using all the mechanisms at its disposal including violent street mobs—the so called 'guarimbas'—as well as mobilizing the large retailers to provoke artificial short-ages. With the aid of the local and international mass media and corporate funded NGOs they accuse the Maduro government of being 'authoritarian'. Self-styled human rights groups have launched a virulent propaganda cam-paign against the government for jailing oppositionists that have been exposed in their plotting of terrorist activity and a military coup–oppositionists like the mayor of Caracas Antonio Ledesma, who, it was revealed, signed a document endorsing a coup programmed for February 2015. The staged propaganda cam-paign is designed to take advantage of the crises to discredit the government by exaggerating the deterioration and labeling the government as incompetent.

The US propaganda campaign has not worked in the region, where it is the US that is isolated—its actions almost universally denounced. The formation of a new political bloc inclusive of all governments in the region with the excep-tion of the two imperial powers, the US and Canada has rejected Washington's intervention and the anti-Venezuelan propaganda of the mass media—BBC, NYT, WP.

All countries in the region and organizations such as CARICOM, and beyond in the United Nations—the group of 77 (now well over 100) non-aligned countries—have supported and continue to support the Maduro government in diverse international forums against the transparent efforts of the US gov-ernment to wield its formidable state power. Unfortunately, none of this appears in the North American mass media, which continue to engage on behalf of the US. The media outlets in the propaganda war continue to present Venezuela's actions in defense of the constitutional order as undemocratic...as constituting a threat to the security of the region and thus to the US.

The Anatomy of a Failed Coup (February 2015)[1]

The second serious attempt to provoke a coup was in February 2015 in the con-text of Operation Jericó, a US operation supported by Germany, Canada, Israel and the UK (Resumen Latinoamericano / Red Voltaire / Por Thierry Meyssan /23/02/2015).

The plan for this operation kicked in on February 12, 2015. A plane owned by Academi (formerly Blackwater), disguised with the insignia of the armed forces of Venezuela, would bomb the presidential palace in Caracas and kill President Nicolas Maduro. The conspirators planned to put into power former congressional deputy Maria Corina Machado and seek the support of several

---

1   This section is a summary and paraphrase of the analysis made by Thierry Meyssan (2015). Our translation.

former Latin American presidents who would acclaim the necessity and legitimacy of the coup as an act of restoring democracy.

President Obama had issued a clear warning. He put it in writing in his new
defense doctrine (National Security Strategy): 'We are on the side of citizens
whose full exercise of democracy is in danger, as in the case of Venezuelans'.
In reality Venezuela, since the adoption of the 1999 Constitution, is one of the
most democratic states of the world. Obama's bellicose rhetoric presaged a
worst-case scenario in terms of the US government's attempts to impede
Venezuela's march on the road of national independence and the redistribution of national wealth—towards the socialism of the 21st century. By February
6, 2015, Washington was in the process of finishing planning the overthrow of
Venezuela's democratic institutions. The coup was planned for February 12.

Operation Jericho had the oversight of the National Security Council, under
the responsibility of Ricardo Zuniga. This 'diplomat' is the grandson of another
Ricardo Zuniga, president of the National Party of Honduras who organized
the military coups of 1963 and 1972 on behalf of General López Arellano. The
Zúñiga Ricardo who now works in the White House directed from 2009–2011
the CIA station in Havana, where he recruited agents and funded a feeble
opposition against Fidel Castro.

As always in such operations, Washington strives not to seem involved in
the events that it leads. The CIA organizes and directs the coup through supposedly 'nongovernmental organizations', or 'civil society': the NED (National
Endowment for Democracy) and its two tentacles on the Right and the Left—
the International Republican Institute (IRI) and the National Democratic
Institute (NDI); Freedom House and the International Center for Non-Profit
Law. Moreover, the US always uses its domestic clients as contractors in organizing or conducting certain aspects of the coup. This time at least Germany
was an active participant, charged with the responsibility of ensuring the protection of citizens of NATO countries during the coup, As for Canada, an avid
supporter of Obama's campaign against Venezuela, it was assigned control
over Caracas' International Airport. And Israel was put in charge of ensuring
the murder of several Chavista personalities, while the UK was put in charge of
propaganda for the coup, putting a 'democratic' spin on it. Finally, the US government planned to mobilize its political networks in securing recognition of
the coup: in Washington, Senator Marco Rubio; in Chile, former President
Sebastián Piñera; in Colombia, former presidents Álvaro Uribe Vélez; in
Mexico, former presidents Felipe Calderon and Vicente Fox; and in Spain, the
former prime minister José María Aznar.

To justify the planned coup, the White House encouraged large Venezuelan
companies to hoard their store of staples and sabotage the economy. The

non-distribution of these products was aimed at causing large queues at the shops and the outbreak of riots provoked by the action of provocateurs infiltrated among disgruntled consumers. But the manoeuvre failed because, despite the artificially induced scarcity during January and February and the queues at the shops, Venezuelans did not riot or attack the shops as was hoped.

To strengthen the planned economic sabotage, President Obama on December 18, 2014, signed a law imposing sanctions against Venezuela and against several of its leaders. Officially Washington said it wanted to punish the persons responsible for the 'repression' of student demonstrations. But in actual fact, since the beginning of the year Washington had been paying a salary—at four times the average income of Venezuelans—to gang members to engage them in assaulting the police. The pseudo student riot led to the killing of 43 people, mostly police and regime supporters, and spread terror in the streets of Caracas.

The military action was put under the supervision of General Thomas W. Geary, from SOUTHCOM headquarters in Miami, and Rebecca Chavez, from the Pentagon. The actual military operation was subcontracted to Academi (formerly Blackwater), currently administered by Admiral Bobby R. Inman (former head of the NSA), and John Ashcroft (former Attorney General of the Bush administration).

According to this part of the plan, a Super Tucano military aircraft, with the registration N314TG, purchased by Academi in Virginia in 2008, was to be used. The plane, to be falsely identified with the insignia of the armed forces of Venezuela, would bomb the Miraflores presidential palace and other targets such as the headquarters of the Ministry of Defense, the intelligence directorate and the headquarters of Telesur, a multinational television channel created by the ALBA. The plane was parked in Colombia, the headquarters of the coup-makers who were installed in the US Embassy in Bogota with the participation of US Ambassador Kevin Whitaker and his deputy, Benjamin Ziff.

Several senior officers, active and retired, had prepared a pre-recorded message to the nation announcing that they had seized power to restore order in the country. They were also expected to underwrite the Transition Plan, drafted by the Department of State and published on the morning of February 12, 2015 in *El Nacional*. The plan included the formation of a new government, led by former deputy Maria Corina Machado Maria, President of SÚMATE, the association that organized and lost the recall referendum against President Hugo Chavez in 2004. Machado's funds came from the National Endowment for Democracy. Maria Corina Machado was received with honours by President George W. Bush in the Oval Office of the White House on March 21, 2005. After being elected in 2011 as a representative from the State of Miranda, on March

21, 2014 Maria Corina Machado appeared before the Organization of American States as head of the delegation of Panama to the continental forum and was immediately dismissed from her post as deputy for having violated Articles 149 and 191 of the Constitution of Venezuela.

Unfortunately for the coup-makers Venezuelan Military Intelligence had under surveillance individuals suspected of having fomented a previous plot to assassinate President Maduro. In May 2014, the prosecutor of Caracas accused María Corina Machado, Governor Henrique Salas Romer, the former diplomat Diego Arria, the lawyer Gustavo Tarre Birceño, the banker Eligio Cedeño and businessman Pedro M. Burelli, of an active role in a pending coup. By tracking the conspirators, Military Intelligence discovered 'Operation Jericho'. On the night of February 11, the main leaders of the conspiracy, and an agent of the Israeli Mossad, were arrested and aerial protection of the Venezuelan capital was reinforced. Others involved were arrested on 12 February. On the 20th, the confessions of those arrested led to the arrest of another accomplice: the mayor of Caracas, Antonio Ledezma, a liaison officer with Israel. The coup had totally unravelled (but not without the attempt of the White House to accuse the Maduro regime of actions to subvert democracy).

Obama's Imperialist Offensive against Venezuela

The plan of the 'opposition' forces was to overthrow the democratically elected Maduro government, by diverse measures including destabilizing the economy, in an effort to provoke street violence and repression by the government. When this 'conspiracy' and attempted coup were discovered and made public, the Washington Post on February 23 and New York Times on February 14, 2015, published editorials denouncing the discovered 'conspiracy' as a 'distraction' engineered by the government to divert attention away from the growing economic crisis, and denounced the government's response (arrest of the plotters) as the actions of a 'repressive government'. They called on the government to resign and supported the coupster opposition's call for Maduro to step down in favour of a regime which would implement the 'transition government program' elaborated and presented by the clearly undemocratic opposition forces.

On March 9, 2015, Obama signed an Executive Order declaring Venezuela to be a threat to national security and US foreign policy. Why did Obama declare a 'national emergency', claim that Venezuela represents a threat to US national security and foreign policy, assume executive prerogatives and decree sanctions against top Venezuelan officials in charge of national security, at this time? To answer this question it is essential to begin by addressing Obama's specious and unsubstantiated charges of Venezuela constituting an 'extraordinary threat to national security and foreign policy'.

First, the White House presented no evidence whatsoever because there was nothing to present! There were no Venezuelan missiles, fighter planes, warships, Special Forces, secret agents or military bases poised to attack US domestic facilities or its overseas installations. On the other hand, the US has warships in the Caribbean, seven military bases just across the border in Colombia manned by over two thousand US Special Forces, and Air Force bases in Central America. Washington has financed proxy political and military operations intervening in Venezuela with intent of overthrowing the legally constituted and elected government.

Obama's claims resemble a ploy that totalitarian and imperialist rulers frequently use: accusing their imminent victims of the crimes they are preparing to perpetrate against them. No country or leader, friend or foe, has supported Obama's accusations against Venezuela. His charge that Venezuela represents a 'threat' to US foreign policy requires clarification. First, which elements of US foreign policy are threatened? Venezuela has successfully proposed and supported several regional integration organizations, which are voluntarily supported by their fellow Latin American and Caribbean members. These regional organizations, in large part, replace US-dominated structures, which served Washington's imperial interests. In other words, Venezuela supports alternative diplomatic and economic organizations, which its members believe will better serve their economic and political interests, than those promoted by the Obama regime. Petrocaribe, a Central American and Caribbean association of countries supported by Venezuela, addresses the development needs of their members better than US-dominated organizations like the Organization of American States or the so-called 'Caribbean Initiative'. And the same is true of Venezuela's support of CELAC (Community of Latin American and Caribbean States) and UNASUR (Union of South American Nations). These are Latin American organizations that exclude the dominating presence of the US and Canada and are designed to promote greater regional independence. Both ELAC and UNASUR, together with the G77 within the UN and China, have denounced the Obama government's decree regarding Venezuela as a threat to regional and national security.

Obama's charge that Venezuela represents a threat to US foreign policy is an accusation directed at all governments that have freely chosen to abandon US-centered organizations and who reject US hegemony. In other words, what arouses Obama's ire and motivates his aggressive threats toward Venezuela is Caracas's political leadership in challenging US imperialist foreign policy.

Venezuela does not have military bases in the rest of Latin America nor has it invaded, occupied or sponsored military coups in other Latin American countries—as Obama and his predecessors have done. Venezuela condemned the US invasion of Haiti, the US-supported military coups in Honduras (2009), Venezuela (2002, 2014, 2015), Bolivia (2008) and Ecuador (2010). Evidently, Obama's 'emergency' decree and sanctions against Venezuela are directed at maintaining unchallenged US imperial supremacy in Latin America and degrading Venezuela's independent, democratic foreign policy. So, to understand Obama's policy toward Venezuela we have to analyze why he has chosen overt, unilateral bellicose threats at this time.

Obama's War Threat a Response to Political Failure

The principal reasons why Obama has directly intervened in Venezuelan politics is that his other policy options designed to oust the Maduro government have failed. In 2013, Obama's relied on US financing of an opposition presidential candidate, Henrique Capriles, to oust the incumbent Chavista government. President Maduro defeated Obama's choice and derailed Washington's *'via electoral'* to regime change. Subsequently, Obama attempted to boycott and discredit the Venezuelan voting process via an international smear campaign. The White House boycott lasted six months and received no support in Latin America, or from the European Union, since scores of international election observers, ranging from former President James Carter to representatives of the Organization of American States certified the outcome.

In 2014, the Obama regime backed violent large-scale riots, which left 43 persons dead and scores wounded (most victims were pro-government civilians and law enforcement officers) and millions of dollars in damages to public and private property, including power plants and clinics. Scores of vandals and right-wing terrorists were arrested, including Harvard-educated terrorist Leopoldo Lopez. However, the Maduro government released most of the saboteurs in a gesture of reconciliation. Obama, on his part, escalated the terror campaign of internal violence. He recycled his operatives and, in February 2015, backed a new coup. Several US embassy personnel (the US had at least 100 stationed in their embassy), turned out to be intelligence operatives using diplomatic cover to infiltrate and recruit a dozen Venezuelan military officials to plot the overthrow of the elected government and assassinate President Maduro by bombing the presidential palace.

But President Maduro and his national security team discovered the coup plot and arrested both the military and political leaders, including the Mayor of Caracas. Obama, furious for having lost major internal assets and proxies, turned to his last resort: the threat of a direct US military intervention.

The Purpose of Obama's 'National Emergency' Declaration

Obama's declaration of a national security emergency has psychological, political and military objectives. His bellicose posture was designed to bolster the spirit of his jailed and demoralized operatives and let them know that they still have US support. To that end, Obama demanded that President Maduro free the terrorist leaders. Washington's sanctions were primarily directed against the Venezuelan security officials who upheld the constitution and arrested Obama's hired thugs. The terrorists in their prison cells can console themselves with the thought that, while they serve 'hard time' for being US shock troops and puppets, their prosecutors will be denied visas by President Obama and can no longer visit Disney Land or shop in Miami. Such are the consequences of the current US 'sanctions' in the eyes of a highly critical Latin America.

The second goal of Obama's threat is to test the response of the Venezuelan and Latin American governments. The Pentagon and CIA seek to gauge how Venezuela's military, intelligence and civilian leaders will deal with this new challenge in order to identify the weak links in the chain of command, i.e. those officials who will run for cover, cower or seek to conciliate, by giving in to Obama's demands.

It should be remembered that during the US-backed April 2002 coup, many self-styled 'Chavista revolutionaries' went into hiding, some holing up in embassies. In addition, several military officials defected and a dozen politicians curried favour with the coup leaders, until the tide turned and over a million ordinary Venezuelans, including slum dwellers, marched to surround the Presidential Palace and, with the backing of loyalist paratroopers, ousted the golpistas (coup-makers) and freed their President Chávez. Only then did the fair-weather Chavistas come out from under their beds to celebrate the restoration of Hugo Chávez and the return of democracy.

In other words, Obama's bellicose posture is part of a 'war of nerves', to test the resistance, determination and loyalty of the government officials, when their positions are threatened, US bank accounts are frozen, their visas denied and access to 'Disney Land' cut. Obama is putting the Venezuelan government on notice: a warning this time, an invasion next time.

The White House's openly thuggish rhetoric is also intended to test the degree of opposition in Latin America—and the kind of support Washington can expect in Latin America and elsewhere.

Cuba responded forcefully with unconditional support for Venezuela. Ecuador, Bolivia, Nicaragua and Argentina repudiated Obama's imperial threats. The European Union did not adopt the US sanctions, although the European Parliament did echo Obama's demand to free the jailed terrorists. Initially Brazil, Uruguay, Chile and Mexico neither backed the US nor the Venezuelan government. Uruguayan Vice President Raul Sendic was the only official in Latin America to deny US intervention. However, on March 16 at an emergency meeting of UNASUR in Quito Ecuador, the foreign ministers of Argentina, Bolivia, Chile, Colombia, Ecuador, Guyana, Peru, Surinam, Uruguay and Venezuela unanimously denounced US sanctions and military intervention.

But what was most important is that President Maduro stood firm. He declared a national emergency and asked for special powers. He called for two weeks of nationwide military exercises involving 100,000 soldiers beginning March 14. He made it clear to the Pentagon and the White House that a US invasion would meet resistance. That confronting millions of Venezuelan freedom fighters would not be a 'cake walk'—that there would be US casualties, body bags and new US widows and orphans to mourn Obama's imperial schemes.

Conclusion

Obama is neither preparing an immediate invasion nor giving up on 'regime change' because his coup operatives failed in two consecutive years. His militarist posture is designed to polarize Latin America: to divide and weaken the regional organizations; to separate the so-called 'moderates' in MERCOSUR (Brazil/Uruguay/Paraguay) from Venezuela and Argentina. Despite his failures thus far, Obama will press ahead to activate opposition to Venezuelan security policies among the Chilean, Peruvian, Mexican, and Colombian neoliberal regimes.

Washington is building pressure externally and preparing for a new round of violent unrest internally to provoke a robust government response. In other words, Obama's military invasion will follow the well-rehearsed scenario of 'humanitarian intervention' orchestrated in Yugoslavia, Libya and Syria—with such disastrous consequences on the people of those countries. Obama, at this time, lacks international political support from Europe and Latin America that would provide the fig leaf of a multilateral coalition and has lost his key internal operatives. He cannot risk a bloody unilateral US invasion and prolonged war in the immediate future, but even so he is inexorably moving in that direction.

Obama has seized executive prerogatives to attack Venezuela. He has alerted and mobilized US combat forces in the region. He understands that his current teams of operatives in Venezuela have demonstrated that they are incapable of winning elections or seizing power without major US military backing. He is now engaged in a psychological as well as physical war of nerves: to run down the Venezuelan economy, to intimidate the faint-hearted, and exhaust and weaken the militants through constant threats and widening sanctions over time.

The Maduro government has accepted the challenge. He is mobilizing the people and the armed forces: his democratically elected regime will not surrender. The national resistance will be fighting in their own country for their own future. They will be fighting an invading imperial power. They represent millions, and they have a 'world to lose' if the *squalidos* (the domestic fifth column) should ever take power: if not their lives, their livelihoods, their dignity and their legacy as a free and independent people.

Epilogue

President Maduro sought and secured Russian military support and solidarity in the form of arms, advisors and an agreement to engage in joint military manoeuvres to meet the challenges of Obama's war of attrition. President Putin addressed a public letter of support of the Venezuelan government in response to Obama's threats. At the same time Obama is engaged in a two-pronged economic and military strategy, which will converge with a US military invasion. The overt military threats issued in early March 2015 are designed to force the Maduro government to divert large-scale financial resources away from meeting the economic crisis to building emergency military defense. Through escalating military and economic threats, the White House hopes to diminish government subsidies for the import of basic foodstuffs and other essential commodities during an internal campaign of hoarding and artificial shortages committed by economic saboteurs.

Obama is counting on his Venezuelan proxies and the local and international mass media to blame the government for the economic deterioration and to mobilize the big protests of irate consumers. White House strategists hope a massive crowd will serve as a cover for terrorists and snipers to engage in violent acts against public authorities, provoking the police and armed forces to respond in a re-play of the 'coup' in Kiev. At that point, Washington will seek to secure some form of support from Europe or Latin America (via the

OAS) to intervene with troops in what the State Department will dub as 'peace mediators in a humanitarian crisis'.

The success of sending in the US Marines into Venezuela on a peace mission will depend on how effective Special Forces and Pentagon operatives in the US Embassy have been in securing reliable collaborators among the Venezuelan military and political forces ready to betray their country. Once the collaborators seize a piece of territory, Obama can mount the charade that US Marines are there by invitation of democratic forces.

Under conditions of explicit military threat Maduro must change 'the rules of the game'. Under emergency conditions hoarding is no longer just a misdemeanour: it becomes a capital crime. Politicians meeting and consulting with representatives of the invading country should lose their immunity and be summarily jailed. Above all, the government must take total control over the distribution of basic goods; establishing rationing to ensure popular access; nursing scarce financial resources by limiting or imposing a moratorium on debt payments; diminishing or selling assets in the US (CITGO) to avoid confiscation or their being made illiquid ('frozen') by some new Obama decree. On the external front, Venezuela must deepen military and economic ties with its neighbours and independent nations to withstand the US military and economic offensive. If Obama escalates the military measures against Venezuela the parliamentary elections scheduled for September should be temporarily suspended until normality is re-established.

Bibliography

Acosta, A. (2009). *La Maldición de la Abundancia*. Quito: Comité Ecuménico de Proyectos/Ediciones Abya-Yala.

Amin, S. (2001). "Imperialism and Globalization." *Monthly Review* 53(2). <http://www.monthlyreview.org/601amin.htm> (Accessed 02 July 2015).

Arellano, J.M. (2010). "Canadian Foreign Direct Investment in Latin America." Background paper. Ottawa: North–south Institute.

Bartra, Roger (1974). *Estructura agraria y clases sociales en México*. Mexico: Ediciones Era.

Bebbington, et al. (2009). "Contienda y Ambigüedad: Minería y Posibilidades de Desarrollo," *Debate Agrario*, No. 44, pp. 31–62.

Bernstein, Henry (2010). *Class Dynamics of Agrarian Change*. Halifax: Fernwood.

Bienefeld, M. (2013). "The New World Order: Echoes of a New Imperialism," in H. Veltmeyer (ed.). *Development in an Era of Neoliberal Globalization*, 105–27. Oxford: Routledge.

Biersteker, T. (1992). "The 'Triumph' of Neoclassical Economics in the Developing World: Policy Convergence and the Bases of Government in the International Economic Order," in James Rosenau and E.O. Czempiel (eds.). *Governance without Government: Order and Change in World Politics*. Cambridge: Cambridge University Press.

Borras, S. Jr., and J.C. Franco (2010). "Towards a Broader View of the Politics of Global Land Grab: Rethinking Land Issues, Reframing Resistance," The Hague: International Institute of Social Studies (ISS), *ICAS Working* Paper, No. 1.

Borras, S. Jr., J. Franco and M. Spoor (2011). "Land Grabbing in Latin America and the Caribbean," Seminar paper, 14 November. Santiago de Chile: Food and Agriculture Organization of the United Nations (FAO) Regional Office.

Borras, S. Jr. Gomez, C. Kay and M. Spoor (2012). "Land Grabbing in Latin America and the Caribbean," *Journal of Peasant Studies*, Vol. 39, Nos. 3–4, pp. 845–72.

Bresser-Pereira, L.C. (2007). "Estado y mercado en el nuevo desarrollismo," *Nueva Sociedad* 210 (July–August): 110–25.

——— (2009). *Developing Brazil: Overcoming the Failure of the Washington Consensus*. Boulder, CO: Lynne Rienner Publishers.

Bulmer-Thomas, V. (1996). *The Economic Model in Latin America and Its Impact on Income Distribution and Poverty*. New York: St. Martin's Press.

CEPAL – Comisión Económica para América Latina y el Caribe (1998). *Foreign Investment in Latin America and the Caribbean 1998*. Santiago: ECLAC. <http://hdl.handle.net/11362/1158> (Accessed 02 July 2015).

——— (2012). Foreign Direct Investment in Latin America and the Caribbean 2011. Santiago: ECLAC. <http://hdl.handle.net/11362/1147> (Accessed 02 July 2015).

Chibber, Vivek (2005). "Reviving the Developmental State? The Myth of the National Bourgeoisie," *Socialist Register 2005*. Verso: London.

Clark, T. (2002). *Canadian Mining Companies in Latin America: Community Rights and Corporate Responsibility*. Conference Report to the Centre for Research on Latin America and the Caribbean (CERLAC) and Mining-Watch Canada, Toronto, 9–11 May.

Collier, P. (2003). "Natural Resources, Development and Conflict: Channels of Causation and Policy Interventions," Paper presented at the Annual World Bank Conference on Development Economics – Europe, Washington, 28 April.

Collier, P., and A.J. Venables (2011). *Plundered Nations? Successes and Failures in Natural Resource Extraction*. London: Palgrave Macmillan.

Cooper, Robert (2000). "The New Liberal Imperialism," *The Guardian*, April 7.

Crouch, C., and A. Pizzorno (1978). *Resurgence of Class Conflict in Western Europe since 1968*. London: Holmes and Meier.

Cypher, J. (2010). "South America's Commodities Boom: Developmental Opportunity or Path Dependent Reversion?" *Canadian Journal of Development Studies* 30(3–4): 635–62.

Dangl, B. (2007). *The Price of Fire: Resource Wars and Social Movements in Bolivia*. Oakland, CA: AK Press.

——— (2010). *Dancing with Dynamite: Social Movements and States in Latin America*. Oakland, CA: AK Press.

Davis, M. (2006) *Planet of Slums*. London: Verso.

ECLAC – Economic Commission for Latin America and the Caribbean (2012). *Statistical Yearbook for Latin America and the Caribbean*. Santiago: ECLAC.

Engler, Y. (2012). *The Ugly Canadian: Stephen Harper's Foreign Policy*. Halifax: Fernwood Publishing.

Esteva, Gustavo (1983). *The Struggle for Rural Mexico*. Greenwood Publishing.

Evans, Peter (1995). *Embedded Autonomy: States and Industrial Transformation*. Princeton: Princeton University Press.

FAO – Food and Agriculture Organization (2011). *Land Tenure and International Investments in Agriculture*. Rome: FAO.

Farthing, L., and B. Kohl (2006). *Impasse in Bolivia: Neoliberal Hegemony and Popular Resistance*. London: Zed Books.

Foster, J.B. (2003). "The New Age of Imperialism," *Monthly Review*, Vol. 55, No. 3, pp. 1–14.

——— (2006). *Naked Imperialism: The US Pursuit of Domination*. New York: Monthly Review Press.

Frieden, J. (2006). *Global Capitalism: Its Fall and Rise in the 20th Century*. New York: W.W. Norton.

Giarracca, Norma, and Miguel Teubal (2014). "Argentina: Extractivist dynamics of Soy Production and Open-Pit Mining," in H. Veltmeyer and J. Petras (eds.). *The New Extractivism*. London: Zed Books.

Golinger, Eva (2006). *The Chávez Code: Cracking us Intervention in Venezuela*. Olive Branch Press.

Gordon, Todd (2010). "Canadian development aid takes on corporate colouring," *Toronto Star*, Vol. 29 (November). <http://www.thestar.com/opinion/editorialopinion/2012/11/29/canadian_development_aid:takes_on_corporate_colouring.html> (Accessed 02 July 2015).

Gudynas, E. (2010). "The New Extractivism of the 21st Century: Ten Urgent Theses about Extractivism in Relation to Current South American Progressivism," in *Americas Program Report*. Washington, DC: Center for International Policy.

Gudynas, Eduardo (2011). "La izquierda de los límites al nuevo extractivismo," *La Primera*, Lima, 11 de mayo. <http://www.diariolaprimeraperu.com/online/columnistas/la-izquierda-de-los-limites-al-nuevo-extractivismo_85841.html> (Accessed 02 July 2015).

Haber, Stephen, and Victor Menaldo (2012). "Natural Resources in Latin America: Neither Curse Nor Blessing," *SSRN Working Paper*. Oxford Handbook of Latin American Political Economy. <http://ssrn.com/abstract=1625504> (Accessed 02 July 2015).

Hardt, M., and A. Negri (2000). *Empire*. Cambridge: Harvard University Press.

Harvey, D. (2003). *The New Imperialism*. New York: Oxford University.

Hayter, Teresa (1971). *Aid as Imperialism*. Harmondsworth: Penguin Books.

Holloway, John (2002). *Change The World without Taking Power: The Meaning of Revolution Today*. London: Pluto Press.

IMF – International Monetary Fund (2000). *International Financial Statistics Yearbook*. New York: IMF.

Infante, B.R., and O. Sunkel (2009). "Chile: hacía un desarrollo inclusivo," *Revista CEPAL*, Vol. 10, No. 97, pp. 135–54.

Kay, Cristóbal (2009). "Development Strategies and Rural Development: Exploring Synergies, Eradicating Poverty," *Journal of Peasant Studies*, Vol. 36, No. 1, pp. 103–38.

Klare, M. (2003). "The New Geopolitics," *Monthly Review*, Vol. 55, No. 3, pp. 51–56.

Klein, Emilio, and Victor Tokman (2000). "La estratificacion social bajo tension en la era de la globalización," *Revista CEPAL*, Vol. 72 (Deciembre), pp. 7–30.

Leiva, Ignacio Fernando (2008). "Toward a Critique of Latin American Neostructuralism," *Latin American Politics and Society*, Vol. 50, No. 4 (Winter), pp. 1–25.

Lewis, W.A. (1954). "Economic Development with Unlimited Supplies of Labor," *Manchester School of Economic and Social Studies*, Vol. 22, pp. 139–91.

Magdoff, H. (2003). *Imperialism without Colonies.* New York: Monthly Review Press.

McLean, David (1995). *War, Diplomacy and Informal Empire.* London: Tauris.

Meyssan, Thierry (2015). "Falla el putsch de Obama en Venezuela," Red Voltaire, Resumen Latinoamericano, 23/02/2015.

MiningWatch Canada (2009). *Land and Conflict: Resource Extraction, Human Rights, and Corporate Social Responsibility: Canadian Companies in Colombia.* Ottawa: Mining-Watch Canada.

Mirowski, P., and D. Plehwe (eds.) (2009). *The Road from Mont Pelerin: The Making of the Neoliberal Thought Collective.* Cambridge: Harvard University Press.

Norman, C.S. (2009). "Rule of Law and the Resource Curse," *Environmental and Resource Economics*, Vol. 43, No. 2, pp. 183–207.

North, L., T.D. Clark and V. Patroni (eds.) (2006). *Community Rights and Corporate Responsibility: Canadian Mining and Oil Companies in Latin America.* Toronto: Between the Lines.

Novo, A., K. Jansen, M. Slingerland and K. Giller (2010). "Biofuel, Dairy Production and Beef in Brazil: Competing Claims on Land Use in São Paulo State," *Journal of Peasant Studies*, Vol. 37, No. 4, pp. 769–792.

Nun, José (2001). *Marginalidad y exclusion social.* Buenos Aires: Fondo de Cultura Económica. <https://www.fce.com.ar/ar/libros/detalles.aspx?IDL=767> (Accessed 02 July 2015).

Ocampo, J.A. (2007). "The Macroeconomics of the Latin American Economic Boom." *CEPAL Review*, Vol. 93 (December), pp. 7–28.

OCMAL – Observatorio de Conflictos Mineros de América Latina (2011). *Cuando tiemblan los derechos: Extractivismo y criminalización en América Latina.* Quito: OCMAL. <http://www.rebelion.org/docs/150198.pdf> (Accessed 02 July 2015).

OXFAM (2008). "Another Inconvenient Truth: How Biofuel Policies Are Deepening Poverty and Accelerating Climate Change," *Briefing Paper.* Boston: OXFAM International.

Panitch, L. (2000). "The New Imperial State," *New Left Review*, Vol. 2 (March–April).

Panitch, L., and C. Leys (2004). *The New Imperial Challenge.* New York: Monthly Review Press.

Peet, R. (2003). *Unholy Trinity: The IMF, World Bank and TWO.* London: Zed Books.

Petras, J. (2000). "Geopolitics of Plan Colombia," *Economic and Political Weekly*, Vol. 35, Nos. 52/53, pp. 4617–23.

Petras, James (2008). "President Chávez and the FARC: State and Revolution," July 3. <http://petras.lahaine.org/?p=1741> (Accessed 02 July 2015).

Petras, J., and H. Veltmeyer (2001). *Unmasking Globalization: The New Face of Imperialism.* Halifax: Fernwood Books/London: Zed Books.

———— (2004). *Las privatizaciónes y la desnacionalización en América Latina.* Buenos Aires: Libros Prometeo.

——— (2005a). "Foreign Aid, Neoliberalism and Imperialism," in A. Saad-Filho and D. Johnston (eds.). *Neoliberalism: A Critical Reader*, 120–27. London: Pluto Press.

——— (2005b). *Empire with Imperialism*. Halifax and London: Fernwood Publications and Zed Books.

——— (2007a). "Neoliberalism and Imperialism in Latin America: Dynamics and Responses," *International Review of Modern Sociology*, Vol. 33, No. Special Issue, pp. 27–59.

——— (2007b). *Multinationals on Trial*. Aldershot: Ashgate Publishing.

——— (2009). *What's Left in Latin America*. Aldershot UK: Ashgate.

Petras, J., et al. (1981). *Class, State and Power in the Third World*. Montclair: Allanheld, OSMUN.

Pilger, John (2002). *The New Rulers of the World*. London: Verso.

Robinson, W. (2007). "Beyond the Theory of Imperialism: Global Capitalism and the Transnational State." *Societies Without Borders*, Vol. 2, pp. 5–26.

Rodrik, D. (1999). *The Global Economy and the Developing Countries: Making Openness Work*. Washington, DC: ODC (Overseas Development Council).

Romero, G. (2014). "Poder adquisitivo cayó 77% en 35 años en México," *La Jornada*, 6 de agosto. <http://www.jornada.unam.mx/ultimas/2014/08/05/cayo-77-el-poder -adquisitivo-en-mexico-en-35-anos-dice-mancera-7860.html> (Accessed 02 July 2015).

Roorda, Erie (1998). *The Dictator Next Door: The Good Neighbor Policy and the Trujillo Regime in the Dominican Republic, 1930–1945*. Durham, NC: Duke University Press.

Sandbrook, R., M. Edelman, P. Heller and J. Teichman (2007). *Social Democracy on the Periphery*. Cambridge, UK: Cambridge University Press.

Saxe-Fernández, J., and O. Núñez (2001). "Globalización e Imperialismo: La transferen-cia de Excedentes de América Latina," in Saxe-Fernández et al. (eds.). *Globalización, Imperialismo y Clase Social*. Buenos Aires/México: Editorial Lúmen.

Sena-Fobomade (2011). "Se intensifica el extractivismo minero en América Latina. Foro Boliviano sobre Medio Ambiente y Desarrollo," 2 marzo. <http://fobomade.org.bo/ art-1109> (Accessed 02 July 2015).

Silva, E. (2009). *Challenging Neoliberalism in Latin America*. New York: Cambridge University Press.

Singh, J. Nem (2013). "Towards Postneoliberal Resource Politics? The international political economy of oil and copper in Brazil and Chile," *New Political Economy*, Vol. 19, No. 3. DOI: 10.1080/13563467.2013.779649. <http://www.tandfonline.com/ doi/abs/10.1080/13563467.2013.779649#.UpO3vaUgUpE> (Accessed 02 July 2015).

Tockman, J. (2010). "Varieties of Postneoliberalism: Ecuador and Bolivia's divergent paths of citizenship, participation and natural resource policy," Paper presented at the 2010 Congress of the Latin American Studies Association, Toronto, 6–9 October.

UNCTAD – United Nations Conference on Trade and Development (1998). *World Investment Report 1998: Trends and determinants.* New York and Geneva: UNCTAD.

——— (2007). *World Investment Report 2007.* New York and Geneva: UNCTAD.

——— (2011). *World Investment Report 2011.* New York and Geneva: UNCTAD.

——— (2012). *World Investment Report 2012.* New York and Geneva: UNCTAD.

Veltmeyer, H. (2005). "The Dynamics of Land Occupation in Latin America," in Sam Moyo and Paris Yeros (eds.). *Reclaiming the Land: The Resurgence of Rural Movements in Africa, Asia, and Latin America.* London: Zed Books.

Veltmeyer, H., and J. Petras (2014). *The New Extractivism.* London: Zed Books.

Vreeland, James (2003). *The IMF and Economic Development.* Cambridge: Cambridge University Press.

Wade, Robert. "Bringing the State Back In Lessons from East Asia's Development Experience," IPG 2 [International Politics and Society].

Webber, J. (2008). "Imperialism and Resistance: Canadian Mining Companies in Latin America." *Third World Quarterly,* Vol. 29, No. 1, pp. 63–87.

——— (2010). *Red October: Left Indigenous Struggle in Modern Bolivia.* Leiden: Brill.

Weisbrot, Mark, and Luis Sandoval (2008). *The Venezuelan Economy in the Chávez Years.* Washington, DC: Center for Economics and Policy.

Wily, Liz Alden (2013). "The Global Land Grab: The New Enclosures," in David Bollier and Sike Helfrich (eds.). *The Wealth of the Commons.* The Commons Strategy Group.

Williamson, J. (ed.) (1990). *Latin American Adjustment. How Much Has Happened?* Washington, DC: Institute for International Economics.

World Bank (2002). *Recent Trends in International Resource Flows.* Washington, DC: World Bank.

——— (2005). *Extractive Industries and Sustainable Development. An Evaluation of World Bank Group Experience.* Washington, DC.

——— (2007). *Meeting the Challenges of Global Development.* Washington, DC, October 12.

——— (2008). *World Development Report 2008: Agriculture for Development.* New York: Oxford University Press.

——— (2010). *Rising Global Interest in Farmland: Can It Yield Sustainable and Equitable Benefits?* Washington, DC: World Bank.

Index